ACROSS THE GREAT DIVIDE

ACROSS THE GREAT DIVIDE

*Between Analytic and
Continental Political Theory*

Jeremy Arnold

STANFORD UNIVERSITY PRESS
Stanford, California

STANFORD UNIVERSITY PRESS
Stanford, California

Printed in the United States of America on acid-free, archival-quality paper

Library of Congress Cataloging-in-Publication Data
Names: Arnold, Jeremy, 1980– author.
Title: Across the great divide : between analytic and continental political
    theory / Jeremy Arnold.
Description: Stanford, California : Stanford University Press, 2020. |
    Includes bibliographical references and index. |
Identifiers: LCCN 2019037477 (print) | LCCN 2019037478 (ebook) |
    ISBN 9781503612136 (cloth) | ISBN 9781503612143 (paperback) |
    ISBN 9781503612150 (epub)
Subjects: LCSH: Political science—Philosophy. | Analysis (Philosophy) |
    Continental philosophy.
Classification: LCC JA71 .A7416 2020 (print) | LCC JA71 (ebook) |
    DDC 320.01—dc23
LC record available at https://lccn.loc.gov/2019037477
LC ebook record available at https://lccn.loc.gov/2019037478

Cover design: Anne Jordan

Typeset by Kevin Barrett Kane in 10/14 Minion Pro

CONTENTS

ACKNOWLEDGMENTS

I would like to thank Paulina Ochoa Espejo, Joel Schlosser, Tom Donahue, and the participants in the Tri-Co Political Theory Workshop at Haverford College for generously responding to and improving the Introduction of this book. I also need to thank my former colleagues at the National University of Singapore, especially Mark Brantner, Donald Favareau, and Peter Vail, for wonderful conversations about everything but political theory. Emily-Jane Cohen took an interest in this project long before it was finished and her editorial advice and commitment to this book has proven invaluable. The reviewers of the book were extremely helpful in their criticism, models of intellectual engagement, and I thank them. Finally, to Mabel Wong, yet another opportunity not taken to answer your question; and to Isaac: read generously, critically, lovingly. Try to live that way too.

ACROSS THE GREAT DIVIDE

INTRODUCTION

The Schism and Its Impact

I AM A POLITICAL THEORIST writing in the early 21st century, in-heritor of a great divide in western philosophy that began in the last century and still shapes philosophy and its penumbral disciplines today: the divide between *analytic* and *continental* philosophy. The goal of this book is to show one approach to navigating the divide within the world of political theory and philosophy, but before we get to that approach and the detailed readings and arguments of later chapters, we need to know how we got here; where things stand now; and where we might go. In other words, we need a story.

HOW DID WE GET HERE?

From March 17 to April 6, 1929, Martin Heidegger, Ernst Cassirer, and a number of soon to be famous philosophers—including Rudolf Carnap and Emmanuel Levinas—met in Davos, Switzerland, for a series of philosophical discussions meant to bridge the German and French intellectual communi-ties. The high point of the conference was a public debate between Heidegger and Cassirer. Michael Friedman described the conference as a "parting of the ways" that marked the division of continental from analytic philosophy (Fried-man 2000).[1] While Cassirer's neo-Kantianism continued to address traditional philosophical problems, Heidegger was a self-conscious revolutionary. His existential-hermeneutic analysis of Dasein sought to overthrow modern phi-losophy: both the epistemological project René Descartes initiated and the sub-ject/object ontology that Heidegger saw as undergirding that project. Although trained by neo-Kantians, and an assistant to Edmund Husserl (himself an inheritor of the Cartesian tradition), Heidegger rejected the presuppositions of modern philosophy and offered a radical reinterpretation of the philosophical tradition in order to revive its most fundamental, yet most repressed, question: the meaning of being.

In the decades prior to Davos, philosophers such as Gottlob Frege, Bertrand Russell, Gilbert Ryle, Franz Brentano, Husserl, Cassirer, Carnap, Ludwig Wittgenstein, and indeed Heidegger himself could and did respond to each other's work. After Davos, so the story goes, engagement between, on the one hand, those committed to the philosophical issues raised by the new logic and the new physics and, on the other hand, those committed to a deconstruction of the western philosophical tradition came largely to an end. Carnap took Heidegger's claims about the Nothing as his example of the pseudo-statements of metaphysics, and Heidegger dismissed symbolic logic as a continuation of the forgetting of being.[2] There were moments of interaction: Cassirer and Heidegger occasionally, and sometimes implicitly, continued their debate in print; Ryle reviewed Heidegger's *Being and Time*; and Wittgenstein and Heidegger revealed some knowledge of each other's work.[3] These important examples aside, as the 20th century proceeded, so did the parting of the ways.

In 1958, a second famous conference, "La Philosophie Analytique," held in Royaumont, France, exposed the rift more clearly. The paper Ryle presented made clear the differences between English-language philosophy and at least some continental philosophy, specifically the work of Husserl. That paper begins with what Ryle calls a "caricature" of Husserl's thought, and Ryle's tone in describing Husserl's work is charitably described as ironic (Ryle 2009, 188). For example, Ryle claims that Husserl's path of investigation into the philosophy of mind "led him into a crevasse, from which no exit existed," whereas English philosophers were led into "morasses, but morasses from which firmer ground could be reached" (Ryle 2009, 188). Husserl was also "bewitched," his use of "Essence" "over-portentous," and his attempt to make philosophy a rigorous science a sign that Husserl had never met a real scientist, nor made a joke. Philosophers at Cambridge and Oxford, though, were frequently in merry "post-prandial" contact with scientists (Ryle 2009, 188–189). One frankly offensive dig was Ryle's repeated use of the terms "Fuehrer" and "Fuehrership" when speaking of Husserl's aim to make philosophy a master science. After all, the latter was a Jewish philosopher once expelled from his university by the Nazis.

Simon Glendinning's useful overview of the debate at Royaumont is far more critical of Ryle than I would be (Glendinning 1999, 8–11). Ryle was no stranger to Husserl's work and he approvingly cites Jean-Paul Sartre later in his talk. Ryle's talk is striking because it reveals how different the *procedures* of philosophy at Oxford and Cambridge had become in comparison to those at Freiburg and Paris. Glendinning argues that Ryle might have been deliberately creating, rather than describing, gulfs between England and the Continent because he knew that many philosophers in France and Germany were attacking the Cartesian subject as well. However, while the *results* of the Oxford and Cambridge philosophers might overlap in interesting ways with the results of the early Heidegger and Maurice Merleau-Ponty, Ryle's talk reveals genuine differences between analytic and continental writers over *how* philosophy should proceed. Ryle did not create the gulf, although he was widening it.

By 1958, then, there was a recognized division between analytic and continental philosophy. The story of the division can be told in other ways, to be sure. One might emphasize the revolutionary modernist impulse of Heidegger *and* Carnap, as well as their associates and followers. Carnap and other members of the Vienna Circle had self-conscious affiliations with the high modernism of the Bauhaus movement, and even though some of Heidegger's many critics see him as an anti-modernist in substance, the formal innovations and destructive intentions of at least Heidegger's work in the late 1920s puts him squarely in the modernist camp (see Galison 1990). The story of 20th-century philosophy, if framed in terms of a debate between modern*ist* philosophers and more traditional, modern philosophers, might be told in a less divisive fashion, even if deep differences between the analytic and continental traditions would remain. Another possibility is to follow those like Richard Rorty, Henry Staten, Samuel Wheeler, and others who, taking seriously the "linguistic turn" in both analytic and continental philosophy, see the more creative philosophers in both traditions converging, at moments, in their substantive philosophical positions. A further complication is that there are many answers to the question what is continental philosophy?, some of which deny that the term is useful at all given its provenance in analytic philosophy and the diversity of thinkers labeled *continental* (see Critchley 2001; Leiter and Rosen 2007, 1–4). The term *analytic* is also problematic, as it is anachronistic and masks the diversity of philosophy in the English-speaking world. The existence of a divide, or a given account of it, is not to be simply accepted. However, anyone working in philosophy is aware of the split.[4] For all of the problems with making clear distinctions between what is analytic and what is continental, there are some consistent differences—whether in procedure or aim, content or form, canonical texts, or linguistic fluency required. These differences are important, and even worth preserving.

If the story so far is relatively familiar, the next part hasn't been properly told. To my knowledge, no historical work has been written on how the analytic-continental split has shaped contemporary political theory and philosophy.[5] My hunch is that the specific consequences of the divide in political thought are, in the United States and to a lesser extent in England and Australia, inflected by the institutionalization of political *theory* within departments of political *science*. On the one hand, political theory became a distinct subfield of political science amid contentious methodological debates. These debates were partly shaped by developments in analytic philosophy (specifically logical positivism), but as historians of political science have argued, the debates originally concerned the axiological and political commitments of American political scientists and theorists. Political *philosophy*, on the other hand, has its institutional home primarily in philosophy departments, which in the Anglophone world are largely analytic.

John Gunnell has shown that the story of political theory in the United States cannot be told outside of the context of the development of political science, for "the issues that arose in the subfield of political theory" in the midst of the behavioral revolution "were determinative with respect to its subsequent evolution" (Gunnell 1988, 71).[6] However, Gunnell argues that *before* the behavioral revolution in the 1950s, a key factor in the debates between political theory and political science was the perception of crisis in, and/or the defense of, liberalism (Gunnell 1988, 74–79; 2006). The sense of crisis was brought to the United States in the 1940s and 1950s by European émigrés we now associate with continental political theory: Leo Strauss, Eric Voegelin, Hannah Arendt, and Theodor Adorno, among others. Nietzschean nihilism, Weberian disenchantment, and a distrust of positivism and liberalism play notable roles in the *story of decline* that characterizes, however differently, the works of Strauss, Arendt, Adorno, and other émigré theorists. Gunnell argues that the introduction of European political theory into American political science split an American consensus on the normative values of liberalism and research goals in both theory and empirical political science. Theory began to be associated with the supposedly anti-liberal and anti-scientific views coming from the Continent, and political science strongly reacted to anti-liberal and anti-positivist theorizing.[7]

The fact that continental *philosophical* ideas precipitated tense debates between American political scientists and political theorists is revealing. Strauss, Arendt, and Adorno were trained as philosophers within the same intellectual milieu that culminated in the Davos dispute. This historical background inspired at least three influential strands of contemporary political theory critical of positivism, liberalism, instrumental rationality, and scientism: critical theory, Straussianism, and Arendtian inspired political theory. All three positions emerge from a constellation of philosophical ideas owing far more to G.W.F. Hegel, Friedrich Nietzsche, Max Weber, and Heidegger than they do to Husserl, much less Frege, Russell, Wittgenstein, and the Vienna Circle.

Beyond the literal continental heritage of European émigrés, a number of American theorists shaped at least in part by continental thinkers developed their accounts of the history and purpose of political theory in the context of attacks by behaviorists and others. Sheldon Wolin is critical of so-called post-structuralist or postmodernist theories, but his criticisms of liberalism and his approach to political theory are far more consistent with the aims and procedures of those now labeled continental than they are, for example, with the work of a Marxist like G. A. Cohen. Wolin's historical method also differs from that of historians of political thought such as Quentin Skinner and J. A. Pocock.[8] Simplified and schematic as all this may be, we can now identify four sources of "continentalish" political theory: Strauss, Adorno, Arendt, and Wolin. Surely there are more strands to be identified, most obviously those theorists associated with the New Left and its aftermath.

This brief account is meant to suggest what a history of the divide within political theory might look like. One complicating factor is that contemporary political theory is not a single enterprise, and approaches to it vary in their relation to the analytic-continental split. Presently, political theory contains within itself a number of subfields: history of political thought, normative political theory, comparative political theory, critical theory, and so on. *Political theory* is a capacious term that names a set of distinct but related practices of reading and writing.

A second complicating factor is that the influence of post-WWII continental theorists such as Jürgen Habermas, Michel Foucault, Jacques Derrida, Gilles Deleuze, Jacques Lacan, Louis Althusser, Jacques Rancière, Alain Badiou, and others, was not fully felt in the English-speaking world of political theory until at least the 1980s. These thinkers constitute a generation of theorists taught both by the earliest continental philosophers still alive and by the generation of Strauss, Adorno, and Arendt. Their work is in part critical reactions to the ideas of Husserl, Heidegger, Freud, the early Frankfurt school, and so forth, and in part contributions to politically charged events and academic discussions in France and Germany during the 1960s. This has had the effect of making the language, sensibilities, arguments, and political commitments of more contemporary continental theorists even more opaque to those not conversant with the continental tradition and the political context of, say, Mai 68. The unintended effect of these successive waves of theorists from the Continent has been to make conversation across the divide even more difficult, but it also makes for difficult conversation *within* contemporary political theory among subfields not easily placed on one or the other side of the divide.

These and other more recent effects of the divide on political theory, shaped by institutional histories, political events, and political commitments, ought to be the subject of historical inquiry. Political theory sits uneasily in departments of political science, and it is conflict *between* theorists and political scientists, rather than conflict *among* political theorists, that has occupied the attention of historians of the discipline of political theory and political science. However, one need only take a look at the disheartening political science blogosphere to see that political theorists from competing approaches, when anonymously posting on rumor mills, repeat the usual criticisms of continental thought as obscure, inane, intellectually irresponsible, and so on. Anonymous blogs might seem to be poor evidence in favor of the effects of the split on political theory, but citation counts from leading journals of political theory tell a similar story of mutual shunning.[9]

If these suggestions are correct, then the effect of the analytic-continental split on political theory is real, although it is inflected by the institutional history of political theory and political science. So far, my focus has been the influence of continental theorists on political theory since the middle of the last century. Let's turn now to political philosophy.

Normative political philosophy has its institutional home primarily in philosophy departments, the majority of which, in the English-speaking world, are analytic. Undoubtedly, many political theorists in political science departments associate themselves with normative political philosophy and do the same kind of work, but most of the influential analytic political philosophers of the last several decades have PhD degrees in philosophy and were or are working in philosophy departments. More importantly, the history of contemporary normative political philosophy was shaped not only by debates between consequentialists and deontologists, liberals and libertarians and communitarians, and more recently involving questions of global justice and the global basic structure, but also by broader developments in philosophy, moral philosophy in particular, in the analytic tradition.[10]

For example, Isaiah Berlin's classic essay "Does Political Theory Still Exist?" begins by rehearsing the analytic-synthetic distinction drawn by logical positivists, before defending political theory and philosophy more broadly as a rational mode of inquiry (Berlin 1999, 143–144). Or take the section "Some Remarks About Moral Theory" in John Rawls' *Theory of Justice*. Rawls defends his reliance on intuitions and considered judgments in reflective equilibrium in part by rejecting the restriction of political philosophy to the analysis of definitions, meanings, and the logical relations that hold a priori between terms (Rawls 1971, 51). Both Berlin and Rawls clear philosophical space for substantive political philosophy within the context of philosophical movements that denied the rationality of substantive evaluative discourses (although metaethics was fine). The logical positivist distinctions between the analytic and the synthetic, fact and value, clearly shaped at least the context within which Berlin and Rawls were writing.[11]

The political context of contemporary analytic moral philosophy is just as important. If Gunnell is right that the anti-liberal tendencies of Arendt, Adorno, Strauss, and the like had important consequences for intra-disciplinary debates within political science, it seems quite likely that the almost ubiquitous pro-liberalism and pro-modernity attitude of normative political philosophy contributes, as much as intellectual disagreement, to the divide as it appears in political philosophy. Thomas L. Akehurst argues that many analytic philosophers—Russell, Berlin, A. J. Ayer, Ryle, Karl Popper, Stuart Hampshire, R. M. Hare, and others—associated continental philosophy of the 18th and 19th centuries with the rise of fascism, citing Jean-Jacques Rousseau, Hegel, Nietzsche, romanticism, idealism, and (in the 20th century) Heidegger (Akehurst 2008). This is bound to have had some effect on normative political philosophy insofar as it affirms modern forms of liberalism whereas many of the most important continental thinkers within political theory today are often highly critical of liberalism.

We can see evidence of the dominant liberalism of analytic political philosophy in the central place given to intuitions and the "considered judgments" of citizens in many works of analytic political philosophy. The intuitions relied upon are almost exclusively the intuitions of members of the liberal democratic

societies in which most analytic philosophers live and work. While normative political philosophers are not uniformly uncritical of liberalism, they are
generally committed to many of liberalism's basic institutions, principles, and
values. Many of these commitments alone distinguish most analytic political
philosophers from many continental philosophers.

More importantly, liberal values and associated judgments are incorporated
into normative arguments as either relatively fixed points or as judgments to
be justified philosophically. It is not only that *liberal* intuitions play a central
role in analytic political philosophy, it is that liberal *intuitions* play a central
role. Continental thinkers are more likely to reject the philosophical role of the
pre-philosophical intuitions of the "common man."[12]

The issues here are quite complicated but the difference in sensibility is clear.
The use of intuitions in analytic political philosophy is an accepted practice,
unlike the deep suspicion of ordinary political beliefs, values, and attitudes
that characterizes some of the most influential strands of continental theorizing. If one begins from the premise that there is something deeply problematic
or ideological in the theory and practices of modern liberal societies or their
citizens, then one's philosophical practice, not just one's politics, is likely to be
very different from much contemporary analytic political philosophy. For these
and other reasons, it is unsurprising that political philosophers who train in
analytic philosophy departments are exposed to a range of ideas and methods,
and to sentiments and suspicions, common to analytic philosophy as a whole.

My suggestion is that the disciplinary history of 20th-century analytic philosophy has shaped the methods, problems, and philosophical concerns of analytic political philosophy. This, along with the latter's normative commitment
to liberalism, distinguishes it from a great deal of 20th-century continental
thought.

That is how we arrived here: with a divide between continental and analytic
political theory.

WHERE ARE WE NOW?

Where has the divide left political theory and philosophy today? We can isolate
three key differences that have reinforced the mutual shunning between continental and analytic political theory.

First, most continental theorists do not see political theory as a *justificatory*
and *analytic* enterprise. Most continental theorists do not attempt to discover
necessary and sufficient conditions for, say, political legitimacy that would then

justify a regime that met those conditions. Much modern continental political theory works in the wake of what William Connolly has called the "Foucauldian reversal," that is, the claim that

> the very problematic of legitimacy, with its associated concepts of the subject, freedom, reflexivity, allegiance, responsibility and consent, is the juridical twin of the problematic of disciplinary order. The former is not, as it sees itself, the alternative to the latter; the two function together to produce the modern subject and to subject it to the dictates of the order. The critique, in Foucauldian terms, sets the stage for the reversal of the problematic of legitimacy. (Connolly 1987, 90)

For those theorists who accept something like the Foucauldian reversal, justifying state legitimacy is no longer an unambiguous enterprise, but the broader point is that justificatory projects that seek necessary and sufficient conditions are rare in the continental tradition regardless of topic.

Continental theorists also tend to rely on a genealogical or etymological analysis of concepts. When Arendt writes about freedom or authority, she is clearly engaging in analyses of the concepts and practices of authority and freedom. Her approach, though, is etymological and genealogical, not logical. This entwines her mode of conceptual analysis with the history of concepts, something quite foreign to logical analysis. Derrida's analyses of concepts like "justice," "forgiveness," the "political," and so on, while often logical—Derrida seeks to articulate the necessary and sufficient conditions for the proper definition and employment of concepts like justice—relies on an account of language and phenomenology that ends in aporias and the impossibility of realizing justice or forgiveness in practice. Arendt and Derrida, to be sure, are trying to *clarify* political concepts and the judgments and practices that employ those concepts. However, their analyses tend to make such concepts, or the logic of those concepts, or the use of those concepts in practice, more problematic and ambiguous. Continental theorists usually take seriously Nietzsche's dictum that only something that has no history can be clearly defined.

Foucault's work, too, has made the analysis of political concepts a more difficult task. Even a "willful liberal" and erstwhile conceptual analyst like Richard Flathman found in Foucault a challenger to the analysis of concepts (Flathman 1992). For Flathman, Foucault's history of the entwinement of freedom and discipline helps us see that while *conceptually* "discipline is one thing and freedom another . . . empirically, perhaps phenomenologically, perhaps ontologically, they are inseparable" (Flathman 2003, 33).[13] Thus, even if conceptual analysis can keep our thinking clear, its usefulness for understanding political phenomena is more questionable the more conceptual distinctions fail to capture corresponding features of politics. The tendency of many continental theorists, and those sympathetic to such theorizing, to make concepts and the logical processes of justification more problematic is not, to be clear, a consequence of taking ambiguity or complexity as desiderata of theorizing. It is, rather, because the phenomena and concepts being explained *are* complex and ambiguous.

Analytic political philosophy still employs conceptual analysis, and the justificatory project is ongoing. Thomas Christiano and David Estlund, for all their disagreements, share a justificatory project (see Estlund 2009a; and Christiano 2009). Christiano defends the idea that "democratic and liberal rights are grounded in the same fundamental principle of political equality" so that "one cannot justify the one without the other" (Christiano 2008, 3). Estlund argues for the legitimacy and authority of democracy from an epistemic proceduralist perspective: democratic procedures tend to produce correct decisions (Estlund 2009b, 8). As we will see in Chapter 1, even the anti-moralist Bernard Williams is interested in justifying state legitimacy because the "basic legitimation demand" demands an "acceptable" answer to the problem of securing political order, and an acceptable answer is required for state legitimacy (Williams 2005, 3–6). What is true of discussions of the concept of legitimacy is often true of analytic political philosophy as a whole: despite real disagreements, many of the most influential analytic philosophers share a commitment to the justificatory project of political philosophy. Part and parcel of that project is clarifying just what is meant by justice, legitimacy, freedom, and the like.

To be sure, not all analytic philosophers seek, in their justificatory practices, necessary and sufficient conditions. A significant feature of post-Rawlsian political philosophy is the turn to public justification, that is, the idea that a justification for coercive state action need not be foundationalist or exhaustive in its uncovering of necessary and sufficient conditions. Justifications of coercive state action require "only" that every citizen has sufficient reasons for endorsing the legitimacy of the state, or of a scheme of justice, or of a particular law. What these reasons are may differ among citizens, but so long as those citizens have sufficient reasons for endorsement, nothing more is needed to justify a political order or some part of it. There are "thin" and "thick" versions of public justification—Rawls' political liberalism is a thin version, Gerald Gaus' justificatory liberalism a thick—but neither Rawls nor Gaus seek necessary and sufficient conditions (Gaus 1996). However, with the exception of Habermas and some of his followers—who straddle the analytic-continental divide in interesting ways—continental theorists are as skeptical toward public justification as they are toward more foundationalist justificatory practices.[14]

Second, and related to the first point, the *modes of acceptable argumentation* within analytic and continental political theory are quite different. We can further identify at least three ways in which different modes of argumentation manifest themselves: style, interdisciplinarity, and canon.

Many continental theorists have been criticized for a style of writing often called "obscure," "difficult," "jargon-filled," and worst of all, "non-argumentative." The latter charge (or term of approbation) is found even in the work of friends of continental theory. Rorty writes that "[n]on-Kantian philosophers like Heidegger and Derrida are emblematic figures who not only do not solve problems, they do not *have* arguments or theses" (Rorty 1982, 93).[15] For Rorty, continental theorists are trying to shake free of the tradition, and this partly explains their non-argumentative, "obscure," "difficult," "writerly" style. Rorty is wrong—although he modified his view somewhat later—but many continental philosophers and political theorists do often appear to eschew argument in order to write *autrement*. There are many reasons why given theorists might choose to write as they do, and to the extent that many theorists mimic the writing of their preferred hero, the result is often frustrating. But charges of obscurity, jargon, literariness, non-argumentativeness, and so on, are misplaced. The first two, for example, apply just as equally to many analytic texts as well as scientific work, and for the same reasons: technical terms are not used solely to distinguish insiders from outsiders but because a word has precise, discipline specific meanings. Imposing terms like *gastrulation*, *supervenience*, or *différance* are perfectly intelligible, so long as one has done enough reading or research in biology, moral philosophy and philosophy of science, or the work of Derrida. It is true that the prose of some continental theorists is often difficult, elliptical, paratactic, allusive, elusive, and the like, and that this inspires comparisons with modernist literature. This does not mean that arguments are not to be found, however. Technical terms and difficult-to-read prose are, for various reasons, part of the rhetorical strategy of many continental theorists, but these theorists are usually still making arguments.[16]

While few analytic texts are devoid of technical terminology, prose in analytic philosophy is rarely difficult to read (the sense of obscurity, if it exists, comes from elsewhere). Yet, clarity does not guarantee anything about the strength of one's argument, nor even that one is making an argument. Moreover, to the extent that clear writing is seen as a virtue, it may misleadingly assume an unwarranted simplicity in the phenomena or problem being discussed. The accusation that the "obscurity" of continental theorists is meant to hide the lack of good arguments is easily countered with the accusation that the clarity of analytic writing is meant to hide the real complexity of the phenomena being discussed. These back-and-forth accusations are common among theorists, and symptomatic of the way in which style, no matter how internally differentiated within each tradition, contributes to the sense of difference in modes of argumentation. What the specific stylistic differences are cannot be reduced to terms of criticism like "obscure," "literary," or "clear," but the differences feel real in the reading, and they mark a present, if not entirely defined, difference in how each tradition writes and persuades.

The roles of interdisciplinarity and canon in differentiating modes of argumentation are related. The continental political theory canon is more interdisciplinary, and in part for this reason, continental theorists have greater latitude in drawing on diverse texts in their approach to political theory. Film, literature, psychoanalysis, neuroscience, complexity theory, aesthetics, history, and more; all of these play roles in many prominent continental theories. This has had the effect of expanding the canon of primary texts of political theory as well as the theoretical resources for understanding both texts and political life. Continental political theory is a broadly interdisciplinary field of inquiry, drawing from the humanities, arts, social sciences, and more recently some of the physical sciences.

The canon of analytic political philosophy is not as widely interdisciplinary as that of continental theory. The canon of analytic political philosophy is largely the canon of ancient, modern, and contemporary western philosophy. Moral philosophy is drawn on extensively, and disciplines such as economics, jurisprudence, and to a lesser degree sociology, political science, and psychology, make appearances in many analytic philosophical texts. For the most part, though, many analytic political philosophers are problem driven and respond to texts that raise the same or related problems, that is, other political philosophical texts. It is tempting to interpret the narrower confines of the analytic canon in terms of the generally different assessments of modernity in the continental and analytic traditions, a temptation I will succumb to in a moment.

Style, interdisciplinarity, and canon play key roles in the modes of argumentation in both traditions of political theory. Add to this the difference over the role of justificatory projects and conceptual analysis, and it is not surprising that theorists on either side of the divide employ different prose styles, incorporate different disciplines, and read and respond to different texts. If a writer is articulating the necessary and sufficient conditions of democratic legitimacy or offering a (hypothetical) public justification, that project likely delimits the writer's style and what disciplines and texts are relevant. If a writer seeks to understand how political regimes constrain sensibility and intelligibility so as to make certain forms of appearance and certain subjects unrecognizable, then how he or she writes and argues, which texts matter, and which disciplines are relevant, will likely be shaped by this concern (see Rancière 2009). All of this contributes to the feeling that what theorists on one side of the divide are doing just isn't *arguing* at all; isn't *political theory* at all; or isn't sufficiently attentive to the *complexity* of political phenomena—at all. This may explain the desire to avoid crossing the divide and, even when the desire is present, the feeling that the barriers to entry are too high given the time we all have spent learning at least one tradition. An aim of this book is to show that to the extent that barriers to entry exist and reasons for mutual shunning are not without merit, they should nonetheless be overcome.

Finally, and to return to the general question of where we are now, the two traditions of political thought differ in their basic sensibilities toward modernity, that is, roughly the period of time that begins with the emergence of capitalism as the dominant mode of economic production and the political era inaugurated by the American and French Revolutions. Another way of naming this time period is to call it the *post-Enlightenment*. Habermas' criticisms of Foucault, Derrida, and the first generation of critical theorists epitomize this second framing of modernity (Habermas 1990). However critical of metaphysical thought, Habermas' "post-metaphysical" philosophy never disavows the redemptive, rationalistic dream of Enlightenment politics, even as it reconceptualizes its philosophical foundation. He accuses Foucault, Derrida, and even the first generation of critical theorists of disavowing the utopic kernel of modern thought and sees this disavowal as politically reactionary. It strikes me that analytic political philosophy shares this Habermasian attitude toward modernity: whatever the problems with the line of political philosophy beginning with Thomas Hobbes and the obvious political disasters of the last few centuries, the enlightenment values and political ideals that shaped the formation of the modern (western) world—both in theory and practice—are to be affirmed.

The pro-modernity attitude of analytic political philosophy likely explains the *relative* disinterest in the political and economic consequences of modernity for the vast majority of the non-western world, that is, those who live outside the North Atlantic regions. While concerns with global justice and capabilities are clear and important exceptions, the framework within which analytic philosophers seek to address the immense economic inequalities and unevenly distributed effects of violence remains the framework of liberalism and/or analytic philosophical justification. The negative effects and consequences of modernization are the subject of a great deal of continental inspired political theory, from the criticisms of secularism in William Connolly, to the varied works of post-colonial theorists like Pheng Cheah and Gayatri Spivak, to the Foucaultian worries about disciplinary and biopolitical regimes in Wendy Brown and Judith Butler, and to the attention to irresolvable paradoxes of democratic legitimacy and liberal values in Bonnie Honig and Chantal Mouffe. Continental political thought is far more ambivalent in its acceptance of liberalism and the moral, political, and epistemic norms that shape normative theories of liberalism. In general, continental theorists have been far more sensitive to, and engaged with, the global costs of modernity than analytic political philosophers; but analytic political philosophers have, perhaps, been importantly reminding us of the benefits of modernity, if not always their unequal distribution across state lines (the same is not true of domestic inequalities, which are a serious, perhaps the foundational, concern of a great deal of contemporary analytic political philosophy).

So far, we have seen how we got here and how things now stand. But where should we go from here?

WHERE SHOULD WE GO NOW? THE NEED FOR CROSS-TRADITION THEORIZING

The chapters in this book are intended to support two big claims. The first claim is that more political theorists and philosophers ought to engage in what I call *cross-tradition theorizing*. The second claim is that what I call *aporetic cross-tradition theorizing* is a viable and attractive mode of cross-tradition theorizing. Given the significant differences between analytic and continental theorizing, an obvious question is why we should bother with cross-tradition theorizing generally, which I will address before arguing for the aporetic mode I prefer.

A basic premise of this book is that many, if not all, fundamental political phenomena are *dense*. Density is, in physics, the ratio of mass to volume, but in political phenomena we can think of density as the ratio of historical mass to simplicity for a phenomenon. For example, the phenomenon of freedom is, presumably, quite simple. To be free, we can learn from the *Oxford English Dictionary*, is, roughly, to be unconstrained (Oxfordians, apparently, all think a great deal of negative liberty). Yet, freedom is a dense phenomenon in the western tradition because of the central place of freedom in political thought and practice since at least the ancient Greeks. Solon's reforms in 594 BC introduced an idea of political freedom and instantiated it constitutionally, and two centuries later the distinction between slaves and free people is made early in Book I of Aristotle's *Politics*. Obviously, freedom continues to be central to our understanding of politics, at least in constitutional liberal democracies. Yet, we have many competing accounts of freedom and its conditions, from the ancient Greeks to the social contract theorists to Isaiah Berlin, Hannah Arendt, and Philip Pettit. The intellectual history of the concept of freedom in political thought is linked to the history of philosophical explorations of metaphysical freedom as well and, more recently, biological and neurological accounts of the questionable freedom of the will. The difficulty of conceptual problems with freedom is perhaps exceeded by the complexity and ambiguities of freedom in political practice. Debates over free speech, civil disobedience, freedom of religion, freedom of the press, the proper form of democratic rule, human rights, and many other issues present obvious instances of this complexity and ambiguity. To be free is to be unconstrained; but in both thought and practice, the density of freedom is apparent. Unpacking that density is difficult, not only because analysis is hard when the constituent features of an object are numerous and so closely bound together but also because political theorists and philosophers are in the business not only of description and analysis but of normative and axiological inquiry. We want to know not only what freedom is—hard enough—but what the value of freedom is and whether we ought to be free or to design institutions that enhance freedom. What is true for freedom is true for justice, equality, legitimacy, coercion, violence, and other fundamental political phenomena.

Dense phenomena are difficult to theorize, and one reason we need cross-tradition theorizing is that we need all the help we can get, from any intellectual tradition that focuses on political thought and practice. This first reason ought to be uncontroversial, although controversy begins when we start to identify which traditions are, in fact, helping rather than harming political understanding. This first reason is, of course, not nearly enough to seal the case for cross-tradition theorizing.

A second and more important reason is that the analytic and continental traditions each respond to a different need, or set of needs, in the face of dense political phenomena. The analytic tradition, in its focus on justification and conceptual analysis, responds to the need, which I think is inescapable, to provide a convincing set of *reasons* why the coercive power of states (or other political institutions) can be used to order our social, economic, and political arrangements. Reason, once it speaks, should be heard. Once we ask "how," "what," and "why" questions—for example, how can primary goods be distributed among citizens?; what is a just distribution of primary goods?; why should we strive for a just distribution of primary goods?—I see no good reason for ignoring those questions. They seem obviously and immediately relevant and, absent a convincing answer to those questions, the whole, often nasty, business of employing coercive power to arrange the world in one way or another becomes deeply suspect. It is unclear, absent a justification, why any of us should accept the way the political world is as more than the arbitrary employment of force for the self-interested purposes of those who have the power to order the world. Perhaps Thrasymachus is right, but we want to *know* if he is right, that is, to be given good reasons for the correctness of his view. The analytic tradition derives its power and persuasiveness from its focus on justificatory issues because coercive power without a justification is deeply, horrifyingly, troubling. We need the analytic project of justification if we aspire to a political life in which we are more than mere objects of power, hostages to the circumstances of our birth and the violent powers that threaten us. The reconciliatory project of political philosophy identified by Rawls is impossible without the justificatory practices of analytic political philosophy (unless a political world without coercion is realized).

The continental tradition—once again keeping in mind the richness and diversity of each tradition that limits what we can say about them generally—responds to the need to recognize the contingent, historical, constructed, reified, and thus often ideological character of our political worlds, and to demand a different, often radically different, political life. There are good reasons to suspect that any justification of a theorized coercive political power bearing any resemblance to the operations of the real coercive power present in our societies is ideological. But there are also good reasons to suspect that any justification will rely on logical analyses of concepts that ignore the density of those concepts, thereby reifying concepts that are, at any moment, products of determinate theoretical and practical struggles. Some continental theorists—Derrida is the most obvious example—are both deeply skeptical and hyper-rationalistic insofar as they strive to go deeper and farther in the quest for justification but, in so doing, come to realize the impossibility of any justification. Starting with

Hegel, though, most continental theorists tend to, in Hegel's words, "tarry with the negative," and in political terms that entails attending to the failings, limitations, contingencies, histories, reifications, and ideologies at work both in theory and political practice (Hegel 1977, 19).

We need cross-tradition theorizing, then, because both the analytic and continental traditions respond to a real political and theoretical need. Of course, the needs I have identified are clearly in tension with one another. One mode of cross-tradition theorizing—what I call the *synthetic* mode—would seek to reconcile the best of both traditions, to respond to both needs. Synthetic cross-tradition theorizing tries to unite the two needs I have identified: the need for justification and the need to take historicity and contingency seriously. I have my doubts about that mode because I think the two needs truly are incompatible. Any justification of political power will have to avoid or repress or reify a contingent historical feature of the society in question; and attention to historicity and contingency cannot but undermine even the desire for justification. The first two chapters of this book are examples of synthetic theorizing intended, in part, to convince you that the synthetic mode is not the way to go. Rather than seeking synthesis, I argue in this book for *aporetic cross-tradition theorizing*.

Aporetic cross-tradition theorizing intensifies, without resolving, the tension between the needs met by the analytic and continental traditions by emphasizing the power, persuasiveness, and incompatibility of a theory of a political phenomenon taken from each tradition. There are at least three good reasons for employing the aporetic mode.

First, and most importantly, if fundamental political phenomena are truly dense, no single theory, or tradition, will be able to analyze phenomena completely. However, no synthesis of theories or traditions will do any better. Synthesis will not work because dense phenomena contain irreconcilable elements, elements we cannot eliminate and cannot unify. This is a consequence of the historical mass unstably held together within a dense phenomenon. Without pushing the atomic metaphor too far, I hope, we can say that a dense phenomenon stabilizes only when it loses one or many of its elements. To take Berlin's famous distinction between positive and negative liberty as an example, we can stabilize our concept of liberty by denying the very idea of positive liberty. If positive liberty requires, as it does in Rousseau, the idea that one can be "forced to be free," and if that idea is a paradox we cannot resolve, then we might think of Rousseauian positive freedom as not liberty at all. While this might stabilize our concept of freedom—in this very simple example, excluding all other accounts of freedom—it does so by changing the phenomenon, by eliminating an influential, historically important definition of freedom. Given an argument, this might be a valid move. However, there are also elements of freedom that cannot be removed from freedom without transforming the phenomenon. This too, of course, requires an argument, and Chapter 3 provides an argument that we can neither dismiss nor fully accept one element of freedom: self-control. Freedom, in short, is an unstable phenomenon, and rather than ignore that fact or transform the phenomenon, we should approach freedom aporetically, that is, theorize freedom as containing incompatible elements or conditions that can be neither eliminated nor reconciled.

If I am right, then we will necessarily arrive at aporias, at blocked paths, paradoxical needs that cannot be met, when we engage in cross-tradition theorizing. This is a bold claim, perhaps too bold, but it is one of the claims of this book. The necessary failure of both individual theories and synthesis is a consequence of the density of political phenomena and the limitations of our intellectual powers. Chapters 3 through 5 are examples of aporetic cross-tradition theorizing in practice, and I hope to show through those chapters that any good theory of a fundamental political phenomenon will capture some necessary feature or property of that phenomenon. I try to show in those chapters that both theories at issue are persuasive and speak to undeniable intuitions about the phenomenon of freedom and of justice; yet they cannot be reconciled. I can see no non-question-begging reason for thinking that one aspect of freedom is more basic or essential than another, nor that one requirement of justice is necessary and another not. Aporetic consequences are due to the density of the phenomenon itself, not just our current intellectual limitations, which, over time, might be overcome through synthesis. We cannot see this, however, without doing the work of putting as many theories into conversation with each other as we can; the more disparate the better. Thus, aporetic cross-tradition theorizing helps us to make sense of dense phenomena by showing us, in the first place, that and how the phenomena are dense.

A second reason for aporetic cross-tradition theorizing is that our intellectual resources are limited—a claim few would seriously dispute—and more importantly and contentiously, must respond to those incompatible intellectual needs mentioned previously. My discussions of the limitations of the synthetic cross-tradition approaches of political realism and Cavellian consent in Chapters 1 and 2 aim to show that we can neither fit the continental need to attend to contingency, history, dissensus, and so forth, into the justificatory mode of analytic theorizing, nor satisfy the analytic need for justifying coercive power by "reading" a justificatory project like Rawls' *Theory of Justice* as a "text." There is a bit of irony in coming to this conclusion thanks to Cavell's reading of Rawls, because it is Cavell's discussion of intellectual needs—drawn from his reading of Immanuel Kant and Wittgenstein—that inspires my own aporetic cross-tradition theorizing. Intellectual needs are discovered by *patiently listening to* Reason's many voices, those polyvocal and often dissonant claims made on our intellect by questions we cannot help but ask in the course of serious inquiry. Not all the voices in our head are entirely sane, of course. To accept an unresolvable tension in our intellectual needs is not to refuse critical analysis of those needs or of their satisfactions. A bad theory is a bad theory, and often we have compelling reasons for criticizing and dismissing both a voice in our head and a theory. An aim of aporetic cross-tradition theorizing, however, is to respond to our competing intellectual needs and their theoretical satisfactions by offering the most persuasive defense of incompatible theories in order to show that the best we can do is discover the limits of our intellect, of both its resources and its needs. This must be *shown* though, not taken for granted, and aporetic cross-tradition theorizing aims to reveal something we need to *know* about our theories and the political world we are trying to understand. It is knowledge that we are seeking, not skepticism. If we must fail to know or understand, that is a positive result, an intellectual advance.

Third, aporetic cross-tradition theorizing reminds us that however abstract and academic political theory might be, in political theory we are explaining and often justifying the all-too-real practices of often violent coercion used on and against the all-too-real embodied individuals with whom we share a political world. Analytic theorizing, in its justificatory mode, *should* remind us that if we are to use coercion against *this* individual, then we ought to have something to say in justification of that coercion. However, the abstract character of analytic theorizing, even in its most political and least metaphysical moments, often ignores—perhaps must ignore—the concrete individuals who are the objects of the practices being justified. A useful test of a justificatory theory, I would suggest, is to imagine offering that justification face-to-face to the real individual affected by coercive power. This may seem cheap, but I often wonder about the emotional fortitude and intellectual self-confidence required to explain to a prisoner one's preferred theory of why he should be in chains. To the extent that continental theorizing returns us—if just as abstractly—to the contingent, embodied, historical life of politics, that theorizing can check the analytic abstraction that blithely justifies some of the nastier realities of politics.

Conversely, if continental theorizing eschews justification, it leaves us with nothing at all to say, normatively, in defense of political practices that many of us are not prepared to give up entirely or at all. I think there is a great deal of evidence that human beings, just to survive much longer, must radically transform their economic and political arrangements. Such a transformation would require, among other things, a massive global expropriation and redistribution of wealth. Whatever else this entails, it surely entails taking things that at present are understood to be the property of some individual or collective, and giving those things in one way or another to another person who, at present, has no property in those things. We also, at present, have the idea that taking things that belong to one person and giving them to someone else must be justified because of the existence of individual property rights. Is an argument against property rights based, for example, on the contingent, constructed, historical character of those rights—the fact that they didn't exist at some time, exist now, and need not exist in the future—enough to justify taking someone's money or other property? I don't see how a critical analysis of the concept of property rights itself could justify taking someone's property unless we make the further argument that any justification of property rights is ideological, that is, a historically contingent justification of a state of affairs that is naturalized by those who stand to benefit from present economic arrangements. However, unless we are relying on a conception of history in which, inevitably, economic arrangements are going to arrive at an economic order without property rights—whether that is metaphysically understood or just the consequence of the psychological, political, and economic consequences of capitalism—then something must be said in justification of a world without property rights and thereby in justification of expropriating the wealth of the few in the service of all. I do not deny that continental theorists can—and perhaps some do—offer such justifications, but if so then they surely have to meet, on the same ground, justifications of capitalism, property rights, unequal distributions of goods, and the like, many of which are found in the analytic tradition.

Aporetic cross-tradition theorizing, or at least my rendition of it, has, at its ethical core the demand of the singular, embodied, all-too-real coerced individual, the simple demand for justification, for an answer to "why?" To remain faithful to the continental need is to remind ourselves of the concrete, lived, contingent, historical realities of *this* individual subjected to political power;

to remain faithful to the analytic need is to remind ourselves that this person has every right to demand a rational, reasonable answer to that question, to demand a justification. I hope the chapters in this book all demonstrate that we must and cannot remain faithful to both demands at the same time. This is the ethical core of aporetic cross-tradition theorizing, and although academic political theory is usually just that—academic—it is nevertheless an academic discourse about contingent employments of power, power that is exercised here and now, but need not be. I would suggest that aporetic cross-tradition theorizing is a powerful expression of the unrealizable but valuable ethical and political ideal of answering to *this* person's subjection to power with reasons *this* person could accept.

Readers of this book in manuscript have raised an important objection that needs to be addressed. The objection is quite straightforward: "You say that we learn, understand, or know, something through aporetic cross-tradition theorizing, but all we come to know is that we don't know, or can't know, enough. Why is this nothing more than setting impossible standards of satisfaction for a political theory? Sure, no theory is perfect, but so what? Moreover, isn't this just a Socratic lesson that teaches us only the limits of what we can know, rather than any concrete, substantive piece of knowledge? I already know that our intellectual resources are limited, but that is true of all intellectual inquiry." This is a powerful objection, and it needs answering, a task this introduction has aimed to accomplish. Let me summarize those answers here.

It is true that aporetic cross-tradition theorizing doesn't itself teach us something new about, say, justice, other than teaching us that no theory of justice is likely to succeed because justice is dense and our intellectual needs are real and in real, unresolvable tension. Only a theory of justice—or a novel, or work of history, or new form of political action or social movement, or some similar endeavor—will teach us something new about justice, and aporetic cross-tradition theorizing doesn't produce new theories of justice, or anything else. To continue with the example of justice, one can read the later Rawls to find out that justice cannot rest, in modern liberal democracies, on metaphysical foundations. And one can read the later Derrida to find out that justice couldn't possibly be fully realized in our polities without metaphysical foundations. Both Rawls and Derrida are right, but if they are both right, then justice both requires and cannot require, for us, now, in our liberal democratic societies (if that is where we live), a metaphysical foundation. If we learn something substantive from aporetic cross-tradition theorizing, it is that dense political phenomena are dense, and we learn more about that density and where it leaves us. Is this too little to learn? Perhaps. However, I don't think so, if only because I think I have learned a great deal more about legitimacy, state violence, freedom, and justice by reading more widely and writing aporetically about those phenomena. The density of the phenomenon of justice came to light only when I put theories from different traditions into conversation with each other, that is, when I wrote about them. We can learn a great deal about justice by writing about Aristotle and Rawls, Rawls and Amartya Sen, Rawls and Thomas Pogge, Rawls and Gaus, and so on. But we learn something very different about justice in writing about Rawls and Derrida. Or so I hope to have shown in Chapter 5.

Does aporetic cross-tradition theorizing set impossible standards for theory-success, only to point out, trivially enough, that the theory fails? Yes, but pointing to the failure of a theory to satisfy an impossible standard is not trivial, because political theories, to say it again, fundamentally concern the imposition of force against individuals. There are things physicists do not understand about the cosmos, and the best physical theories are surely not complete. Is anyone's pain or suffering or deprivation legitimized by the failure of those theories? No (yes, I can think of counter-examples too, but to what end?). Things get a little trickier when we come to economic and moral theory, because a flawed and limited economic or moral theory might very well lead to deprivation or pain; but does the economic or moral theory justify that deprivation? If so, then economic and moral theory share something with political theory. The point remains the same: if we believe, as I do, that intentionally causing pain and suffering and deprivation is prima facie wrong, then political power must be justified. Can a flawed theory of legitimacy satisfy the "why?" of the prisoner? Must it? Can we say to the prisoner, with a straight face, "Yes, yes, I know that this justification of state violence is not perfect, but it's good enough to punish you"? I can't think of a single political theorist whose work explicitly acknowledges this response; but I can think of many ultimately flawed political theories that would have to say as much. I cannot accept that response; it is not good enough, not when we are talking about the flaying of flesh or the destruction of minds. If aporetic cross-tradition theorizing sets impossible standards for political theories, that is because those theories attempt to justify, directly or implicitly, the intentional imposition of pain, suffering, and deprivation. Good enough is not good enough. The commitment to impossible standards of theory-success is ethical, not intellectual. There is no problem with a limited physical theory; such are the limits of human knowledge. A limited political theory that justifies violence, however, is a real problem: an ethical problem.

That brings me to the end of the story: how we got here, where we are, and where we should go. The burden of this book is to show that aporetic cross-tradition theorizing is a viable strategy for navigating the analytic-continental divide, and a valuable mode of political theory. I have found myself unable to shake either tradition, and rather than being faithful to one tradition or drawn and quartered by inescapable ties, I have chosen, in this book, to bring both traditions together and to remain suspended between them, in a tolerable amount of pain, but without being dismembered.

THE STRUCTURE OF THIS BOOK

I have chosen to focus on five thinkers and one "movement" in political theory. The continental side of things is represented by Arendt, Derrida, and in the first chapter, by Cavell's synthetic mode of theorizing. The analytic side is represented by political realism (as an example of a synthetic mode), Pettit, and Rawls. Some might question my choice of Pettit to represent the analytic tradition, but his work is undoubtedly in that tradition, both in aim (it intends to justify both a theory of political freedom and a form of government) and in method. Given the wealth of theorists in both traditions, my choices say as much about my interests in political theory as they do about the divide more broadly. I hope those convinced by this book will carry out their own cross-tradition work, whether in an aporetic, synthetic, or some other possible mode.

Chapters 1 and 2 explore two synthetic cross-tradition possibilities, although only one of the possibilities, Stanley Cavell's interpretation of consent and the social contract, is self-consciously a crossing of traditions. While the central focus of each of these chapters is the theory itself, each chapter begins by showing how Cavell and political realists are engaging in synthetic cross-tradition theorizing. The chapters end with a discussion of how, and why, the synthetic mode fails to get a grip on a central political phenomenon: state violence. These "bookends" foreshadow my discussion in the final chapter.

Chapter 1 is a discussion of the *political realism* we find in contemporary political theory. Inspired by the work of Bernard Williams and Raymond Geuss, the distinctive claim of realists of all stripes is the rejection of "moralist" approaches to politics, on display most prominently in philosophers such as the early John Rawls, G. A. Cohen, and Robert Nozick. Realists today are working to develop a "political" rather than moralist theory of legitimacy, relying on

values and norms internal to politics. Any realist theory of legitimacy will likely
find itself in trouble, however, when it turns to the problem of state violence, a
central practice within any state. A realist theory of legitimacy will fail to find
political norms that can justify state violence and ensure a distinction between
legitimate force and illegitimate violence. The chapter ends with my suggestion
for realists dealing with the problem of violence: give up the attempt to find a
realist theory of legitimacy, and thereby become even more "realist."

Chapter 2 turns to the philosopher Stanley Cavell, who occupies a unique
position between the analytic and continental traditions. His work—informed
by Wittgenstein and J. L. Austin, Nietzsche and Heidegger, and Ralph Waldo
Emerson and Henry David Thoreau—attempts to expand upon the problems
and solutions of both traditions in philosophy of language, epistemology, moral
philosophy, and political theory. Cavell's unique interpretation of the social
contract tradition, seen in the light of the putative legitimacy of state violence,
is far more problematic than it might at first appear. If a crucial aim of classical
consent theory and the social contract is to legitimize state violence, Cavell's
interpretation not only fails, *in fact*, to respond to that aim, it also cannot, *in
principle*, respond to the moral problem of state violence. Like realist legitimacy,
Cavellian consent runs into significant problems when confronted with the
legitimacy of state violence. This chapter reinforces the conclusion of the first,
both on the substantive issue and, more broadly, with respect to the possibilities
of synthetic cross-tradition theorizing.

Chapters 3 and 4 offer a detailed discussion of the two most powerful contemporary theorists of political freedom: Hannah Arendt and Philip Pettit. Both
theorists offer the two most attractive alternatives to freedom as conceived in the
liberal tradition. The centrality of freedom in both Arendt's and Pettit's work is
not the only link between them. They both share a commitment to republican
political ideas and institutions. However, in a variety of important, and perhaps
ultimately incommensurable, respects, Pettit and Arendt disagree greatly about
the "ground" of freedom, its description, and the relation of these philosophical and phenomenological accounts of freedom *as such* to political freedom.

In Chapter 3 I argue that these two accounts, however opposed, each point
us toward a crucial aspect of freedom downplayed, undertheorized, or simply
ignored in the other account. Bluntly stated, there is a tension between freedom
as control of the self by the self and freedom as the initiation of newness through
action, an experience of non-sovereign, spontaneous activity that requires the
absence of all control. There is a tension because Arendt and Pettit can both

appeal to intuitions and ordinary language to support their claims, and yet it seems clear that freedom cannot both require, and not require, control.

I first examine Pettit's and Arendt's theories of freedom *as such* in order to show the place of control in each account and, at least in the case of Arendt, to reconstruct an at times unclear set of descriptions and claims into a coherent phenomenology of freedom. The aim of the chapter is to show that the place of control in freedom is something we can neither accept fully nor do without, because the experiences and values associated with freedom as control and freedom as spontaneous activity are too central both to our conceptions of freedom and to our individual and collective lives.

Chapter 4 builds on the previous chapter by demonstrating that the standoff between Pettit's and Arendt's conclusions about freedom *as such* shapes and produces a conflict between their accounts of political freedom as well. Once again the issue is control, but the political consequence of control is a conflict between two ways of conceiving the relationship of freedom to the structure of rule. For Pettit, non-dominating freedom is not only possible under legitimate rule but enabled and protected by a legitimate democratic regime. Arendt, however, suggests in a number of places that *isonomy*—which she defines as a structure of "no-rule"—is the "regime" most conducive to freedom.

Both Pettit and Arendt face real difficulties, though, in their arguments for republican democracy and isonomy. On the one hand, Pettit cannot successfully distinguish his version of republicanism from the moralized versions he opposes in Rousseau and Kant. This raises serious questions about the possibility of distinguishing legitimate from illegitimate government interference without reference to a moralized conception of the common good and freedom. On the other hand, Arendtian isonomy faces real difficulties when we think seriously about how to institutionalize a condition of "no-rule." For whatever the value of freedom as disclosive action, without a stable space for political action freedom is only the fleeting experience of a lucky few. Arendt's attempts to think through the institutionalization of the political reveal just how problematic isonomy becomes as a stable structure of "rule."

In Chapter 5 I explore Rawls' and Derrida's accounts of the concept and various conceptions of justice because when read together, Rawls and Derrida expose a deep, and often recognized, difficulty in modern political thought: can we do without metaphysics in political theorizing?

Rawls and Derrida navigate this debate, albeit from opposite directions: they both try to articulate a post-metaphysical conception of justice by tying it to the specific legal and political *history* of the West. The central innovation in Rawls' views, from *Theory of Justice* to *Political Liberalism*, is to replace "metaphysical" foundations for justice as fairness with historical "foundations." Rawls, in an attempt to dispense with metaphysics, turns to a specific historical tradition. Drawing upon a Kantian lineage, Derrida argues that justice is *unconditional* but *must* be rendered, however impossibly, in *law*: specifically, and explicitly, the law as it has developed in the western constitutional tradition.

In both cases, history *cannot* provide normative validity to justice without presupposing a metaphysic of history that neither Derrida nor Rawls can endorse. In both cases we are left with a compelling problem that has no obvious answer: we can neither dispense with metaphysics nor, for familiar Rawlsian reasons, use it to ground politics and law in modern liberal democracies. If this claim is correct, then we political theorists face some serious difficulties.

The concluding chapter makes three claims in defense of aporetic cross-tradition theorizing, and summarizes the reasons why the synthetic mode is not as viable an alternative. It also "applies" the results of Chapter 5 to the problem of reparations for America's long and continuing history of brutal enslavement and oppression of black Americans, considering specifically Ta-Nehisi Coates' influential "The Case for Reparations." I argue that Coates' case betrays his reliance on a specific American jeremiadic tradition and can succeed only if we accept metaphysical presuppositions of the jeremiadic tradition. His argument's power rests on those presuppositions, but cannot succeed because of them. The aporia of justice in its relationship to history and metaphysics can no more be mastered by Coates than by Rawls or Derrida.

1

POLITICAL REALISM, LEGITIMACY, AND STATE VIOLENCE

POLITICAL REALISM **NAMES** a diverse but overlapping set of theories that offer a serious and challenging alternative to what Bernard Williams calls "political moralism."[1] On the realist account, moralists—John Rawls (arguably), Robert Nozick, G. A. Cohen, and many others—see the political as a sphere to be, at least in theory, understood in terms of, and constrained by, moral theory and pre-political moral commitments.[2] Realists reject political moralism and embrace a mode of political theorizing attentive to what they take to be inescapable in politics: deep and often irresolvable conflict. Realists disagree, however, over the prospect and conditions of a realist theory of legitimacy. Many realists share with moralists a concern with a *normative* conception of state legitimacy, even though realists cannot appeal to pre-political moral conceptions of justice, fairness, equality, freedom, or fundamental rights.[3] Realists must find within the concept and practices of politics itself the materials to construct a normative conception of legitimacy. Williams outlines this project in his influential essay "Realism and Moralism in Political Theory," and those realists interested in legitimacy have been inspired by Williams' work.

Political realism is fascinating on its own, but its pertinence to this book goes beyond the inherent interest of the movement. Political realism largely operates within an analytic philosophical idiom, yet many realists emphasize phenomena and concepts more commonly attended to in continental political theory. Political realism, I argue, is a type of *synthetic cross-tradition theorizing.* Consider that the substance (although not the rhetoric) of the following statement from the French theorist Jacques Rancière is fully realist: "We will be testing the following hypothesis: that what is called 'political philosophy' might well be the set of reflective operations whereby philosophy tries to rid itself of politics, to suppress a scandal in thinking proper to the exercise of politics. This theoretical scandal is nothing more than the rationality of disagreement" (Rancière 1999, xii). Rancière's focus on disagreement as proper politics; Carl Schmitt's emphasis on the friend/enemy distinction as the basic political relationship; Bonnie Honig's critique of political philosophy as evading or displacing politics: these themes, common enough in the continental political theoretical literature, are political realism's point of departure. Just why political realism has emerged now, and in implicitly cross-traditional form, is likely a consequence of the work of realism's ur-theorists: Bernard Williams and Raymond Geuss. Williams' metaethical, ethical, and political ideas, as well as his humanistic and historical approach to philosophy, put him at odds with many mainstream analytic views even though he is undoubtedly an analytic philosopher. Geuss shares with Williams a deeply historical approach to philosophy and has always engaged works in the continental tradition, especially critical theory. Realists influenced by Williams and Geuss, whether methodologically or substantively, are well placed to move beyond the confines of the analytic tradition because they take seriously the contingent expressions of political identity, value, and institutions found in everyday political life.

Realism presents one possible synthetic mode of cross-tradition theorizing, and beyond the merits of political realism itself, I want to see whether or not cross-tradition theorizing in a synthetic mode is a possibility worth pursuing. Evidence for the plausibility of a synthetic approach would be its ability to get a grip on the continental problems of historicity, contingency, and ideology that often slip through the grasp of analytic theory, while nonetheless working in an analytic idiom.

To that broader end, but with more local concerns, this chapter focuses on a surprising absence in the realist literature: a concern with the normative legitimacy of practices of state violence.[4] Political realism echoes themes from realism in international relations but it does not appear to share a similar interest in state violence.[5] Yet, the concept of state legitimacy is inseparable from the problem of state violence. This problem is most acutely posed in, but not confined to, the classical contract theorists. In the absence of pre-political foundations for the state, something must justify the state's use of violence if that use is to be normatively distinguished from illegitimate uses of violence.

It does not appear that realists have taken up the question of the legitimacy of state violence in their attempts to theorize legitimacy in a realist mode.

Realists will find that state violence is a stumbling block in their cross-tradition synthetic attempts to justify state legitimacy without appeals to morality. The threat of violence is one of the primary reasons politics is called for, at least in realist theorizing of the sort we find in Williams. Any attempt to justify state violence to those individuals or groups targeted by it must therefore pass a justificatory bar that is, I will argue, too high to reach. Realists must show that state violence is of a different normative order from the violence a citizen faces outside of politics, and yet they must do so without appeals to pre-political moral ideas and theories. If this is right, then there is no possible normative *political* justification of state violence to the individual being treated violently by the state. Any realist justification of legitimacy will fail to justify state violence and thus fail to account for an essential reason why we want justified legitimate states in the first place. Realists cannot synthesize the two intellectual needs described in the introduction: the justificatory need to answer the "why?" of the coerced and the need to take seriously the concrete, all-too-real individuals who suffer from state violence.

What follows is a three-part argument. First, I show that state violence is importantly different from other forms of state coercion and raises a special problem for political realism. Second, I turn to realist theories of legitimacy—primarily Williams' seminal version—in order to show that a justification of state violence and, thereby, state legitimacy cannot succeed when offered to individuals subjected to state violence. Third, I propose a *Hobbesian principle* as a way to clarify just why realist theories of legitimacy will not be able to justify state violence, and argue that realists should accept this Hobbesian principle.

COERCION AND VIOLENCE

A key premise of my argument is that violence is qualitatively different from other forms of coercion.[6] Coercive acts—leaving aside threats—logically require that the coerced are resistant to whatever is being demanded of them.[7] It makes little sense to speak of coercion when paying an income tax that funds various government programs one supports even if, ceteris paribus, one would rather not pay any taxes and still get the benefits. Free-riding might make for a happier citizen, but coercion is not at issue in that example. Some citizens might, however, be resistant to taxation as such or to the programs supported by tax revenue. In that case, the state's enforceable demand that taxes must be paid is coercive and the threats of non-compliance pertinent and a constraint upon choice. So much is fairly uncontroversial.

A subset of coercive state actions is violent coercion. Defining violence is a contentious issue, but let's assume that domestic actions like imprisonment and the death penalty are obviously violent insofar as they meet the *Oxford English Dictionary* definition of violence as the "deliberate exercise of physical force against a person, property, etc.; physically violent behavior or treatment." Some state activities in international affairs are also violent, but the focus here will be on the domestic context. There is a difference in kind, a difference that makes a difference for our understanding of state legitimacy, between violent and non-violent coercive acts.

Violent state acts target basic features or aspects of an individual, of both their body and their mind: let's call these features *minimal conditions of normal human agency*.[8] Without getting lost in the philosophy of action, we can identify at least four plausible conditions of normal human agency: (1) life itself, (2) freedom of movement, (3) freedom of choice, and (4) psychological integrity.

Conditions 1 and 2 should be uncontroversial. On a roughly Davidsonian account of agency and action, a dead human being is not an agent because post-mortem movements cannot be truly described as intentional actions (Davidson 2001, 46). As for 2, if an agent is constrained in movement then agency is constrained along a spectrum ranging from a restriction on performable actions to being unable to act in any meaningful sense at all.[9]

Conditions 3 and 4 may appear more controversial, but only at first glance. We all face constraints on our choices, but attending to the limitations on choice faced by the prisoner are revealing. The constraints on choice faced by the prisoner are more elemental for they are severe constraints on quotidian choices that a typical adult rarely confronts. For example, the prisoner has little to no choice over which clothes to wear or when to go inside or outside the cell. The mundanity of the actions limited by imprisonment reveals a significant and pervasive loss of agency when freedom of choice is so constrained. Much of what an adult takes for granted as within their power of choice is lost under conditions of imprisonment.

Condition 4, a loss of psychological integrity, is documented in research on the negative psychological and physical effects of imprisonment. At one extreme are "supermax" prisons and solitary confinement. Craig Haney writes that "there is not a single published study of solitary or supermax-like confinement in which non-voluntary confinement lasting longer than 10 days . . . failed to result in negative psychological effects" (Haney 2003, 132). These effects, ranging in severity but with generally high prevalence rates (over 50% of inmates), include hallucinations, suicidal thoughts and behavior, uncontrollable anger, and depression. Even in normal prison settings *prisonization* takes place, that is, the adjustment to the "abnormal" norms of prison life. These adjustments include loss of independence and initiative, loss of self-regulation of behavior, heightened distrust and suspicion of others, diminished self-worth, and other impairments (Haney 2002, 79–84). Prisonization takes a toll on the self of the prisoner, and while the negative effects are not necessarily irreversible, within the prison it is clear that the majority of inmates must negotiate a significant change in their sense of self in order to survive the institution. The loss of spontaneity and initiative is a significant diminishment of normal adult human agency.

These conditions, and their being unfulfilled or restricted, give us reason to see a clear and significant difference between violent and non-violent coercion. Tax policy might annoy individuals deeply attached to their money and its purchasing power, but barring a manifestly unfair system of taxation, it is hard to associate any significant harm to the minimal conditions of agency with the enforcement of tax codes. Tax policies do not directly target freedom of movement or autonomy in decision making, much less psychological integrity or life itself. The same holds true for legislation passed against a citizen's personal wishes, or for the outcomes of elections. A citizen may disagree with a particular piece of legislation and yet the harm done does not—under normal circumstances—threaten the minimal conditions of agency. Even extremely controversial issues like abortion may deeply offend a citizen's political, moral, and religious sensibilities, but it is hard to imagine, much less assess, what significant harm is done to the agency of the citizen forced to abide the legalization of abortion. This holds true even for the anti-abortion tax-averse citizen who must abide their tax dollars supporting a government program subsidizing abortion. The "harm" may be spiritual or moral as well as economic, but provided the tax in question is not obviously unfair, the "harm" done leaves the citizen's agency intact.

Violent coercion, however, attacks the minimal conditions of agency and it does so not for the sake of the individual but for the sake of other individuals. Imprisonment is not an example of a coercive act in which the coerced individual can be expected to say, "All things considered I would rather not be imprisoned for the sake of other people, but insofar as I desire a safe, secure society; and I am a threat to that; I should go to jail." Some convicted individuals might say something along those lines, but that makes of going to jail a supererogatory act, a species of martyrdom or self-sacrifice for the good of others. There is no reason for incredulity in hearing a convicted murderer on the way to the death chamber or a professor on the way to the drunk tank assert that they are being *wrongly* harmed. Why is incredulity not out of order here whereas we have good reasons to be suspicious of cries of significant harm when the state takes a bit of someone's income to support programs they abhor?

The answer will come out more fully in the next section, but briefly: there is no possible *normative political justification* of state violence to the individual being treated violently by the state. *Political justification* should be understood in the sense intended by realists, that is, an *acceptable* justification of state violence addressed to the object of state violence that draws mainly (perhaps solely) on normative *political* concepts, not pre-political moral concepts. If we take the latter requirement seriously and imagine what we *really* could or would or must say in the way of justification to the object of state violence, we will find not only absurdity, but horror, the political equivalent of "the beatings will continue until morale improves." That is why violence is different. Violence harms any and every individual in obvious and undeniable ways. Jeremy Bentham rightly insisted that "all punishment is mischief: all punishment in itself is evil" (Bentham 1988, 170). Punishment harms and it must be accounted for *as such*.

Violence is a different kind of coercion. The only kind of justification that *could* legitimize violence is moral. This is why the difference of violence from non-violent coercion makes a difference in theorizing state legitimacy. Political realists must either turn to moralism or give up on justifying state violence. If the former is not an option, and the latter is essential to any plausible theory of state legitimacy, then realist theories of legitimacy must look left to rocks and right to hard places. The rest of the chapter defends this conclusion.

REALIST THEORIES OF LEGITIMACY

The main outlines of a realist theory of legitimacy—seminally found in Williams—will be quickly glossed here so that we can focus on two specific features of the theory.[10] Williams identifies a "first political question," the question of how to secure order, protection, safety, trust, and the conditions of cooperation (Williams 2005, 3). This question is prior to questions of justice because securing the conditions of cooperation and security is the precondition of answering questions about justice. A legitimate regime must satisfy the "basic legitimation demand" (BLD): the solution to the first political question must be acceptable to, at least ideally, *each* member of the polity.[11] A minimum requirement for acceptability is that the solution to the first political question is better than the problem it is meant to solve, and insofar as any political order must coerce some of its members, any members coerced by the state can demand a justification for why and how that coercion is better than the problem. An axiom of politics, Williams asserts without argument, is that might does not make right. The sheer fact of being able to coerce is no justification for the coercion. The BLD can only be met in certain ways, but how the BLD is met in a particular time and place cannot be determined by universal, pre-political moral ideals.

A possible objection might be raised now, and it is worth getting it out of the way. Williams is offering a realist theory of the legitimacy of the *state*, not of the *violence* of the state, or any other coercive practice. It might seem that my argument is a non sequitur because it is focused on a specific state practice, violent coercion, rather than on the state as such. This objection, while understandable, fails, and it is important to see why. What is legitimate when we say "the state is legitimate"? The state of course. For Williams, at least, this appears to mean something quite different from, for example, the "person" of the state that we find in Hobbes. If the state is Hobbes' "artificial man," then it makes sense to distinguish between the person and the actions of the person. Any individual's action might be illegitimate or immoral even though the person's own legitimacy or authority is not thereby challenged. Thus, a state can wrong a citizen of the state, or a subset of citizens, without the state becoming obviously illegitimate.

Williams, however, seems to equate state legitimacy with meeting the BLD, which is met by providing an "acceptable" answer to the demands of those *coerced* by the state (Williams 2005, 4–5). He writes: "meeting the BLD can be equated with there being an 'acceptable' solution to the first political question," and later he adds, "if the power of one lot of people over another is to represent a solution to the first political question, and not itself be part of the problem, *something* has to be said to explain (to the less empowered, to concerned bystanders, to children being educated in this structure, etc.) what the difference is between the solution and the problem" (Williams 2005, 4). In short: we find out whether a state is legitimate by listening to the state's justifications of coercion and, further, by finding out whether the audience finds that justification acceptable. If this is right as an account of Williams, and perhaps realist theories of legitimacy more broadly, then it makes no sense to speak of a legitimate state unless its *coercive* actions are acceptably justified. In short, what needs justification for Williams is not the state's non-coercive activities, but *what the state does coercively*. This is why the objection fails: if what the state can say to its citizens/subjects can never satisfy the realist demands for a political justification of violent coercive state actions, then the state cannot offer an acceptable answer to the first political question, and hence cannot be fully legitimate in realist terms. With that objection out of the way, let's look more closely at two features of Williams' theory: (1) the criterion of acceptability, and (2) the requirement that a justification of legitimacy must "make sense" (MS) as an *intelligible* order of authority (Williams 2005, 10).

Before moving on to MS we should take seriously the criterion of acceptability itself. Matt Sleet criticizes Williams for offering a moralistic conception of acceptability insofar as the idea of the BLD being acceptable to *each* person implies a moral conception of the equal moral mattering of each person (Sleat 2010, 496). Why else would we need to justify the BLD to each individual if each individual has no moral claim on our, and the state's, attention? Sleat points out that the constituency for whom the BLD must be acceptably met at any one time is itself a normative political question that can be answered only within a historical context, and therefore who must be provided with an acceptable justification is not clear in advance. However, once the constituency is determined, then each member of it must be given an acceptable justification of the state's legitimacy. As Sleat puts it, a necessary but not sufficient condition of legitimacy is satisfying the BLD, but we also need a determination of the contextually variable constituency to whom a justification must be given (Sleat 2010, 497; 2014, 38–39).

If the constituency to whom the BLD must be acceptably met is variable and often itself a political matter, then what about those who do not accept the state's response to the BLD but are within the pertinent constituency? Answering that question turns on

1. whether the answer to the BLD must be (a) accepted or (b) simply acceptable (and if acceptable, then according to what criteria of acceptability);
2. assuming 1a and a lack of unanimity, how many must accept (see Horton 2010, 443)?
3. assuming 1a, must the acceptance of the justification of legitimacy be total, or can individuals "partition" their acceptance so that some features of the state are legitimate, some not?

Assuming 1a for now and moving on to 2, it is surely inevitable that not everyone will accept the justification offered by a state. For those individuals, John

Horton is right in arguing that even though some may not accept the legitimacy of the state, that viewpoint, while important, should not be authoritative: that is, it need not force us to call into question the legitimacy of the state (Horton 2010, 443). What matters, as Paul Sagar points out, is that the state *offers* a justification, for in the absence of even the attempt to justify the state *there is no political relationship at all* between the state and a subject or group, but only sheer domination (Sagar 2016, 371).

Williams' example of a non-constituent group experiencing non-political domination within the state is the Helots in Sparta, and to them, Williams argues, there is nothing to be said. The Helots have every right and reason to revolt (Williams 2005, 5). For those individuals or groups who are incorporated into the state but are radically disadvantaged vis-à-vis the state—that is, are reasonably fearful of coercion, pain, torture, humiliation, suffering, and death at the hands of the state—the BLD cannot be met (Williams 2005, 4–5). Examples of such radically disadvantaged individuals or groups have included slaves, various racial and religious minorities, and certain classes of workers (and this list is hardly exhaustive). One quite problematic answer to 3 is to follow Williams in thinking that a state's authority might be "imperfectly" legitimized relative to a radically disadvantaged group (Williams 2005, 5).

For my purposes here the question is: does a *political relationship* exist between the state and an individual when the state employs violent coercion? Or: is anyone subject to state violence radically disadvantaged so that no justification of the legitimacy of the state is acceptable, or "perfect"?

Given what we know about the effects of state violence, are those subjects harmed by it no longer in a political relationship with the state at all? How one answers this question depends, in part, on what one makes of Foucault's analyses of "the great confinement," or Giorgio Agamben's post-Foucaultian account of bare life in the state of exception and the further question of how to define a political relationship (Foucault 1988; Agamben 1998). The issue, in short, is whether an incarcerated population is incorporated into the state at all. Any answer will be context specific, but it is plausible that in many states prison populations are not, or are no longer, constituents within the state, and thus are not in a political relationship with the state at all. If that is correct, then on realist grounds, incarcerated individuals are, in Hobbesian terms, in a state of war with the state. To them, the violence of the state has no acceptable justification.

If incarcerated populations are incorporated into the state, it is more than plausible—is it even deniable?—that prisoners and those facing corporal and capital punishments are radically disadvantaged with respect to the state, for the state *is* the source of coercion, pain, and in some cases torture, humiliation, suffering, and death. The state no longer protects prisoners and death row inmates from fear, pain, and death, but inflicts it. How, or why, a prisoner can or ought to find such treatment "acceptable," even when offered a justification, is unclear.

The conclusion to draw from these considerations is that in the face of state violence, the requirement that such violence could or would, much less ought to, be accepted by the objects of that violence fails to be satisfied. On Williams' own argument for what is an acceptable justification of state coercion, it is unclear how the BLD can be met when raised by individuals subjected to state violence. For those subjected to state violence, the solution to the first political problem is usually no better than the problem, hence the state will not (cannot?) be accepted as legitimate.

Moving on to MS, let's assume that the BLD can in principle be met even for those facing state violence. How would the justification proceed? A key idea in many realist theories of legitimacy, including Williams', is the hermeneutic necessity of interpreting politics and practices of politics in order to identify those political norms to be later employed in political justifications of the state or its practices. Andrea Sangiovanni argues for a practice-dependent institutionalism in which justifications of a conception of justice (and not only its implementation) must consider the nature and purpose of the institutions to be regulated (Sangiovanni 2008; 2016). Central to Sangiovanni's approach is an interpretation of the point and purpose of an institution (Sangiovanni 2008, 148).

It is telling that Sangiovanni, following Ronald Dworkin, draws on analogies with aesthetic interpretation without seriously reflecting on the issues raised by the differences between interpreting a work of art and a social institution:

> In achieving both tasks, the interpreter seeks to understand the institution (or set of institutions) as an integral whole, whose parts work together in realizing a unique point and purpose. This constraint is given by the task of interpretation rather than by the practice itself; the various elements that make up the main social and political institutions of a system—like the various elements of a work of art—may not immediately seem to cohere or work together at all. Trying to connect and arrange them as parts of a coherent whole is a requirement of interpretive charity. (Sangiovanni 2008, 149; see also Sangiovanni 2016, 19–20; and Dworkin 1986, 52)

Leaving aside questions about aesthetic interpretation itself, Robert Cover, in a blistering criticism of Dworkin that applies equally to Sangiovanni, made clear just what is missing from an aestheticized hermeneutics of legal judgment: the practices of state violence set in motion by legal interpretations and decisions (Cover 1986). In law and politics—but not (we hope) in museums and art history seminars—interpretations justify the infliction of pain and suffering. If we can have reasonable disagreements about the point and purpose of an institution, what consequences for the persuasiveness of a justification of state violence follow given that political interpretations justify real violence?

The absence of attention to violence justified by a justification of state legitimacy is equally apparent in the recent work of Enzo Rossi. Rossi draws, albeit critically, on Sangiovanni's hermeneutical practice-dependent view to further his attempt to articulate a viable realist theory of legitimacy. For Rossi, a viable realist theory of legitimacy requires us to bracket the problem of justice and focus on a justification of legitimacy reliant on a hermeneutical account of the point and purpose of politics in a given context. The question of legitimacy focuses on "why we need politics in the first place" (Rossi 2012, 157). Nobody can seriously dispute that the question what is politics for?—even asked of a specific polity—admits of competing reasonable answers: it is, as realists accept, a matter of interpretation. But once again, how can we rest a justification of something as impactful and grave as state violence on nothing more than an interpretation?

Returning to Williams, his introduction of MS is meant to serve two purposes. First, it undermines the tendency of political moralism to universalize norms of legitimacy internal to modern liberal polities, which norms are then used to show the illegitimacy of non-liberal states. Second and more importantly, "our" justifications of legitimacy must MS and be *normative* for us. What counts for those of us living in liberal polities as an acceptable justification of state legitimacy must be intelligible to us as an order of authority with normative force (Williams 2005, 11). Liberal states, for example, usually exclude justifications reliant on specific religious beliefs and on distinctions between citizens based on race, class, caste, gender, sexuality, and so on. But why are such justifications not only unlikely to succeed in liberal states but also excluded as intelligible orders of authority?

The answer is not to be settled by moral theory. Just as in the later Rawls (see Chapter 5), the answer depends on the distinctive and disputed political history of Western Europe and North America. What MS to us makes sense in light of our interpretations of the history that has brought us to this point in time and space. Of course, the concept of the political is itself open to interpretation, so any axioms we might extract from the concept are as contestable as the lessons we might draw from the history of a given political culture. Interpretation plays a central role in a realist theory of legitimacy because the norms appealed to must be political norms. Insofar as there are and have been a wide variety of different polities—a fact realists take seriously—we are unlikely to find many, if any, universal political norms. We must instead interpret the historical development of polities themselves: their theories, institutions, practices, and transformations.

To take the United States as one example, we should look to constitutional history, the development of political institutions in the pre-independence colonies, the growth of capitalism, the institution of chattel slavery and post-reconstruction racial injustice and violence, the extermination and encampment of indigenous peoples, American imperialism, and so on. These developments don't reveal their own purposes clearly and incontestably, and therefore the realist must interpret those developments so as to discover the point, the purposes, of these developments and related political practices. These purposes are the raison d'être of a polity, and they provide norms on the basis of which we understand what makes sense to Americans as an acceptable justification of the legitimacy of the United States. Given the contestable nature of any interpretation, any justification of the state will be far less than obvious even to those living within the state.

Two problems emerge from the centrality of interpretation in a realist theory of legitimacy if we consider how a state must be acceptably justified to each member of the polity, especially those who are the objects of state violence. First, there is the obvious difficulty in employing what is, at best, a powerful and persuasive *interpretation* of political history and political norms in the service of a justification of state violence. The problem is most acute in the context of a polity with a racist and genocidal past. To return to the United States, here are two plausible sketches of American political history. Drawing on local political practices in New England towns, resistance to British rule, a revolutionary war, the Declaration of Independence and the United States Constitution, the Civil War, the civil rights movements, and so on, we can tell the story of a flawed, always imperfect, realization of a deep and legally instantiated commitment to individual freedom and equality, a history of halting progress in the actualization of core human rights, self-government, political freedom, and private liberty. Or, starting with the legalized brutalities of chattel slavery and the genocide of indigenous peoples, settler colonialism in the West, Jim Crow, violent suppression of labor movements and strikes, imperial ambitions and expansionism from the Monroe doctrine to the Philippines, Korea, Vietnam, Iraq, and so on, we can tell the story of a polity founded in genocide and committed to the global domination of capitalism, white straight men, and Christianity. Each story is plausible, each story selective, each story support for very different political norms.

Now, imagine that we are trying to justify violent coercion, say imprisonment, to an African-American man in a major American city in the year 2017. And let's imagine that the justification involves recourse to the first of the stories briefly outlined here. Do we have any reason to expect, much less a right to demand, that the order of authority will MS to this man? He might, as a matter of fact, accept that story. But what if he finds the second story far more intelligible, far more sensible: for him, *that* story MS? It is not unreasonable to say of this man that, given his plausible interpretation of the polity and its political norms, he is already "radically disadvantaged" not only by the "incompetence" of the state to protect him, but by the very norms of the polity itself (Williams 2005, 5). If the man refuses to accept the state's justification of the legitimacy of its violence even before the question of state violence arises, is that unreasonable? What is a realist theory of legitimacy to do in this situation?

More broadly, even in the best of circumstances, resting a justification of state violence on an interpretation of the political norms of a community opens that justification to reasonable contestation via alternative interpretations. If what is at stake in a particular act of coercion is a tax, or even a more contentious issue like abortion or the death penalty or euthanasia, there is room for the realist point that those who are coerced are neither morally wrong nor wrong at all: they have simply *lost* a political battle (Williams 2005, 13, 83–87). Having lost politically is not, in a reasonably democratic state, a political, much less literal, death sentence. The fight can continue and, meanwhile, the "losers" can live their lives roughly as they have before.[12]

In the case of state violence, however, the minimal conditions of agency are at stake. If the violence of the state is to be more than domination then that violence must be justified to the object of state violence. A contestable interpretation of political history and the norms drawn from it is too weak a support on which to rest that justification, for state violence returns the object of that violence to the condition that raises the first political question. In what sense can one say to the victim of state violence that their condition now is better than the condition of insecurity that the political is meant to solve? Or that their treatment is justified because of a mere interpretation?

Moving on to the second problem, are we likely to find a political norm to the effect that the polity exists *for the sake of* violence? The idea that a state does or is likely to have as a *purpose* of its existence the enactment of violence against some or all or any of its citizens is not only historically rare but such a state cannot satisfy the BLD, at least to those who are the object of the violence. If this is correct, no realist theory of legitimacy can rely on political norms to justify to the object of state violence the state's monopolization on and employment of the means of legitimate violence. This is a strong claim and might appear objectionable for a number of reasons, at least one being that the same conclusion holds true of coercive actions, like taxation. After all, taxation is not a, or the, goal of political organization, at least on most understandings of politics.

Taxation and punishment, the objection continues, are not goals of the state but *instruments* in the service of goals and purposes like security and the provision of basic services. The realist need not appeal directly to a political norm in order to justify taxation or state violence so long as those who will the ends will the means. If money is required for a political goal then taxation is an effective and potentially fair means of raising funds. If security against violent threats is a political goal then violent punishments are an effective means for realizing that goal.

While this may be true of taxation, violence is different because the harm posed to the object of state violence is incontestably a harm *to that individual*, to the minimal conditions of agency. A direct tax to support public education may "harm" an individual if they send their kids to private schools, because they now have less money than before on account of supporting a service from which they do not directly benefit. However, the causality is complex, and what constitutes a benefit and a harm is not always clear in such cases. With state violence the harm done is clear, and the set of beneficiaries of the violence necessarily excludes the object of state violence. A prisoner going to jail enters, as it were, a different society. The prisoner doesn't benefit, even indirectly, from imprisonment.

One might raise a different objection at this point because the prisoner can be understood to benefit from being imprisoned if, for example, they are "rehabilitated" or if, through punishment, they are treated with the respect due to them as an autonomous, free, rational being. This objection fails, however, at least from a realist perspective. For these justifications of imprisonment are obviously pre-political *moral* justifications, not political justifications. The Kantian appeal to moral respect holds outside of politics as well and enters into politics only through the institutionalization of that moral ideal. It is as clear a case of "applied ethics" as one can find. The same holds true for the rehabilitation argument because it implies a conception of the moral person and of better and worse moral states that are applied to punishment in order to justify it.

The difference made by the difference of violence from other forms of coercion is clear: in other cases of coercion even what is a benefit and what a harm of the coercion is always contestable. The opposite is true of state violence: the object of violence is incontestably harmed, the community as a whole (although not necessarily each individual) surely benefits from the removal of a criminal, and the imprisoned does not benefit at all (excepting the moral ideas of benefit cited a moment ago). The maxim that a criminal should not profit from their crime should be, for the realist, as true of the criminal's soul as it is of their bank account.

Any realist theory of legitimacy must discover how a justification of state violence to the object of that violence can be acceptable. If a realist theory of legitimacy draws from existing political norms and enacting violence is not itself a political norm, and if the instrumental uses of state violence cannot benefit the object of violence, then how can a realist theory of legitimacy show how a political justification can possibly justify, to each individual, the legitimacy of the state's use of violence?

This section focused on two aspects of a realist theory of legitimacy: its acceptability criterion and the hermeneutical concept of MS. In both cases a justification for state violence fails because, first, the object of state violence either ceases to be in a political relationship with the state or is radically disadvantaged with respect to the state and, second, resting a justification of the state on a contestable interpretation is too weak a ground for the practices of state violence thereby justified. In short, a realist theory of legitimacy cannot successfully manage what I call the *Hobbesian principle*.[13]

THE HOBBESIAN PRINCIPLE

The Hobbesian principle states that *every individual has the right to resist any act of state violence and has no rational obligation to accept any justification for, or the legitimacy of, state violence.* Hobbes defines the right of nature as "the liberty each man hath, to use his own power, *as he will himselfe,* for the preservation of his own Nature; that is to say, of his own Life, and consequently of doing any thing, *which in his own Judgement, and Reason, hee shall conceive to be the aptest means thereunto*" (Hobbes 1997, 72; emphasis added). The key idea here is that the right of nature includes not only a liberty to preserve one's own life but liberty of will, judgment, and reason. These clauses imply that an individual is at liberty to contest any justification of state violence, no matter how rational or reasonable, with whatever reasons they like. A strong version of the Hobbesian principle is that any argument for the legitimacy of state violence made to an actual or potential object of that violence can be met, rationally and/or reasonably, with "I disagree!" A slightly weaker version of the principle is that the justification can be met with "I disagree because . . . " where any reason that supports the claim that one's life is at risk is good enough.

It may seem odd to interpret Hobbes' reference to will, judgment, and reason in terms of *justifications* of violence offered by the state. After all, the right of nature exists in the state of nature, and polity is not yet at issue at this point in Hobbes' argument, much less justifications of state violence. So, what connection is there between the right of nature and justifications of state violence?

It should be noted that the reference to judgment and reason is seemingly unnecessary. If the right of nature is a right to self-preservation, the most obvious cases of a threat to one's life are clear enough to obviate the need for justification or a response to it. A gun pointed at my head, for example, doesn't demand any significant judgment or reason to count as a threat to my life. Now, the gunman may ask for a reason why he shouldn't blow the victim's head off, but in such cases it is more than merely plausible that the individual whose life is at risk need not respond to the question with good reasons before doing whatever possible to get out of that situation.

Liberty of will, reason, and judgment are most pertinent when the threatened individual is confronted not only, or at all, with a gun, but with reasons justifying the threatened violence. In other words, freedom of will, reason, and judgment is required, to give the relevant situation, when the state threatens the individual not only with weapons but with justifications: for example, the justification, "You agreed to give up the right of self-government," or "You violated the law." At that point, given Hobbes' reputation, one might think that there is nothing for a citizen to say in support of their right to resist. But Hobbes does provide the subject not only with a right to resist the violence but a right to resist the justification.

Recall that the right of nature cannot be renounced or transferred, only "laid down," that is, only not exercised in the hopes of receiving some benefit or another (Hobbes 1997, 73). Given that any laying down or transferring of a right is instrumental, for some benefit or other,

> therefore there be some Rights, which no man can be understood by any words, or other signes, to have abandoned, or transferred. As first a man cannot lay down the right of resisting them, that assault him by force, to take away his life. . . . The same may be sayd of Wounds, and Chayns, and Imprisonment; both because there is no benefit consequent to such patience; as there is to the patience of suffering another to be wounded or imprisoned; as also because a man cannot tell, when he seeth men proceed against him by violence, whether they intend his death or not. (Hobbes 1997, 74)

Hobbes, after a lengthy discussion of all the rights of the sovereign, including the right to make, judge, and enforce law, repeats the same point: individuals have no obligation to submit to the violent enforcement of the law, nor to confess to the sovereign, nor to be conscripted into the military (Hobbes 1997, 119–120). Finally, putting an exclamation point on the whole issue, Hobbes claims that the "Obligation of subjects to the Soveraign, is understood to last as long, and no longer, than the power lasteth, by which he is able to protect them. For the right men have by Nature to protect themselves when none else can protect them, can by no Covenant be relinquished" (Hobbes 1997, 121).

If the inalienable right of nature includes the liberty to deliberate and judge for oneself what is the "aptest means" for preserving one's life, then the implication of Hobbes' argument is that one is *always* at liberty to disobey the sovereign and for *any* reason supporting the claim that one's life is in danger (on the weaker version of the Hobbesian principle) or with no reason at all (on the stronger version). What counts as a sovereign's inability to protect us is for each individual to decide because each individual is always at liberty to reason and judge the aptest means for preserving their life. For my purposes here, the point is that no justification of the violence of the state to the actual or potential object of that violence must succeed. No state violence, from the perspective of the reason and judgment of the object of state violence, is necessarily justified and thus the individual has no obligation to submit to the state, either physically or, as it were, rationally.

It may seem surprising that Hobbes would be so explicit in his rejection of any attempt to *politically* legitimize state violence. Strictly speaking, the sovereign has no *political* right, in the realist sense, to the use of violence against citizens. No political norm justifies state violence, nor does the sovereign receive any rights through the covenant, nor is the sovereign part of the covenant. Rather, the sovereign's right to violence is only the right of nature left unchecked by citizens who agree with each other to lay down their unlimited right of nature for the sake of ending the state of war. The right of nature—a pre-political moral right—is the ground for the "legitimacy" of sovereign violence in Hobbes, but the right to violence is always equally held by everyone. For these reasons, Richard Flathman rightly argues that Hobbes' Leviathan is a paper tiger at best; at worst, it is just the continuation of the state of war (Flathman 1993, 124).

Hobbes the ur-realist is too realistic even for contemporary realists unless they are willing to accept the Hobbesian principle. Hobbes' commitment to the central reason for political order requires him to accept that no object of state violence has any obligation to submit to either the violence itself or to a justification for it. In short: if individuals enter politics to prevent both the threat and the realization of violent attacks, there can be no reason for submitting to or accepting justifications for violence directed at them, even the violence of the state. No political norm can justify state violence to the object of that violence.

Must the realist accept the Hobbesian principle, especially as the right of nature is surely a moral right possessed by individuals outside, as well as inside, the state (Douglass 2016, 7)? The realist has good reasons to accept the Hobbesian principle, because it can be restated in a non-moral fashion, in two parts: (1) no legitimate political order can have as one of its political purposes, one of its norms, the subjection of any of its citizens to violence; and (2) no individual can be required, or even expected, to accept a justification of state violence directed at them. Part 1 captures the Hobbesian and realist idea that we enter politics to avoid violence, not to be subjected to it. Part 2 captures both the idea that if state violence attacks the minimal conditions of agency, this harm is so basic as to be unjustifiable from the perspective of the object of violence, and the idea that those subjected to state violence are either not in a political relationship with the state or are radically disadvantaged with respect to it.

Suppose that the argument so far is correct, that is, that realists ought to accept the Hobbesian principle and thus cannot provide an acceptable justification of state violence to those who are objects of that violence. Should realists be bothered? Does this significantly impact the project of developing a realist theory of legitimacy?

Realists should take the failure of a realist theory of legitimacy to justify state violence seriously because it cuts to the core of why anyone has ever pursued a theory of legitimacy at all: to justify state actions that are prima facie morally questionable, actions that are in some cases the very actions that prompt individuals to enter, or remain in, the state. This is as true for Plato's *Crito* as it is for John Locke's *Second Treatise*, Rousseau's *Social Contract*, Kant's *Metaphysics of Morals*, and Rawls' *Political Liberalism*. A recurring impetus for a theory of legitimacy is the need to justify the use of coercion, especially violent coercion, by the state. If there is no possible non-moral justification for state violence, then any a realist theory of legitimacy faces a serious difficulty: it cannot answer, in realist terms, to the desire for a justification of state violence that distinguishes it from non-state violence and is acceptable to each member or subject of a polity.

How should a realist theory of legitimacy handle the violence of the state? Trying to cut the problem of state violence out of any, but especially out of a realist, theory of legitimacy is a non-starter. My suggestion, to conclude, is that realists should accept both the impossibility of a political normative justification of violence and, as I have argued elsewhere, the impossibility of a moral justification of state violence (Arnold 2017). State violence, in short, is never legitimate. If a significant responsibility of, and fact about, states is the use of violent coercion to promote various legitimate or desirable political ends, then we should accept, with Walter Benjamin, that there is something inescapably *rotten* (*Morsches*) in law (Benjamin 1978, 286). At the core of the state there is always decay, decomposition, putrefaction, death: something about politics always stinks. No theory of legitimacy can eliminate, by justifying, the rotten violence that politics requires. That suggests that no theory of legitimacy can ever fully succeed, be fully acceptable, whether it is moralist or realist.

However, this is only a necessary problem for the moralist, not for the realist. A realist theory of legitimacy that accepts its own inability to fully legitimize the state is a really realist theory of legitimacy.

REALISM AS SYNTHETIC CROSS-TRADITION THEORIZING

I claimed earlier that strong evidence in favor of a synthetic cross-tradition mode of theorizing like political realism—not that all or any realists are trying to be cross-tradition theorists—would be its ability to analytically justify a political practice like state violence while remaining faithful to the continental focus on contingency, historicity, ideology, and conflict. Political realism, I have shown, can no more solve the problem of state violence with synthetic cross-tradition theorizing than can any theory from a single tradition. State violence remains dense. Yet that failure alone is not sufficient evidence against synthetic cross-tradition theorizing in general, or a reason to give up on political realism. I want to end this chapter by suggesting why political realism, as a synthetic cross-tradition mode of theorizing, doesn't do any better with state violence than a single tradition theory.

The first reason is that state violence is what it is: a dense political phenomenon. Realism's failures help us to see that, although many realists might be unhappy with this negative result, if they even accept it.

The second reason, more pertinent to my concerns, is that there are deeper tensions between the analytic and continental traditions than style or thematic focus. Realists share with moralists an analytic political philosophical project, a justificatory project, whether the justification is of legitimacy or justice or anything else. Realists differ from moralists in their emphasis on accepting and perhaps even affirming discord, conflict, modus vivendi, and so on, but these political realities do not, for realists, undermine the justificatory project. The justificatory project of realism maintains, at least implicitly, a presumptive commitment to philosophical agreement, that is, to the goal, value, and capacity of rational argumentation to achieve consensus at the theoretical level. The conflictual political reality realists theorize does not translate into inescapable conflict in theory. This is a laudable assumption of analytic theorizing, and without it the important questions analytic theorists pose could hardly be asked, much less answered. However laudable, the goal and assumption of possible theoretical agreement limits the usefulness of analytic theorizing for explaining discordant political realities. Politics, on the realist account, may be messy and conflictual, but it must assume that politics is not *that* messy, so untidy that no serious theorizing could contain and clarify it. Political realities, on this view, are susceptible to theorization according to the usual norms of reasoning, of commonsense observation, of more sophisticated social scientific observation, of interpretation, and so on, even if those realities are resistant to the ideal theoretical aims of political moralism.

A great deal of continental theory accepts the conflictual character of politics, but it often goes further than realists in denying that we can understand or best understand politics with the rationalistic resources of normative analytic theorizing. The analytic assumption that political reality, however messy, may be tidied up by normative theory assumes a powerful but contestable picture of the political theorist as politically neutral, as non-partisan, at least when that theorist is engaging in exploring the necessary and sufficient conditions of political legitimacy. My metaphor of "tidying" suggests that one is not engaging in the political world one is cleaning up, for if politics is necessarily messy and conflictual, then how could tidying things up be a political act? Rather, one is simply identifying what is what and putting it in its proper place in order to accurately see the political world.

However, seeking and providing justifications of state legitimacy *is* a political move because, first, states are not necessary features of politics and, second, certain practices of statehood follow from, or simply constitute, a state's legitimacy. States are not a necessary fact of politics—a point returned to in Chapter 4—and to endorse a state by calling it legitimate, or to even seek to find what makes a state legitimate, is in part to reject the alternatives or to see those alternatives as not politically viable. *That* is a political move, not merely a theoretical one, for it is to decide, and to persuade others, to accept both that other modes of political organization are not worth investigating and that the state form is virtually or actually necessary.

The political maneuvering continues when we justify a state's legitimacy, because it is at best extremely odd to claim the legitimacy of a state but deny that *practices* of state violence are legitimate. If one identifies a state as meeting the criteria of legitimacy, one is surely also claiming that those practices necessary to statehood are legitimate. Once again, there is a process of reification at work that makes some practices appear necessary even though they are not. The limits of the state are not coincident with the limits of politics, and when necessary state practices intervene in or foreclose non-state political practices, that is a political decision that the theorist of state legitimacy would seem obligated to endorse.

If this is correct, then we have a reason why at least one mode of synthetic cross-tradition theorizing is unlikely to succeed: the assumption of political neutrality that enables the analytic justificatory project—even in political realism—is irreconcilable with the recognition that politics is, as it were, political: dissensual, conflictual, partisan, and so on. Conversely, the "politicization" of political theorizing, in which to engage in political theory is assumed to have, or to issue in, political consequences, is as troublesome an assumption as the analytic assumption of neutrality. It is worthwhile to maintain a distinction between the "politics of political theory" and the "politics political theory theorizes," even though in some instances political theory and political theorists do have an effect on "real" politics. I am not taking sides here, only suggesting why one synthetic mode of cross-tradition theorizing is limited in its abilities to handle a dense problem like state violence. Political realism is evidence for the likelihood that synthetic cross-tradition theorizing cannot work.

In the following chapter we will see another example of synthetic theorizing that, for very different reasons, also proves insufficient for the problem of state violence.

2

CAVELL, CONSENT, AND STATE VIOLENCE

THE FOREWORD TO STANLEY CAVELL'S *The Claim of Reason* acknowledges the analytic-continental divide and announces Cavell's as yet unrealized hope that the divide, at least in his work, might begin to be overcome (Cavell 1999, xvii). Cavell's consciousness of the divide and his self-consciousness about his relation to both traditions shapes all of his work, including his occasional engagements with canonical texts in political philosophy.

Cavell's approach to synthetic cross-tradition theorizing differs from that of the political realists discussed in Chapter 1. Many readers liken his "literary" approach to reading and writing to the work of French philosophers like Jacques Derrida, and that approach was, and is, at odds with standard modes of reading in analytic (and a great deal of continental) philosophy. Cavell is no "deconstructionist," but his method of reading and writing embraces the "textuality" of the philosophical text, even when the text at issue is from the analytic tradition. This mode of reading enables provocative and original interpretations of canonical works of political philosophy that challenge readers to rethink texts like John Rawls' *A Theory of Justice* and Rousseau's *Social Contract*. If Cavell's practice of reading and his drawing on continental themes in his interpretations of political philosophy can help us understand, or even solve, political problems like state violence, then we will have a strong reason to think that other political problems might be solved in the same way. However, Cavell's reading of the social contract tradition and of what I call *social violence* does not get to the political problem of state violence central to the social contract.

Cavell's version of synthetic cross-tradition theorizing is part of the reason the problem of state violence eludes him, a point explored further at the end of the chapter. But now, on to Cavell.

For many political theorists Cavell is now a significant point of reference. Focusing on his discussions of the social contract, consent, and moral perfectionism, recent writing on Cavell has, in the main, been an exegetical project intended to bring a new thinker into contemporary political theoretical debate.[1] There is ample appreciation *and* criticism of Cavell's contributions to epistemology and the philosophy of language, but there have been few attempts to identify the limitations of Cavell's most explicit contribution to political theory: his interpretation of consent and the social contract.[2]

Cavell's readings of John Locke, Rousseau, and Rawls turn our attention away from or significantly modify concepts of authority, legitimacy, obligation, justice, and natural and positive law. Cavell points us toward a hitherto undetected concept and discouraging fact exposed by the social contract theorist: that we are morally *compromised* by our consent to unjust societies, raising the question of whether and how a citizen can continue to consent to a society in which some measure of injustice continues to exist. Cavell shifts the social contract theorist's question from "why ought I to obey?" to "can I continue to consent to my society, and how might I justify such consent to those who are treated unjustly?" Much is gained in this shift from political obligation to moral responsibility and responsiveness, and what Cavell has discovered in the social contract tradition is of crucial importance for political theory. This chapter, though, explores what might be lost in such a shift, specifically whether Cavell's analysis of the moral complexities of life in unjust liberal democracies, and his call for a "conversation of justice" to respond to these complexities and compromises, can make sense of a more "traditional" aim of the social contract and consent: to justify state violence.

Cavell's interpretation of the concept of consent founders on the problem of justifying state violence. Cavell not only does not, but cannot, deal with this distinctively political problem because his analysis of consent is explicitly an analysis of human community *as such*, not the political community specifically. One cannot deny the political relevance of Cavell's work—the polis is, after all, a human community—yet *Cavellian consent* forecloses attention to the political and moral problems common to political communities. That we should take seriously whether or not Cavell's moral perfectionist understanding of consent can adequately respond to more common concerns in politics and political theory is a reasonable extension of his caveat in *Conditions Handsome and Unhandsome*: "Restricting my attention to those in positions of relative advantage means that I am not attending to the condition of poverty, say economic victimization. I assume that justice is bound to attend without fail to these conditions, so that if the perfectionist position I adumbrate is incompatible with this attention of and to justice, the position is morally worthless" (Cavell 1990, xx). Although Cavell is here defending Emerson, Thoreau, and himself from charges of moral indifference to the "herd," one can easily extend his concern about economic victimization to the issue of state violence and other central questions of political theory. If Cavell's reading of consent and the social contract cannot make sense of the justness of state violence and its relation to consent and contract, then something is wrong with Cavell's reading. Cavell is inviting us to see whether his perfectionist interpretation of consent is compatible with the functions of consent in social contract theory.

To this end, I argue for two claims. First, within Cavell's writing and in the growing secondary literature on political aspects of that writing, the concept of community central to *The Claim of Reason* and informing Cavell's later essays on moral perfectionism is too general to be useful and relevant for understanding political communities. In short, Cavell and his readers fail to take seriously how the specificities of politics delimit and transform concepts and practices of consent.[3]

Second, Cavell's interpretation of consent fails to consider the supposed power of political consent to legitimize the state's use of violence. In most versions of consent theory, consent is taken to be the necessary and/or sufficient act that legitimizes state violence. Insofar as Cavellian consent does not account for this function of consenting and political consent raises a set of problems that Cavellian consent cannot resolve, then, at the very least, Cavellian consent is deeply problematic.

If, for Cavell, consenting to human community entails being compromised by existing injustice, the violence or violation that the consenting human bears witness to and responsibility for is a violence or violation possible in any form of human association. This violence is *social violence*, defined here as the violence of demands for conformity and the possible negative consequences of non-conformity. Broadly speaking, this form of violence is a facet of what Cavell calls *acknowledgment* and *avoidance*. Social violence is undoubtedly terrible; but consenting to modern political societies also requires consenting to practices of *physical political violence* that, in order to be used legitimately, must be normatively distinguished from other forms of physical violence. It is part of the "grammar" of political consent that it authorizes and legitimizes, that is, normatively distinguishes, state violence. However, consenting to legitimate state violence raises different moral problems from the problems engendered by conformity/exclusion.

The main difference between the two forms of violence is that social violence is an inescapable feature of human life because of the normative constraints of language and social life more generally. To consent to community is to be party to, *implicated* in, *responsible* for, acts of social violence. The legitimate violence of the state, however, is not inescapable, although it is an essential, *grammatical*, feature of the political in the contract tradition. State violence is a useful but optional way of enforcing order in a political society; thus it stands in need of justification if it is to be distinguished from domination. Consenting to state violence *authorizes* that violence. To be *implicated* by one's consent to a society in which there are significant costs to inclusion or exclusion and to *authorize* suffering in one's society through one's consent are two different moral/political matters. If part of the grammar of consent is that it authorizes state violence, then it is unclear to me how Cavell's work can deal with this grammatical political problem.

THE ABSENCE OF THE POLITICAL IN CAVELL

Claiming that there is a neglect of the specifically political in Cavell's work implies that there is a domain of human experience or action that is distinctly political. Demarcating the political requires both phenomenological and axiological considerations. Aristotle saw the political as the natural telos of human community, a space in which speaking animals with a perception of good and evil, just and unjust, could share a view in these matters for the sake of the good life. Hannah Arendt understands the political as a space of self- and world-disclosive free action in which there is neither ruler nor ruled. Both Aristotle and Arendt divide the political from the private realm, and Arendt distinguishes both the public and the private from the hybrid realm of the social. The public, private, and social are domains of human experience in which different needs are met, different forms of rule appear, and different values prevail. Carl Schmitt claimed for the political an extremely confined space and time: the political is defined by the transformation of non-political associations into friends and enemies in the moment of decision on the enemy. What is of utmost value—continued existence and the meaning of existence itself—is at stake in politics, whereas in the economy, in religion, in aesthetics, and in other domains, different values, and different fundamental antitheses take prece- dence (Schmitt 1996, 25–37). Rawls takes the political to be distinct, at least in part, insofar as the political is neither like other voluntary associations nor is it based on affection as personal or familial relationships are. The political allows for the full moral development of the individual, a life lived in the presence of justice and recognized as worthy of respect by one's fellow citizens (Rawls 1996, 137, 201–206). One could multiply examples of claims to the autonomy or dis- tinctiveness of the political. There are also theorists—Freud and Marx for ex- ample—who either explicitly or implicitly give us reason to think that politics is shaped, if not determined, by non-political forces. Finally, there are examples of thinkers like Michel Foucault who see politics or political problems of power as pervasive features of multiple domains of human life.

Although it is doubtful that the political is autonomous in the ways Arendt, Schmitt, and others suggest, there are distinctively political problems, problems that many of us expect or hope politics will solve, rather than the market, the family, or the individual. In modern liberal polities the political is imagined to be associational, often contractual, and relied on to solve a set of problems while leaving other problems to the private or social sphere. A specific political problem is the use of force or violence to maintain social order, a problem that requires the violence of the state to be morally distinct from the violence the state is punishing or trying to prevent. It may be that the legitimacy of state violence is a question that any polis must answer, but for modern liberal polities putatively based on consent, this problem is central.

Thus, one can begin to see the absence of the distinctly political problem of state violence in Cavell's work by, first, briefly attending to the nexus of issues addressed by many philosophers and political theorists interested in consent theories. For A. John Simmons "*political power* is *morally legitimate*, and those subject to it are *morally obligated to obey*, only where the subjects have freely consented to the exercise of such power and only where that power continues to be *exercised* within the terms of the consent given" (Simmons 2001, 129; empha- sis added; see also Simmons 1993). Joseph Raz sees valid consent to the authority of the law as a possible way of creating an obligation to obey, for "consent to the *authority* of a *just government* is noninstrumentally *valid* if given as an expres- sion of an attitude of identification with [the citizen's] society" (Raz 1981, 129; emphasis added). Hanna Pitkin distinguishes four questions asked by consent theorists seeking to discover when consent *obliges* us to obey; to *whom* we owe such *obligations*; whether there is a real difference between *legitimate authority* and *mere coercion*; and why one is obligated to obey, what are the *justifications* for obligation (Pitkin 1965, 991). C. S. Nino argues, vis-à-vis the more specific issue of justifying *punishment*, that if an agent performs a voluntary act with the knowledge that this act would necessarily entail a loss of his legal immunity from punishment, then the agent has consented to the punishment (Nino 1983, 298). The italicized words and phrases form a series of concepts familiar to political theorists: power, legitimacy, law, obligation, authority, justice, validity, justification, coercion, punishment. The texts just cited are representative of a unity of themes and concepts in political philosophical accounts of consent and/or the social contract, and they largely follow the range of issues raised by Hobbes, Locke, Rousseau, and Kant. Although many of these concepts are not unique to political philosophy or politics, the inflections of those concepts in the writers cited and in political theory generally are political insofar as they emerge from attention to, and with an aim to resolve, problems within political communities. In Cavell's work many of these concepts play an integral role in both his epistemological and his moral thinking, but they do not—except in passing, and that only rarely—take on the usual political theoretical inflections.

I focus attention now on the concept of community: first, because of the central role that concept plays throughout Cavell's writing, particularly in his discussions of consent; and second, because community is, for political theory, a central idea. Cavell's most evocative reference to community is found early in *The Claim of Reason*:

> The philosophical appeal to what we say, and the search for our criteria on the basis of which we say what we say, are claims to community. And the claim to community is always a search for the basis upon which it can or has been established. I have nothing more to go on than my conviction that I make sense. It may prove to be the case that I am wrong, that my conviction isolates me, from all others, from myself. That will not be the same as a discovery that I am dogmatic or egomaniacal. The wish and search for community are the wish and search for reason. (Cavell 1999, 20)

The transcendental overtones in this passage are not accidental because, for Cavell, Wittgensteinian criteria and grammar—the search for which is the search for community—constitute "the knowledge Kant calls 'transcendental'" (Cavell 1969, 64). If so, then the search for community and the basis of it is the search for the transcendental itself. The identification of community with the transcendental is a pervasive feature throughout Cavell's writings. Whether the issue is how ordinary language philosophy can invoke the first-person plural, what insures our mutual attunement, or the seeming necessity of the imposition of or desire for conformity; whether the thinker is Austin, Wittgenstein, Emerson, Thoreau, or Mill; or whether the text is a remarriage comedy or *A Doll's House*, in the foreground or in the background is the idea of community as the transcendental.[4]

When Cavell seeks to explicate further the concept of community cited here, he turns to the concept of consent as it appears in social contract theory. Contract theory provides an answer to a question Cavell asks about how language might be conventional even though there never was a convention in which individuals agreed upon the grammar of a language. It is as an analogy to this question about language that Cavell turns to the social contract, for it is in social contract theory that one finds ideas about original conventions that never did take place. Tellingly, Cavell gives sustained attention to the social contract in order to answer a question asked not of political society but of community, of language, of the human, *as such* (Cavell 1999, 22).

Cavell does, to be sure, immediately begin to address specifically political issues: how consent means membership in a polis, which requires a shared conception of political equality and political freedom; what is wrong in Hume's attack on the idea of a social contract; tacit consent in Locke. However, Cavell sets the terms of his later writings (in *Theory of Justice, for example*) by interpreting the social contract question "why ought I to obey?" in a unique manner: "What the question in fact means therefore is, 'Given the specific inequalities and lacks of freedom and absence of fraternity in the society to which I have consented, do these outweigh the 'disadvantages' of withdrawing my consent?'" (Cavell 1999, 24). But, one is obliged to ask: how does this answer, or even expand, the social contract theorist's question, "why ought I to obey?"[5] Cavell here seems to repeat the conclusion, if not the justification or meaning, of Thoreau's having "rejected" the question and the subject of obligation within the social contract (Cavell 1992, 88). In order to see why we cannot reject this question, we must look at the grammar of consent-based political communities.

Given the context and Cavell's use of these political terms and texts, it is hard to see how Cavell, in spite of his reference to "actual" societies and "specific" injustices, is really discussing distinctively political societies, or even the "imagined" cities of words we find in political theories. Entering political community, at least in liberal polities, also requires one or all of the following: the institution and protection of private property; the constitution and enforcement of a system of law; a government bureaucracy; the recognition of specific rights and duties; taxation; and so on. These are political realities Cavell almost never addresses in anything more than a sentence or two. Cavell's concept of community is relevant to political concerns because the polis is a community, but to the extent that community is transcendental we should be careful to note what happens to community when it is realized as a polis. That Cavell can employ the concept of consent to illuminate the conventionality of all language in *The Claim of Reason*, and also the young adult's response to the demand for conformity in an essay on Emerson; Thoreau's discovery of the mysteriousness of society and the melancholy that pervades it; problems in Rawls' *Theory of Justice*; problems in Kripke's reading of Wittgenstein; and finally, what is expressed by those who, compromised by the failures of democracy, choose to live in an "illustrious monarchy" suggests that the concept of consent is being employed in a far broader manner than is usual (Cavell 1992, 82; 1990, 125).

The broad scope of Cavellian consent is repeated in the work of two of his best readers, Andrew Norris and Stephen Mulhall. For Norris, it is Cavell's distinctive and illuminating mapping of the transcendental conditions for the sharing of our words and lives—that is, community—that makes Cavell's work so relevant to political theory. However, if Cavell is speaking throughout his earlier work of the transcendental conditions of community and language, then it seems clear that Cavell is not, in these works, taking into account the important distinctions between kinds of communities: the social club, the sports team, the union, and the political community.

For Norris, Cavell's discussion of the social contract addresses the "distinctively *political* community" of speaking beings. In spite of Norris' emphasis on "political," it is unclear what is so distinctively political about beginning "with speaking beings in a context within which their speech with one another is intelligible" and then asking "how they will elaborate or evade that basic community" (Norris 2006, 12). If Aristotle is correct, then one condition of possibility for political community is speech; but this is also true for other forms of human association. Where is the distinction that makes political community different? For Aristotle, the distinctiveness of the political rests not simply upon the fact that human beings *can* speak, but in *what* they speak about and why they speak in this way: it is in the political that we speak of and practice justice, and we do so not solely for the sake of better securing the necessities of life, but in order to pursue the good life (Aristotle 1992, 1252b27–1253b1; discussed in Norris 2006, 80–97). Yet, the distinctiveness of political community, even in Aristotle, is not exhausted by its condition of possibility and the subject matter of its conversations. Aristotle identifies the task of political theory as an investigation into both ideal and real constitutions, that is, distributions of power and offices, laws, and the location of sovereignty.[6] Cavell does, as Norris has shown, follow in an Aristotelian line, not only in his attention to human speech but also in what Cavell calls the "conversation of justice." However, even Cavell's use of "justice" here exceeds the boundaries of the political.[7] To be sure, justice is not an exclusively political concept; but the fact that some renderings of justice are violent, and that the violence of state punishment is justified has led some—Blaise Pascal, Walter Benjamin, and Derrida come to mind—to think extensively about the relationship of justice to violence. Cavell alludes to this problem only briefly, while questioning whether the "sword" of justice is raised in attack or defense (Cavell 2004, 172).

Norris notes that although Cavell "expresses almost no interest in political institutions such as the state or in the violence to which it claims a monopoly," he is, like Foucault, Judith Butler, and Alasdair MacIntyre, "more interested in political subject formation than rules of governance" (Norris 2006, 15). Yet, Cavell is distinct from at least Foucault and Butler because their investigations of the construction of political subjectivity are inseparable from an analysis of the important role of the state, law, violence, punishment, and political justification. Norris is correct that Cavell's work ignores political institutions and state violence; my aim is to show why this is a problem.

Mulhall's reading of Cavell may pose a challenge to my claim that there is no attention to distinctively political communities or problems in Cavell's writings. Mulhall delineates an aesthetic, moral, and political community within Cavell's writing, even as he rightly notes that "Cavell's work embodies from the outset a unified vision of modern western culture—one in which its various domains or spheres appear as differing inflexions of a single pattern or structure" (Mulhall 1994, 55). However, the distinctions between these three domains of human life are, for Mulhall, largely a function of the different ways an individual discovers and negotiates, through the making of claims—about the beauty of an object; about what is the right thing to do; about the content of the social contract—a relationship to community. In aesthetics, what is at stake is a particular object and whether or not it is beautiful. An aesthetic community is one in which a possible but not guaranteed agreement is sought through the giving of relevant reasons. The individual's claim to the beauty of an object is a claim to speak for all others in that community, even if that claim might be rejected (Mulhall 1994, 28). In a moral community, in contrast, while there is equally no guarantee of agreement in conclusions about what is to be done or the rightness of an action, "I need make no claim to speak for others when declaring my own position on the rightness or wrongness of an action, and when I do attempt to speak for another, I can only do so if I confront her declared position in terms of her own cares and commitments" (Mulhall 1994, 50). In the moral life, what matters is taking seriously the other person, their needs, their cares, and their commitments. Moral claims assert what the other ought to do or must do, revealing both my own position vis-à-vis the other and leaving open the possibility that even if the other rejects my claims, we can remain in community. In morality "community does not constitute a denial or repression of individuality because it consists in a respect for individual differences—it can be attained even if our differences remain" (Mulhall 1994, 50). If this is an accurate account of the moral life, then the kinds of reasons one can give within that community will be different from those reasons one can give within an aesthetic community. Mulhall's account of these different communities in Cavell's work is quite nuanced, but it is already clear that the fundamental differences between aesthetic and moral communities are a consequence of their distinctive claims, the different reasons given for those claims, and how the individual relates to others in each community. In Mulhall's convincing reading of Cavell, the differences between moral and aesthetic communities are grammatical, that is, they are differences in what *counts* as moral or aesthetic, as being a moral being or a critic, as making an aesthetic judgment or moral judgment, and so on. They are "inflexions" of the search for community, the search for the transcendental.

What, then, about the political community? Mulhall, following Cavell, fails to articulate a distinct sense of political community, because at the grammatical or transcendental level, political claiming and community appear as almost an *Aufhebung*, a complex synthesis, of the aesthetic and moral communities:

> Whereas Cavell's interpretation of aesthetic discourse tended to foreground the establishment of achieved communities of response, and his interpretation of moral discourse tended to focus on the achievement of self-knowledge, his interpretation of political discourse gives equal weight to the two themes. . . . In this respect, therefore, political discourse seems to epitomize the ways in which the grammars of these three criterially governed and constituted modes of human interaction closely parallel the grammar of philosophical practice. (Mulhall 1994, 65)

Political community seems to be the "epitome" of the procedures of ordinary language philosophy at the same time that it combines grammatical features of both the aesthetic and moral communities. What, then, is distinctive about the political community? If it is not its grammatical features—and the fact that political community epitomizes ordinary language philosophy procedures already suggests that in Cavell and Mulhall the community in question is community *as such*—then might it not be the "content" of political speech? For if aesthetics deals with certain kinds of objects, and morality deals with certain kinds of actions, then might not politics deal with a certain kind of . . . something, say, justice? But justice is, seemingly, as much an object of morality as it is of politics, for according to Cavell, justice "is a concept concerning the treatment of *persons*; and *that* is a concept, in turn of a creature with commitments and cares," that is, of a moral being (Cavell 1999, 283).

Both Cavell and Mulhall fail to acknowledge that in political communities, unlike in either aesthetic or moral communities, there are procedures in place—procedures legitimated by consent—to stop discussion and conversation, to "realize" a judgment through the execution of a policy or law. The use of legitimate force is a grammatical feature of consent-based political communities. Law and the violence it uses, authorized and morally legitimated through the consent of citizens, is one of the "institutions" that is part of the grammar of consent-based polities. Law and its justified violence distinguish consent-based political communities from other forms of human association, and it is the reason why nearly any contract theorist must offer an account of how the state has the right to forcefully execute the law. This moral problem is not one which a "conversation of justice" can help us sort through because consenting to practices of state violence does not *implicate* us in something that, were our polis perfect, we wouldn't have to feel compromised by. Rather, consent gives *authority* to the deliberate infliction of pain upon fellow beings even in a perfectly just state, often in order to achieve a just state. This is an entirely different matter.

I have criticized Norris and Mulhall because they get Cavell right, so right that they follow Cavell's apparent indifference to the distinctive features of political communities. The lack of attention to legitimate state violence in Cavell's writings is problematic because Cavellian consent might not be able to respond both to social violence and to political violence at the same time. I will now outline how the absence of the distinctly political in Cavell is manifest in his account of the relationship of community to what I am calling *social violence*.

THE NORMATIVITY OF LANGUAGE AND SOCIAL VIOLENCE

Let's define *social violence* as (1) the physical and psychological effects of the demands for conformity to communal norms, and (2) the possible negative consequences of non-conformity. While there is evidence within Cavell's work for defining conformity and exclusion as a kind of "violence," the term *social violence* is mine, a consequence of taking seriously Norris' association of Cavell with theorists like Foucault and Butler. Whether social violence is rightly called violence is a genuine question, but I assume that social violence is violence because it is a coercive force with significant physical and psychological effects.

For Cavell, the possibility, perhaps necessity, of social violence is a consequence of the normative force of language. The normative force of language and the importance and power of norms in the process of initiation into a linguistic community is a concern throughout Cavell's work. The arguments Cavell gathers to justify his understanding of the normative power of language and the issues involved are clearly stated in a debate between Mulhall and Steven Affeldt, precluding the necessity of summarizing the arguments here (Affeldt 1998; Mulhall 1998). Instead, pertinent citations will demonstrate the normative power of language, setting up a more detailed discussion of how this normative power can lead to social violence.

Responding to criticisms by Benson Mates of the validity and value of ordinary language philosophy—specifically the normative connotations of saying that *this* is what we (must) mean when we say *that*—Cavell writes that "the normativeness which Mates felt, and which is certainly present, does not lie in the ordinary language philosopher's assertions about ordinary language; what is normative is exactly ordinary use itself" (Cavell 1969, 21). Roughly speaking, what is normative in ordinary language is in part that "something does follow from the fact that a term is used in its usual way: it entitles you (or, using the term, you entitle others) to make certain inferences, draw certain conclusions. . . . *Learning what these implications are is part of learning the language. . . .* We are, therefore, exactly as responsible for the specific implications of our utterances as we are for their explicit factual claims" (Cavell 1969, 11–12). To learn a language—to learn to speak normally—is to learn that when we say something we are also saying, implicitly, other things for which we can be held responsible. Normal language use warrants others to infer that when we say something we must be using the words in a normal way, a way always connected to related concepts, words, situations, intentions, and so on. For example: if you say "your laces are untied," normally this is not, or not only, a description. It is also a warning ("you might trip"), an exhortation ("tie your laces"), and so on. If I then tie them and you run off in a huff claiming I ruined your day, then I have every reason to question your behavior, for your use of that sentence clearly differed from its normal use. One may be able to make sense of this behavior as unimportant or revelatory idiosyncrasy. One can imagine, however, other examples that might raise a question as to whether or not the other is using the same language as I am, is part of the same community as I am.

Language is thus also normative because the "ground" of our community and our language is the conventional, yet nonetheless natural, result of what Wittgenstein called "natural history." In other words, if language is conventional it is not the case—just as with the social contract—that the conventions of language once required a convention of people to institute them. Rather,

> [t]hat *that* should express understanding or boredom or anger—(or: that it should be part of the grammar of 'understanding' that *that* is what we call "his suddenly understanding") is not necessary . . . someone *may* be bored by an earthquake or by the death of his child . . . or *may* be angry at a pin or a cloud or a fish. . . . That human beings on the whole do not respond in these ways is, therefore, seriously referred to as conventional; but now we are thinking of convention not as the arrangements a particular culture has found convenient, in terms of its history and geography, for effecting the necessities of human existence, but as those forms of life which are normal to any group of creatures we call human. . . . Wittgenstein's discovery, or rediscovery, is of the depth of convention in human life; a discovery which insists not only on the conventionality of human society, but, we could say, on the conventionality of human nature itself. (Cavell 1999, 111)

This picture of human community and language is one in which to say something normally is to be included in and by a *normative* conception of a human being. This normative conception of the human is not "merely" conventional in the sense that it is a social construct, contingently and perhaps arbitrarily constructed to exclude some humans from the human community. Cavell wants to argue the far more powerful and unsettling idea that the normal is closely linked to the natural: to be normally human is to be naturally human, to have the same natural history as other humans. More precisely, to be normally human is to share with others the recognition of certain practices and uses of language *as* natural to the human (Cavell 1989, 40–52). Not all practices and usages of language within human communities need to be seen as natural, for there are different practices in different cultures. But as Richard Eldridge has argued, drawing upon Cavell, there are certain practices that we have a deep *need* to see as naturally human, as true for any human being (Eldridge 1986, 573). For Cavell, so much of human interaction depends upon the other's "natural understanding," "natural reaction"; and "it is astonishing how far this takes us in understanding one another, but it has its limits" (Cavell 1999, 115). When another being fails to respond naturally, fails to respond as others we see as human naturally respond—or if I fail to respond naturally—then questions arise: is the other part of my world?; are they part of the *human* world?; am *I* part of the human world? Language and community are normative because they depend upon a distinction between normal and abnormal use, a distinction intimately linked to natural and unnatural reactions and responses. To fail to speak normally, to respond naturally, poses the risk of falling outside of, or being pushed out of, the human community.[8]

These two views of the normativity of language—as being responsible for the implications of what one says and as being normally, naturally, human—return in Cavell's reading of Emerson's essay "Fate." Emersonian fate, Cavell writes, is shown to be "irresistible dictation," where "we do with our lives what some power dominating our lives knows or reveals them to be, enacting old scripts" (Cavell 1988, 38). Drawing upon the etymology of "dictation," Cavell goes on to identify fate's dictatorial powers with language itself: "It sounds as though the irresistible dictation that constitutes Fate, that sets conditions on our knowledge and our conduct, is our language, every word we utter" (Cavell 1988, 39). This conditional finding is, in Cavell's next paragraph, more categorically asserted: "Now it [Emerson's essay] says openly that language is our fate. It means hence that not exactly prediction, but diction, is what puts us in bonds, that with each word we utter we emit stipulations, agreements we do not know and do not want to know we have entered, agreements we were always in, that were in effect before our participation in them" (Cavell 1988, 40). And there we are, back, more or less, to "Must We Mean What We Say?"

In referring to the normal and the natural we have laid the grounds for Cavell's close attention to social violence, to the normative power that puts us in shackles, conditioning our lives wherever and whenever we live them. If the normal and the natural set limits to the human community, creating the line separating who is in and who out of the community, the violence of those limits affects both those inside and those outside. Scenes of social violence appear throughout Cavell's work,[9] and it is in the constellation of concepts like conformity, normality, naturalness, humanity, exclusion, recognition, and so on, that we can appreciate Norris' useful association, mentioned earlier, of Cavell with Foucault and Butler.

However, while social violence can take a political form, the adjective "social" reminds us that the normative force Cavell is referring to applies to human beings as such because to be human is to be part of a community, of a society, of a form of life. We should distinguish, then, between (1) social violence, (2) political social violence, and (3) non-political social violence. All humans grow up in specific communities with their own norms, initiation practices, languages, and so on. To be human is to be subject to the normative force of language and community, and the coercive power of that normative force affects all humans regardless of language or community: it is what we call "growing up." To the extent that growing up is a coercive process in any human community and for all individuals, it is not domain-specific: for example, specific to political life. In growing up, we experience many types of social violence. Social violence can, however, become a form of *political social violence*. For example, while the normative force of language demands conformity to specific norms, not all the norms are "transcendental," applying to all human beings. It is not written into the natural and conventional history of humanity that any one race, or gender, or caste, or class, is of a lower order of humanity than another. These specific forms of exclusion can be either political social violence or non-political social violence, depending on the exclusion at work. If citizenship is restricted to property-owning white men, then we have political social violence, because the in/out decision is realized in the political terms of citizenship. If "propriety" requires members of one race to never look at women of another race, then we have non-political social violence, because the in/out decision is realized in terms of different norms of behavior and interpersonal engagement. No doubt, political social violence and non-political social violence often reinforce each other; but there are good analytical reasons to keep different inflections of social violence apart, for in so doing we can make better sense of why, if we are seeking racial justice, it may not be enough to simply end one form of political social violence while maintaining other forms of non-political social violence, and vice versa. The important point is that all forms of social violence share the inclusion/exclusion opposition, that is, they decide who is in, and who is out, of a community.

Earlier I made one further distinction: between physical political violence, that is, state violence, and social violence. It is just as important, analytically, to keep state violence distinct from social violence, even from political social violence, as it is to keep different forms of social violence analytically distinct. There are a number of reasons why we should keep state violence and social violence distinct, but for my purposes now the main reason is that they have a very different relationship to the concepts of community and consent, specifically within discussions of the social contract. Collapsing the distinction between state violence and social violence is a mistake because we will miss the distinctive political and moral implications of consenting to the state if we identify state violence with social violence or think of the latter as the former. A pertinent and complex example of this misidentification of state violence and social violence is Cavell's criticism of *A Theory of Justice*, returned to later in this chapter.

DIFFERENCES BETWEEN SOCIAL VIOLENCE AND STATE VIOLENCE, AND THE DIFFERENCE THOSE DIFFERENCES MAKE

If, for Cavell, the social contract asks whether one can continue to consent to one's society given its injustices and other failings, then the temporality and critical function of the social contract and our consent to it changes significantly. Hobbes and Locke turned to the social contract in response to problems about the origin of the legitimacy and authority of a state. In the absence of natural or divine foundations, what could possibly ensure that historically constituted polities had the sovereign rights and powers necessary to legitimately demand obedience from the citizenry? The figure of the social contract and consent to it provided a powerful and persuasive answer to that question.

It is no accident that Cavell turns to Rousseau, rather than Hobbes or Locke, when he turns to the concept of the social contract and consent in *The Claim of Reason*. Rousseau is still interested in origins, but he shifts the critical function of the social contract from a focus on constituting legitimate political authority in the absence of pre-political grounds to rectifying *existing* injustices in existing polities. Two sentences after the famous opening line of Chapter One, Book One of *The Social Contract* ("Man is born free, and everywhere he is in chains"), Rousseau writes: "How did this change occur? I do not know. What can make it legitimate? I believe I can answer this question" (Rousseau 1978, 46). Rousseau is not telling us how to return to our newborn freedom, so the issue here must be how to legitimize our chains rather than remove them, and that requires us, as Rousseau writes a few sentences earlier, to take men as they are and laws as they can be. If we take Rousseau at his word—something we are often wise not to do—then the point of turning to the origin of political society is not to show us how to create, *de novo*, legitimate polities, but how to transform and legitimize the illegitimate, unjust, polities we already live in. Cavell's interpretation of the contract theorist's question is foreshadowed in Rousseau, but not in Hobbes or Locke.

The philosophical significance of social contract theory is to impart a political education:

> it is philosophical because its method is an examination of myself by an attack on my assumptions; it is political because the terms of this self-examination are the terms which reveal me as a member of a polis; it is education not because I learn new information but because I learn that the finding and forming of my knowledge of myself requires the finding and forming of my knowledge of that membership (the depth of my own and the extent of those joined with me). (Cavell 1999, 25)

Rousseau is the "deepest" contract thinker, Cavell continues, because "what he claims to know is his relation to society" and this epistemological problem becomes the problem of discovering "my position with respect to these facts [the facts of society]—how I know with whom I am in community, and to whom and to what I am in fact obedient" (Cavell 1999, 25).

Cavell's interest in the social contract is not in the foundations of state authority, legitimacy, political obligation, and the like, but in the capacity of contract theory to raise, philosophically, questions of who is in and who is out of one's community, especially whether the questioner is in or out. Contract theory also helps us think through whether we desire to remain in or out of our communities. Reflecting on consent becomes a matter of whether or not one wishes to be in or out of a community, a fraught decision because withdrawal from political community, however unjust the community may be, is nothing less than the acceptance of a kind of silence, of having nothing to say (politically at least) to anyone (Cavell 1999, 28). Consenting to a community, warts and all, poses its own challenges to the self because one then bears the responsibility of making sense of, and perhaps even justifying oneself to, those who are treated unjustly.

It follows from Cavell's interpretation of the lessons of social contract theory that individuals are to learn how to understand and respond to social violence. While, ideally, consent to the social contract means consenting not only to obey but also to be an equal member of a community of autonomous individuals, Cavell quickly returns us to political realities, where equality, autonomy, and justice are often lacking. In those circumstances, being answerable *for* and *to* our community leads us back to the issues of belonging and exclusion already noted, issues that involve how and why the polis treats some of our fellow citizens unjustly and whether we can continue to consent to the society as it stands.

Cavell nowhere turns, however, to state violence and thus to the problem of legitimate state violence that is putatively solved in classical contract theory, whether in its Hobbesian, Lockean, or Rousseauian form. Cavell ignores the admission of a reticent Rousseau that consenting to the social contract justifies the sovereign power to punish and kill, a power that the sovereign holds absolutely and, apparently, without limit. Although the sovereign cannot exercise that power, if the Prince thinks it expedient to kill a citizen, then that citizen ought to be killed (Rousseau 1978, 64). The issue here is state violence, not social violence, and although no contract theorist endorses the wanton killing of citizens, the classical contract theorists all endorse the sovereign right to violently punish, and they ground that right in consent. State violence presents a different problem than social violence does because consenting to the social contract *authorizes* the state to punish, gives the state the moral legitimacy required to use physical force that for the most part, for any non-state actor, would be morally and legally wrong. When the state uses state violence, it does so with, as it were, the authority of one's moral signature. Our consent is the moral source of legitimate state violence.

Cavellian consent to membership in an imperfectly just polis does not *authorize* anything, whether state violence or social violence, nor does it certify the moral justness of a society, or whitewash the failings of a polis. On the contrary, continued consent to an unjust polis *implicates* citizens in the injustice, *compromises* their integrity, their ability to stand apart from society, and their claim to be "above reproach." Citizens are morally stained, compromised, by consent to a good enough society, not relieved of moral responsibility as in the case of consenting to the state and authorizing its use of violence

Traditional consent to state violence and Cavellian consent to social violence are very different because consenting to state violence justifies state violence and thus can, in principle, wash away the putative sins of state violence and a citizen's complicity in it. Cavellian consent, in contrast, implicates citizens in the injustice of social violence, ties them to it, makes them responsible to those whose unjust treatment is not a reason for them to reject their society.

These are very different problems, and if Cavellian consent cannot, in principle, address the problem of state violence, then it is, at best, limited in its political relevance. The place to test Cavellian consent is in Cavell's criticism of Rawls' *A Theory of Justice.*

Cavell emphasizes that in Rawls' original position, one consents not to society as such, as in classical contract theory, but to the two principles of justice: briefly and roughly, (1) that each individual is entitled to the most extensive set of basic liberties compatible with a similar liberty for others; and (2) that any inequalities in society are in fact to everyone's advantage and a consequence of equality of opportunity. The relevant principle for Cavell is the "difference principle" because it justifies inequality (Cavell 2004, 170–171). Cavell draws out a curious consequence of Rawls' original position and the focus of consent on the two principles of justice rather than society as such. If the maximin principle would be chosen by a rational actor in the original position, but in actual societies inequalities are present, then the choice of the difference principle in the original position in effect relieves the better off in that society of any responsibility for inequality. If those who happen to end up worse off than others complain of injustice, or express resentment toward those with more resources, Cavell finds that Rawls' implicit response to those complaints is to claim that the better off are "above reproach" and that the complainers are suffering from a morally suspicious case of envy (Cavell 2004, 171). The implicit Rawlsian idea Cavell elaborates is that insofar as everyone agrees or would agree to the maximin principle, the worse off choose not their fate—for they are ignorant of their fate in the original position—but the conditions that make possible that fate. Individuals, in other words, are rational in their choice of an unequal society even though they would not, and did not, choose to be worse off. The point is that they were right, that is acting rationally, in choosing those conditions, and thus individuals who are in fact worse off have no real grounds for complaint. It is just a simple twist of fate, and not the structure of the polity and its administration, that has left them on the bottom rung of the economic ladder. Neither the better off nor political institutions are justly blamed for one's lower station in life if the difference principle is realized in practice.

Cavell's sensible expectation is that resentments and frustrations, cries of injustice and unfairness, are nonetheless likely to be heard even in the most just of unequal societies. Cavell's other sensible expectation is that "how I respond, as a member of the favored family, to your outburst of resentment and indignation is fateful to what I want of my society, to its democratic aspirations"

(Cavell 2004, 180). One response an individual might make is to follow Rawls and claim that one is above reproach, not responsible, and thus morally in the clear. The justification for that response *is* the two principles of justice: if they are realized in practice, then it is true that individuals, and society as a whole, are above reproach because no wrong has been committed. That response, Cavell argues, in effect treats fellow citizens as moral and political idiots, irrational and morally suspect because they cannot see that the rational choice behind the veil of ignorance was to choose the principles that govern the society they currently live in (Cavell 2004, 177–178). The response treats fellow citizens as though they don't understand what justice is, what principles of justice are, what a rational choice looks like; in short, the response treats other citizens like incompetent children. To give that response to one's fellow citizens is to sever moral relations with those citizens, to create a different sort of hierarchy in the heart of a supposedly democratic society: the rational and the irrational, the ones who understand the rules of the game and the ones who, either out of incompetence or resentment and envy, refuse to understand the rationality and justness of the rules.

To dismiss fellow citizens in this way is obviously to engage in social violence because one is using consent as a justification for rejecting both a claim to injustice and, most importantly, the *claimant*. It is to once again see consent in terms of exclusion and inclusion. For Cavell, the Rawlsian response ends a relationship with a fellow citizen and excludes, or threatens to exclude, some set of citizens from the community, or denies them full membership. To respond to one's citizens with "I am above reproach" is to end a potential "conversation of justice," an ongoing commitment to make clear to oneself and to others just what our society is, where we each stand in it, and where we hope to take it. It is to see oneself as no longer responsible, as no longer obligated to respond, to others with whom one was once in community.

Cavell encourages those better-off citizens who continue to consent to their society to respond differently: in Wittgensteinian fashion they ought to say, "This is simply what I do, where I am, and reasonably happily. I find that I do consent to this society as one in which to pursue happiness" (Cavell 2004, 185). This "weak" response is meant to continue a conversation of justice, to remain in community with the worse off, not by refusing to consent but by accepting one's compromised moral position as a member of the community.

The important point for my purposes should already be clear: Cavell's criticism of Rawls is focused on social violence, not even political social violence, and Cavellian consent is meant to counter social violence by refusing to deny one's complicity in injustice, hence refusing to deny one's moral responsibility toward those one is in community with. The issue, in short, is inclusion and exclusion, and the violence feared is social violence, not state violence.

To see how different are the issues raised by consenting to state violence, we can imagine a scenario analogous to that proposed by Cavell: an imprisoned individual expresses resentment or decries the punishment for its injustice. How, that individual might ask, can we still consent to a society that imprisons fellow citizens, exposing them to real acts of violence? For those of us who are not going to prison, who are "better off" in this respect, what are we to say, and how will consent shape our response?

The standard contract theory response allows us to say: "We, including you, are the reason why the state can punish you, can treat you in these ways, because we all consented to the social contract." And *that* is all that needs to be said. So long as justice is administered impartially, then to point to everyone's consent, including that of the punished, is a sufficient response to anyone complaining about a punishment they are receiving. If they continue to complain, to express resentment, it is quite difficult to understand why any of us who have not committed a crime are morally suspect for refusing to converse with them any longer. It is just obvious why the punished are going to be punished: because they agreed to be coercively bound by the same rules as we are. Our consent settles in advance the limits of our responsibility for the pain and violence the state causes in the name of justice, because consent authorizes that violence. So long as everything is relatively just in the society, then there is no obligation to be responsive to criminals complaining of their fate. State violence, and the consent that legitimizes it and authorizes the state to employ state violence, doesn't concern who is in and who out of community. It concerns only what we all, rule-breakers included, agreed to do to those who break the rules, and insofar as we all agreed to it, there is nothing more to say.

Can Cavell find anything wrong with that response analogous to what he finds wrong with Rawls' supposed response to the complaints of the worse off in a relatively just society? There is nothing problematic, in Cavellian terms, with the response, especially, but not only, if we take a Kantian line in justifying punishment. We can say to the punished individual "you consented to this," and feel above reproach because the criminal has broken the rules they agreed to follow. Their situation was not fated, not just bad luck, but the consequence of a choice, at least ideally. To agree to the maximin principle is, under realistic conditions, to expect that some will be worse off for reasons that are not a consequence of their own activity or choice. To reply to their complaints with "I am above reproach" is to question their moral and political adulthood, their competence and rationality. To agree to punish rule-breakers in reasonably just legal systems is to take human activities and choices seriously, to take the agency of fellow citizens seriously, to take their moral autonomy seriously: to treat our citizens precisely like equal adults. That is why Cavell surely cannot find anything wrong with answering the criminal's question with "I am above reproach." Suffice it to say that I don't agree with any of the "contract" reasoning just offered, but that is not the point. The point is to see that Cavell cannot complain about consent in its relation to state violence and the cries of the "unjustly" treated criminal in the way he can complain about Rawls' "above reproach" as a response to the worse off. The reason is simple: social violence and state violence are not the same, therefore consenting to one is not the same thing as consenting to the other.

Cavell's interpretation of consent clearly has nothing to do with the traditional problems of legitimacy, authority, law, punishment, and so forth, and it is *almost* clear that Cavellian consent and "classical" consent are not just different but incompatible. I will return in a moment to that qualifying "almost." Cavellian consent is incompatible with "classical" consent because Cavell ignores the deep, revolutionary insight of the classical contract thinkers, Rousseau included: the political community, the commonwealth, is an *artifice*, made by humans. The classical contract thinkers did not deny that human beings were social animals, but they did deny that human beings are political animals, and this difference makes a tremendous difference.

Polity and citizenship are human constructions, on the contract view, and that raises a number of problems, but for my purposes now a key implication of the "artificial" view of polity is that *political* relationships between citizens, even in a democracy, are different from other forms of social relationships. If the classical contract and consent view is correct, then citizenship is an institutional role with "institutional obligations." As A. John Simmons (and Rawls) argue, institutional obligations are far more impersonal and indirect than obligations owed to friends, family, or other close acquaintances (Simmons 2001, 65–92). The classical contract perspective sees politics as Cavell explicitly warns us not to: as a system of humanly instituted rules that bind us insofar as we consent with others to be bound, a consent we give because we think the condition of polity is better than a condition without it. If the contract is broken, the polity unjustly administered, then there is cause for complaint, dissent, rebellion, or perhaps even self-exile. If the contract is not broken, if things are more, rather than less, going according to the terms of the contract, then there are no grounds for complaint, there is no standing in the legal sense.

Further, classical consent is consent to create a polity with distinctively political institutions, like a legal system, an executive power to enforce the laws, a judicial system, and whatever else is required for the terms of the contract to be fulfilled. The whole point of creating the polity, on the classical view, is to stabilize social life, to bring authoritative decisions and rules to bear on everyday practices so as to rid human communities of the inconveniencies of the state of nature. These institutions, in order to serve their purpose, cannot be constantly called into question just because one or another individual finds himself unfairly treated even though no institution is to blame. We know the effects of processes of delegitimization on political institutions, and they are quite dangerous.

Cavellian consent is incompatible with classical consent because it demands that we ignore or deny central ideas in the classical contract view: that polity is an *artificial* construction consisting of *institutional* relationships between individuals holding the *role* of citizen, *obligated* to obey a number of *enforceable rules* because they *consented* to those rules in order to better secure their own advantage. If fellow citizens, at least in a democracy, are really to be seen not as role-holders but as people to whom we *must* say something in response to their sense of injustice, then Cavell is rejecting citizenship as an institutional role in favor of citizenship as *fellowship*. Fellowship is then the goal of community, hence of political community. On this view, if fellow citizens complain of injustice, even with no institutional cause, then we must reconsider, at the very least, the nature of our consent and whether we can consent to the polity as it stands. And if, as is likely to be true, upset citizens are never hard to find, we are likely to be continually rethinking our consent, hence threatening political stability.

I am endorsing neither the classical view nor Cavell's, but if the classical view is appealing in its picture of politics as artifice, of consent as grounding political power, of citizenship as a role, then Cavellian consent is likely to undermine all three of those features. Cavell's "picture" of politics is not a continuation of the classical contract and consent theory of polity, but a radical departure from it. It is neither designed to solve problems of political authority and state violence nor, in its proposal of a very different picture of polity as fellowship achieved or lost, does it share the presuppositions of the classical contract view of politics.

I hedged several paragraphs ago because classical and Cavellian consent are not necessarily mutually exclusive. The reason is that if state violence and social violence often reinforce each other in order to maintain a system of injustice, then we might have a reason to think that both classical and Cavellian consent must be mobilized to understand that system. For example, racism in the United States is clearly found in state violence and social violence, not just in parallel but in conjunction. State violence and social violence are targeted at specific minority communities in a multitude of ways, such that poor health outcomes, poverty, social and geographical isolation, dehumanizing representation in media, imprisonment, police violence, and so forth, are all visited on the same communities. One cannot, except for the sake of analysis, really distinguish state violence and social violence in the context of American racism, and that suggests, at any rate, that with enough thought one might find that Cavellian and classical consent are not as incompatible as they appear to be.

But state violence and social violence are different, and Cavellian consent not only cannot account for the former but must also assume a vastly different picture of politics than the picture we find, despite many differences, in the classical contract thinkers. To the extent that the two pictures of politics are opposed, then Cavellian consent is incompatible with classical consent, and we have the answer to the Cavell-inspired question posed above: is Cavellian consent incompatible with classical consent? The answer is yes, and that should force us to seriously question whether Cavell continues, departs from, or even rejects, the contract tradition.

CAVELL, READING, AND SYNTHETIC THEORIZING

If Cavell is a synthetic cross-tradition theorizer, it is because he is not only trained in analytic philosophy but also takes seriously Nietzsche, Heidegger, Derrida, Lacan, Levinas, Blanchot, Benjamin, and others. Nor is it only because he questions the distinction between literature and philosophy in ways akin to Derrida. Cavell is, and sees himself as, a reader and writer of *texts*:

> I have wished to understand philosophy not as a set of problems but as a set
> of texts. This means to me that the contribution of a philosopher—anyway of
> a creative thinker—to the subject of philosophy is not to be understood as a
> contribution to, or of, a set of *given* problems, although both historians and
> non-historians of the subject are given to suppose otherwise. (Cavell 1999, 3)

Cavell's emphasis on "given" implies his modernist leanings insofar as what marks a great text of philosophy is its manner of upending philosophical problems rather than answering existing questions. To see philosophical works as texts is to see those texts as needing to be *read*. This is a common enough premise of a great deal (although by no means all) of continental philosophy, and it explains in part why Cavell so often reads "against the grain." If one takes a philosophical work to be a text subject to textual criticism, and not just argumentative rebuttal, then the interpreter is going to focus on quite different aspects of the text than a more traditional "analytic" philosophical reader.

Consider, for example, the two most important citations from *A Theory of Justice* that we find in Cavell's criticism of it. Cavell quotes Rawls as saying, "Whenever social institutions satisfy these principles [of justice] those engaged in [those institutions] can say to one another that they are cooperating on terms to which they would agree if they were free and equal persons whose relations with respect to one another were fair" (Cavell 2004, 172). There are two things to say here. First, Cavell misleadingly cites the passage from Rawls; and second, why he cites as he does explains why we should still care about Cavell's criticism of Rawls. Cavell cites from mid-sentence; here is the part he left out: "Moreover, assuming that the original position does determine a set of principles (that is, that a particular conception of justice would be chosen), it will then be true that whenever social institutions . . . " Rawls' point is that if we actually do discover which principles of justice would be chosen in the original position—and this is what Rawls sets out to do, that is, make the discovery— then when citizens of a polity realizing those principles say that their polity is just, what they say will be *true*. Rawls is giving us the "truth-conditions" of the statement "our society is just": a society is just if and only if it realizes the principles of justice that would be chosen in the original position.

On the one hand, Cavell's unacknowledged ellipsis changes the meaning of the passage quite significantly, for now it seems as if Rawls is claiming that citizens of a just society can say something that they cannot say in an unjust society, as if the point is that conversations in a just society are different from conversations in an unjust society. That is exactly how Cavell does read the passage: "I call this idea of the communication made possible by the sharing of just institutions the *conversation of justice*" (Cavell 2004, 172). Rawls, though, wasn't claiming that a just society is the condition of a unique type of conversation. His point was only the "deflationary" point that "my society is just" is true if, and only if, my society is just. It seems clear that there is no further conversation to be had at this point, because what is said is true, no longer subject to debate. Cavell misquotes Rawls, and the misquotation matters.

On the other hand, Cavell's misquotation generates a line of critique that would not be possible otherwise, and that critique is, to my mind, quite powerful. The same is true of the second of the two citations alluded to above, the citation of "above reproach," which Cavell does admit is taken out of context. Cavell's critique is really a critique of the whole conception of politics we find in Rawls and, more broadly, in liberal theory: the classical contract idea that polity is a system of enforceable rules and citizenship a matter of specific obligations consented to in order to better secure one's individual interests. Cavell generates a criticism of a liberal *conception* of politics, justice, and citizenship by misquoting Rawls, and he does so by *reading* otherwise, by attending to and emphasizing passages, even words, like "say," that other readers would not lean on as heavily. This makes Cavell's criticism more immanent than it might otherwise seem. Cavell reads his way into a problematic Rawlsian sensibility that is otherwise not apparent, but that sensibility is internal to the contract view of politics, not just to Rawls. Or perhaps you disagree. That is not what interests me right now.

Even if one finds Cavell's readings of philosophical texts illuminating and textually justifiable, in focusing on texts rather than on politics Cavell's critique fails to help us understand the political reality contract and consent were meant to help us see more clearly. Many political theoretical works are no doubt texts, and we have much to learn from taking them as texts, but we often learn far more about the text than we do about politics if we take the Cavellian method of reading seriously. It is not always clear how a reading of a text is also going to be a reading of the political realities that text confronts and theorizes, and barring an explicit connection between reading a text and understanding that reality, we are likely to mistake having criticized a text with criticizing politics.

Cavell's practice of reading is especially problematic vis-à-vis works of analytic political theory. Unless one subscribes to a Derridean view of language, then we can distinguish between *texts* and things that "happen to be texts." Don't worry, I understand perfectly well how Derrida, or a Derridean, would criticize the distinction, but that is just begging the question. Taking seriously the textuality of Plato's *Republic*, or *Hamlet*, or *The Gay Science*, or *Madame Bovary*, or *Philosophical Investigations*, or *The Claim of Reason* is important because those works demand that we take them as texts: we misunderstand them to the extent that we ignore their textuality, their needing to be *read*. Is

A Theory of Justice best understood as a text? Is *Justification and Legitimacy*? *Anarchy, State, and Utopia*? *Democratic Authority*? "Two Concepts of Liberty"? Some of these texts are well written, but none of them demands to be taken as a text, and for this reason we misunderstand them if we take their textuality too seriously. Few analytic works of philosophy, much less political philosophy, even aspire to be texts.

If *A Theory of Justice* is trying to do anything, it is just the obvious: to get us to identify those principles of justice governing the distribution of primary goods that we would rationally endorse if we were unaware of our actual place in society. Rawls is trying to show us a coherent and reasonably realistic vision of a just society under modern conditions, including liberal institutions and capitalist modes of production. *A Theory of Justice* does so through arguments, thought experiments, criticisms of competing theories, and reliance on moral psychology, economic theory, rational choice theory, and so forth. Nothing in Cavell's interpretation of Rawls takes those goals and methods seriously because the real aim of Cavell's interpretation is to expose the Rawlsian project as resting on a restricted conception of politics and justice that forecloses a deeper, richer, and ultimately more just form of polity. This makes Cavell's reading—and many "continental" readings—a fascinating and provocative non sequitur.

That is why *reading* texts in analytic political philosophy is often not a viable mode of synthetic cross-tradition theorizing. It is not a criticism to say that the vast majority of analytic philosophical books and essays are not *texts* at all, in the sense of the term invoked by Cavell. To the extent that we read them as texts we will often fail to take them seriously, on their own terms, in light of their aims, respecting their modes of persuasion and argument.

While my discussion here and in Chapter 1 has not been exhaustive of the possibilities, I hope to have given some argument for a point I return to in the conclusion: synthetic cross-tradition theorizing is unlikely to be a viable method of cross-tradition theorizing. The next three chapters employ my preferred mode: aporetic cross-tradition theorizing.

3

PETTIT AND ARENDT ON FREEDOM I

Freedom, Spontaneity, Control

THE NEXT THREE CHAPTERS are examples of aporetic cross-tradition theorizing in action. They take on freedom and justice—two of the densest political concepts—through the work of Hannah Arendt and Philip Pettit, and John Rawls and Jacques Derrida. In each chapter I show that a crucial feature of the concept theorized by a representative of one tradition cannot be harmonized with another crucial feature of that concept when theorized from the other tradition. This creates an aporia: two necessary but incompatible features of a concept must be, but cannot be, reconciled. I will postpone further discussions of aporetic cross-tradition theorizing until the Conclusion, but suffice it to say that I hope these chapters are strong evidence for the viability and productivity of my preferred aporetic approach.

Freedom, Hannah Arendt claims, is the raison d'être of politics. It is the concept of justice, however, that has dominated political theory in the decades following the appearance of Rawls' *Theory of Justice*. From an Arendtian perspective, emphasizing the just distribution of primary goods is unsurprising because modernity is characterized by the rise of the social, that is, the increasing rationalization, bureaucratization, and "privatization" of the public sphere. When the public sphere is overrun by the social, public life is dominated by economic and administrative problems; problems of internal and external security, as well as precarious struggles for recognition and social equality by previously excluded and/or marginalized groups. Arendt was extremely wary of these tendencies, although her criticism of the social goes hand in hand with a deeply ambivalent affirmation of the value and progress made by laborers and workers, oppressed groups, the poor, and so on. The question of how to justly distribute rights, goods, wealth, responsibilities, education, and other "primary goods" is prompted by the rise of the social and answered through considerations about justice. Lost in these concerns, for Arendt, is freedom, that for the sake of which politics exists and individuals enter the political sphere.

The primacy of freedom links Arendt to the revision and endorsement of republicanism we find in the work of Philip Pettit.[1] Pettit's central thesis is that the republican tradition endorses a view of political freedom as non-domination, that is, the view that political freedom consists in not being subject to a power of arbitrary interference by governmental and non-governmental, collective or individual, actors. Arbitrary interference is interference in the affairs of an individual that does not "track the interests" of the individual interfered with. One's status as free depends upon being free from even the possibility of arbitrary interference, and that status is valuable and desirable in part because it enables a free individual to stand on an equal footing with others. Pettit argues that the supreme value of freedom as non-domination ought to orient our criticisms of existing political regimes, and he offers outlines of how to institutionalize republican freedom in contemporary states. Justice, while a part of such a conception, is in service of freedom as non-domination.

The centrality of freedom for both Arendt and Pettit is not the only link between them. They both share—for Arendt intermittently and perhaps not full-throatedly—a commitment to republican political ideas and institutions, and they both endorse a concept of freedom that challenges negative and positive freedom. However, in a variety of important and ultimately incommensurable respects, Pettit and Arendt disagree about the "ground" of freedom, its description, and the relation of philosophical and phenomenological accounts of freedom *as such* to political freedom.

I argue in this chapter that looking at Pettit and Arendt together enables us to see a crucial aspect of freedom downplayed, undertheorized, or simply ignored in the other. Bluntly stated, there is a tension between freedom as control of the self by the self—what Pettit calls "discursive control"—and Arendtian freedom as the initiation of the new through action, an experience of non-sovereign, spontaneous activity that requires the absence or severe delimitation of control, even self-control. The tension exists because both Arendt and Pettit can appeal to intuitions and ordinary language to support their claims; and yet, it seems clear that freedom cannot require and not require control.

This chapter focuses on Pettit's and Arendt's theories of freedom *as such*. The next chapter turns to the political consequences of the place of control in freedom, and problems that raises for both Pettit and Arendt.

PETTIT'S THEORY OF FREEDOM AS FITNESS
TO BE HELD RESPONSIBLE

Pettit's most extensive account of freedom as such is *A Theory of Freedom*. Pettit begins a bit oddly from an understanding of freedom as "being fit to be held responsible" for one's action (see Knowles 2003; and Gorr 2005).[2] He takes this route as opposed to two other connotations of freedom: (1) freedom as *ownership* of one's action, where a free action is one that the agent can identify as their own; and (2) freedom as *underdetermination*, where an action is free insofar as it is not fully determined (especially by things such as drugs, psychoses, and the like, but also by physical laws). In short, we can understand freedom starting from the *person* in their intersubjective relations (the responsibility path), from the *self* in its relation to its own actions (the ownership path), or from the *action* itself (the underdetermination path).[3] For Pettit, any theory of freedom will have to deal with the freedom of the person, the self, and the action, but he chooses the responsibility path because it enables him to account for both of the other accounts of freedom, whereas the other two cannot account for the agent's responsibility (Pettit 2001a, 6–7).

Freedom as responsibility presumes that "we engage with other human beings in a distinctive manner that involves the spontaneous attribution of responsibility, and we conceive of freedom as that property of human beings, and of the actions performed by human beings, that makes such an attribution appropriate under the rules of the practice" (Pettit 2001a, 13). This responsibility is further understood in light of three conditions: an agent is fit to be held responsible, hence free, only insofar as (1) they can be held responsible from a perspective prior to choice, (2) they are held personally responsible, and (3) they are fit to be held responsible (Pettit 2001a, 14).

The first condition insists that we cannot hold someone responsible solely for the way an action turned out, but only insofar as the agent could have been held responsible prior to the action. Pettit's example is the individual who doesn't crack under torture. While we may praise such an individual, Pettit argues, we certainly wouldn't blame them for cracking under the violence of torture.

Being subject to torture, no matter how the agent acts subsequently, forecloses the attribution of responsibility. Such an agent is not free. One can extrapolate from this that many agents who act under various forms of compulsion or oppression more mundane than torture nonetheless might not be fit to be held responsible. For example, poverty, racial violence, or widespread homophobia might foreclose attributing responsibility to some agents who act "irresponsibly" under these conditions.

The second condition forecloses attributing responsibility to an individual on the basis of assimilating the individual actor to a social class or group. Thus, we might be tempted to treat *anyone* suffering from extreme poverty as not responsible for, say, the normally wrong act of stealing food to survive. However, Pettit argues that in so doing we overlook the individual agent and the potential difference of their actions from the general class of actions or actors to which we assimilate the agent and the act. Perhaps stealing, even by those in desperate need, is wrong; but in a particular case, we should judge the individual as fit to be held responsible solely on the basis of the specific case. The same point holds if we condone stealing by those in desperate need: we should still judge the individual as responsible or not on the basis of the specific case. Only in this way can we insure that the agent is truly fit to be held responsible or not.

The third condition is familiar enough from moral and political philosophy: an agent can only be held responsible if they are actually capable of responsible action. Thus children, the insane, those with mental disabilities, and so on, are often excluded from the realm of responsible action, at least in part. To be truly free is to have the capacity to act freely where this means one can be held properly responsible, not *as if* one is properly responsible (Pettit 2001a, 14–16).

With this analysis of the concept of freedom as responsibility in tow, Pettit moves on to argue for the advantage of conceptualizing freedom as fitness to be held responsible. The argument begins from the fact that we do impute responsibility to others and their actions, and the only way we can understand such responsibility is by assuming that the agent is free. There is, in other words, an a priori conceptual link between freedom and responsibility such that "someone who did not see why that connection had to obtain would fail to understand what freedom was or what holding someone responsible was" (Pettit 2001a, 18). The point is worth emphasizing: an account of freedom that denied the a priori link between freedom and responsibility would fail to be a theory or conceptualization of freedom *at all*. As we will see, Arendt does appear to deny this link, and for this reason we have the beginnings of an aporia. But we will get there.

The a priori link between freedom and responsibility is something freedom as ownership and freedom as underdetermination cannot explain, Pettit argues, because it is unclear why the fact that an action is mine or the fact that an action is underdetermined makes the actor responsible for the action.[4] The intuition that individuals are responsible leads to the claim that freedom is fitness to be held responsible.

Pettit adduces ten further reasons for his analysis of freedom as fitness to be held responsible, but there is no reason to detail them here. He also addresses "conundrums" of freedom that trouble any conceptualization of free action, but that too would take us to issues irrelevant to the main purposes of this chapter. For now we will just accept Pettit's conclusion: freedom is best understood as fitness to be held responsible.

DISCURSIVE CONTROL

If freedom is fitness to be held responsible then we must theorize what kind of control over an action accounts for that responsibility. Pettit raises and rejects two possible theories of freedom. The first is freedom as rational control, which argues that an action is free insofar as the action "materializes in a rationally required way on the basis of rationally held beliefs and desires" even where such rational control is only "virtual," that is, not actively controlling the action (Pettit 2001a, 38). A first problem with this theory is that an action can be rationally controlled without the agent being fit to be held responsible. For example, if rational control is all that is required for freedom, then an individual held up at gunpoint and told to give the attacker their wallet is nonetheless free insofar as in giving up their wallet they might be acting on the basis of rational beliefs and desires (Pettit 2001a, 45–47). Moreover, on the rational control account many animals might be said to be free even though we would not hold them responsible for their actions (Pettit 2001a, 40). Rational control is necessary, but not sufficient, for freedom as responsibility.

The second theory Pettit rejects is freedom as "volitional control." On this view, an action is free if it is both rationally controlled and volitionally controlled, that is, if the agent desires, at a higher-order level, to be effectively moved by a desire the agent has at a first-order level (Pettit 2001a, 50–53). In desiring to be moved by one's desires, the theory argues, the agent can identify fully with their actions—that is, own them—and thus the actions are free from an "ownership" perspective. The problem with this second theory, Pettit argues, is, first, that there is no reason to think that even a second-order desire to be effectively moved by a desire requires ownership of an action, for second-order desires might not be the agent's either. If, to use Pettit's example, there is a first-order desire to clean one's desk and a second-order desire to be effectively moved by that desire, one might nonetheless know that the second-order desire comes from a detested Victorian upbringing and its demands for order and cleanliness. And yet, one may still have the second-order desire. Even if one *approves* of the second-order desire to be effectively moved by the desire to clean one's desk, one may not "own" that desire because the approval itself may be something that "happens" rather than something actively desired and approved of. Moreover, the same difficulty that afflicts the rational control theory returns: if attacked at gunpoint one might very well have a second-order desire to be moved by the first-order desire to hand over money, but how can that entail one's being responsible for the action? Surely when held at gunpoint one is not to be held responsible even if one has rational beliefs and desired desires. Again, though, Pettit sees volitional control as necessary but not sufficient for freedom.

The theory of freedom as discursive control begins from the free person rather than from an account of a free action or a free self. Personhood can be broadly understood as indicating the intersubjective relations each individual maintains with others and, in a sense, even the "intersubjective" because "intertemporal" relations between individual "selves" over the course of a life. The concept of "person" is a "forensic concept that is tied up with questions of who is responsible for what and that personal identity is nothing more or less than the relationship, whatever it is, that propagates responsibility across time" (Pettit 2001a, 83). To be a person one must be able "to square what one does or claims or feels on any occasion with what one did or claimed or felt at earlier times," and thus to be a person is to be capable of maintaining and providing reasons for even contradictory or divergent relationships between one's current and past attitudes, beliefs, and desires (Pettit 2001a, 82). Drawing, like Arendt, on the etymology of "person" from the Latin *persona*—the mask worn by an actor—we can see how a person is the "public face" of an individual, the identity presented to others and the continuous self-identity of the individual over the course of their life.

We can identify a free person by looking at their discursive interactions with others.[5] In discursive debate and deliberation we can make sense of freedom as fitness to be held responsible because in discursive debate one can genuinely say that even if one is under the influence of another person, the nature of that influence leaves one fit to be held responsible. Discursive influence is the influence of *reasons* that the individual can freely accept and endorse as a reasoner (Pettit 2001a, 68). For example, in discussing whether a country should go to war, one might be deeply influenced by the argument of another discussant. This position may be influential, but the influence is a consequence not of blind obedience, but of the rational persuasive power of the reasons provided. In such a case, one can be held responsible for one's beliefs and any consequent action even though the belief is held on the basis of the influence of another person. Discursive interaction conducted on the basis of reasons and procedures all agree to allows discussants to be influenced without losing their freedom. Thus,

> an agent's freedom as a person will naturally be identified . . . with the form of control that people enjoy in discourse-friendly relationships. An agent will be a free person so far as they have the ability to discourse and they have the access to discourse that is provided within such relationships. That someone is free in this sense will be consistent with their undergoing the discursive influence of others. (Pettit 2001a, 70)

Discursive control, then, provides us an account of the free person. How, then, does this theory deal with some of the problems Pettit has previously identified?

First, insofar as discursive control requires others to engage with the individual in "discourse-friendly" ways, there are a set of social constraints placed on persons within discourse. Thus, in order to ensure individual freedom, others can only act in ways that maintain the agent's discursive control. This means that in a situation such as the attack at gunpoint, it is clearly the case that the person is no longer in discursive control. No matter how rational their actions, nor how desired, the agent cannot be held responsible because the agent is not a free person. Other discourse-unfriendly forms of influence that reduce or eliminate the person's freedom include relationships of domination in which one speaker has more social power than another, although what Pettit calls "friendly coercion" is not at odds with free personhood (Pettit 2001a, 78). Such coercion is friendly—crucially for Pettit's republican conception of political freedom—to the extent "that what happens between coercer and coercee is controlled by the coercee's avowable interests and those interests are the discursive considerations that are intuitively relevant to what should happen" (Pettit 2001a, 76). Coercion that "tracks the interests" of the coerced is not a denial of freedom. In general, the possession of discursive control can tell us whether a person is free or unfree in the face of various kinds of coercion.

Second, discursive control accounts for the ownership connotation of freedom insofar as possessing discursive control requires the agent to relate themselves to their own actions, both past and present, such that they "sign" their actions. As we have already seen, to be a person requires the agent to take responsibility even for past actions, that is, to answer for them. A person answers for their past even if they have changed their mind; that is what personal identity is (Pettit 2001a, 82–84). A self—as opposed to a person—is more "presentist" in conception: one may have multiple selves, that is, multiple first-person identifications with beliefs and desires, over time. Identity as a self depends not on answering to past and present actions and beliefs, but actively owning those beliefs and desires (Pettit 2001a, 85). One may, after all, answer for one's past as a religious person—that is, see that past as related to a present self that takes responsibility for it—without thereby identifying now as a religious person. With these conceptions of personal identity and self-identity, Pettit argues that possession of discursive control requires the agent to identify with their past and live up to it. In other words, discursive control requires a committed self, one that answers for what one has said and done and follows through on one's commitments. A self that neither answers for its past nor follows through on its commitments is either an elusive or a weak self, and neither self can be held responsible in the true sense of the term (Pettit 2001a, 86). If one disowns one's past—that is, looks at it as if it happened to someone else—then how can one be held responsible for it? Without reliably following through on one's commitments, why should one be taken seriously by others and held responsible for promises and other obligations?[6] The free self is a self that takes ownership of its past and follows through on its commitments, and is thus fit to be held responsible.

Third, discursive control can account for free action because an action is free insofar as it is performed as a result of either actual or virtual discursive reflection and control. Broadly speaking, an action is free insofar as it can or could pass the test of discursive reflection, performed either publicly or privately. Such actions are free even if the reflection is only virtual, that is, the reflection could be or could have been performed and could serve or could have served as the basis of the act. Thus, Pettit is not committed to the view that free actions must be actively and consciously controlled by reasons and desires fully affirmed and owned by the agent. It is enough for the free act to be capable of discursive support (Pettit 2001a, 90–93).

The theory of freedom as discursive control claims that an individual is free, hence fit to be held responsible, insofar as they stand in discourse-friendly relations of non-domination with others, own their past and follow through on their commitments, and act on the basis of actual or possible discursive reflection. Only if the agent is a free person and self and the action performed a free act, can the agent be free. Under the theory of freedom as discursive control, Pettit argues, we can solve the conundrums each connotation of freedom poses, but the solutions—which are quite problematic—need not concern us here. What is and will prove to be important for the comparison with Arendt is that Pettit's basic account of freedom requires control: the assurance that others cannot dominate you or control you, the control one possesses over one's self, and the control one has over one's actions. Freedom is found in control: a point that Arendt will challenge.

SOME QUESTIONS

Before moving on to Arendt's work it is worth raising a few questions that will shape my reconstruction of Arendt's views on freedom.

First, while the theory of discursive control may give us a good sense of the conditions of freedom as responsibility, the *value* of freedom as such is unclear. In "Freedom in Belief and Desire," Pettit and Michael Smith argue that if freedom is construed as the ability to have done otherwise than what one did, then "[f]reedom in such an unqualified sense—if, indeed, it deserves to be called 'freedom' at all—would not be particularly attractive from our point of view. If an agent believes or desires rightly according to the evidence and the values, then there will be nothing attractive in itself about being such that he could have believed or desired otherwise" (Pettit and Smith 1996, 444). This view is part of Pettit's broader endorsement of "orthonomy," or being ruled by the "right," because it is not enough, and not desirable on its own, to be "metaphysically" free. Worthwhile freedom consists in discursive control, in acting on the basis of reasons and desires one rationally affirms in contexts of non-dominating relations with others (Pettit and Smith 1996, 442–444; 1993, 76–77; Pettit 2007a, 238–242). However, the value of freedom as responsibility or orthonomy is not clearly identified and explained. As we will see in the next chapter, the value of *political* freedom, of freedom as non-domination, is so great that it is a primary good, something anyone ought to possess. But what is the good of freedom as responsibility? Obviously, there may be an instrumental social good or value to responsibility—say, in inculcating habits and/or beliefs that tend toward secure relations among members of a community—but what is the value of being fit to be held responsible for the individual? Is it that one's freedom, or lack thereof, enables a defense against criticism of one's actions? Is it that we can hold others responsible for what they do either to us or to others and blame or punish them? But surely there are a number of ways to secure a society that require no notion of moral, as opposed to causal, responsibility. Moreover, we can surely protect ourselves from domination or unjust accusation without relying on claims about our freedom and responsibility (buy a gun, or several), just as we can respond to others without taking their responsibility into account (buy a gun, or several). Is there something the agent gains simply by being free and responsible? Or is there an intrinsic value in being free? Lacking such an account, why should an agent desire to have discursive control, to be responsible, to be free? On Pettit's account we are not fated to be free, for we are often un- or non-free. The value of freedom as responsibility is not clear.

Second, Pettit's account avoids connotations of freedom that just as easily—and perhaps more obviously—make sense of our intuitions about and experiences of freedom.[7] For example, the concept of *spontaneity* plays no real role in Pettit's theory of freedom, for underdetermination is not quite the same thing as spontaneity, and even if it were the same thing, Pettit deflates the underdetermination problem and "solves" it without any metaphysical argument (see Pettit 2001a, 93–97). Kant, in a passage Arendt refers to, defines spontaneity in the third antinomy in *The Critique of Pure Reason*: an "absolute causal spontaneity" must be a kind of causality such that the cause of an act is not itself caused; the act is, as it were, "self-caused" (Kant 1998, A446/B474). An absolutely free spontaneous act, then, is an act that is not *under*determined by a previous cause or set of conditions, but *un*determined. Kant's idea combines the modality of contingency and the assignment of causal agency to a free agent. A spontaneous act is one for which an agent alone is the cause and one that might not have taken place. For Kant, the possibility of such a causality must be assumed because it is essential to morality and indeed to our investigations into certain objects in the natural world; but it remains for all that an idea only practical reason can really work with. So, one might reject on Kantian grounds any possibility of a phenomenological investigation of an absolute causal spontaneity. What, then, of a *phenomenologically* spontaneous act, where that means something like "an act that is genuinely experienced as new and surprising both by the agent and any spectators."[8] This equally removes us from metaphysical worries, but what might such an act be?

Consider one realization of freedom as relative spontaneity: improvisation. An improviser is free insofar as they are not bound by or acting on the basis of rules. However, successful improvisatory actions are partially made sense of by and thus bear undeniable relations to those rules. The obvious examples here are the jazz musician and the athlete at the top of their game. For both athletes and jazz musicians a great deal of rule-bound and rote technical practice is required, and competitive sports (explicitly) and jazz (more often implicitly) are both rule-bound practices. Improvisers are not fully free to improvise if they cannot physically play their instrument or dribble a ball without closely concentrating on technique. Freedom to improvise musically or athletically also requires a "theory" of music or of a sport, whether that knowledge has been explicitly learned or is implicitly understood.

However, the jazz musician and the athlete—and artists generally—often speak as if, when they are playing well, they are not in control at all but "in the flow." They are almost passive; inspired; freed from decisions, beliefs, desires; open to influence and free for expression and performance. In improvisation freedom is spontaneous invention or composition, often but not always in con- formity with rules. What takes place when we listen to a great jazz solo or watch Magic Johnson lead a fast break is legible, comprehensible; but it is not planned or predictable. We seem fully aware that a guiding mental representation of a progression of quickly played notes is not the cause of the action, nor are the angles and velocities of objects required to make a successful bounce pass from fifty feet away. And yet, such performances make sense *as if* they were consciously and rationally chosen.[9] Even we lesser mortals experience this in ordinary conversations at their best because they often take on the same freedom of improvisation, of call and response. These possibilities will prove to be central to Arendt's own account of freedom as initiating newness, and they suggest that Pettit might have unduly limited the possible connotations of freedom in ad- vance. If one begins from freedom as responsibility—especially if one supports such a starting point on the basis of ordinary experience—then only certain aspects of freedom will be examined, some of which might be in conflict with other ordinary and intuitively plausible accounts of freedom.

Finally, one might raise serious doubts about Pettit's reliance on "virtual control," which enables him to escape the charge that on his theory of freedom we are free only when we consciously and actively possess, and act on the basis of, discursive control. Pettit's account of virtual control is central to his thinking about human action and freedom because it enables him to maintain a commitment to the rationality and causal efficacy of belief and desire in action—and thus to a freedom worth honoring and valuing—without ignoring the fact that human beings are often on what I have been calling "cruise control" as they go about their lives, and hence potentially unfree most of the time. Virtual control plays an important role in Pettit's reconciliation of the economist's view of human behavior and common sense; it is also important in taking seriously neuroscientific results that appear to show the ambiguity or even absence of human will; and it plays a crucial role in Pettit's theory of freedom as discursive control (see Pettit 1995; 2007b).

However, Pettit's examples of virtual control are not persuasive. A police officer walking a beat, for example, is surely often on cruise control. But, Pettit suggests, the appearance of someone on the verge of a breakdown or engaging in a crime will cause the officer to switch over to discursive control immediately. For Pettit, the explanation for this is that the officer was in "virtual discursive control" because the possibility of discursive control was "on standby" (Pettit 2001a, 92). Similarly, although an individual may not always consciously be the rational, self-regarding utility maximizer of economic theory, such a possibility is virtually present if, like the police officer, the usual ways of being more or less other-regarding begin to threaten self-interest (Pettit 1995). This seems wrong.

If Pettit were arguing that *habits* were developed during active discursive control but over time habitual control becomes unconscious, that would be one thing. But Pettit denies that virtual discursive control is "unconscious" active control; it really is on standby (Pettit 2001a, 92). Virtual control is, by analogy with certain implicit beliefs, "hovering" on the "edge of realisation" (Pettit 1995n6). Virtual control is present, but not actual. Pettit's argument for virtual control is that if, on the one hand, a controlling factor, a C-factor, *directly* causes a result, R, such that if C_1 then R_1, then there is active control by the C-factor. On the other hand, if C_1 *usually* causes R_1 on the basis of an independent or collateral causal order, but in a specific case R_1 does not follow from C_1, then a *correction* will be forthcoming. It is this capacity to more or less instantly "correct" for a deviation from the standard, habitual relation of C_1 to R_1, that Pettit calls "virtual control" (Pettit 2001a, 38). The reason there is still *control* is that the C-factor remains in control over the results.[10] Virtual control is like a full-time lifeguard, ready to step in and take active control if something goes wrong. Just as a lifeguard is virtually in control of the pool even when sitting in a chair, so is virtual discursive control controlling the situation even when it is on standby.

On this account, though, virtual control is hardly "control" in the same sense as active control, and we may have here a fallacy of equivocation. Virtual control is entirely *reactive*; it steps into the breach, but only when and where there is a breach. Imagine: a lifeguard is on duty at a public pool and, for the sake of simplicity, let's assume there is just one not entirely water-worthy swimmer in the pool. The role of the lifeguard is to make sure this person doesn't drown. One way for the lifeguard to control the situation, that is, to make sure the swimmer doesn't drown, is to physically hold the swimmer above water at all times. This, I take it, is active control of the swimmer. Most of the time, though, the lifeguard is sitting in the chair. If the swimmer starts to drown, the lifeguard notices and jumps into the pool to hold the swimmer above water; sometimes it is too late. Before the swimmer begins drowning, the lifeguard is virtually controlling the pool and he switches to active control when things go awry.

However, whereas in active control the lifeguard is *in* control, in virtual control the lifeguard must *take* control, and these are importantly different if we want to make sense of the responsibility, hence freedom, of the lifeguard. If the swimmer drowns while the lifeguard is actively holding the swimmer up or if the swimmer drowns after the lifeguard reactively jumps out of the chair and swims to the swimmer (perhaps the swimmer is at the other end of the pool), then surely the fitness to be held responsible is different. If there is no negligence on the part of the lifeguard—just bad luck or limits to human swimming speed—then surely the lifeguard is not fit to be held responsible for the drowning in the virtual control scenario because it is unclear how we can ascribe a meaningful sense of control to the lifeguard. Agents in virtual control are *capable* of reacting to what happens, that is, capable of taking control of an action that has in one way or another gone awry. But the very fact that the agent has to *take* control suggests—and not just for verbal reasons—that the agent was not *in* control at all.

The issue is important for a theory of freedom as responsibility because Pettit's view implies a view about moral luck that needs defense. We are often in virtual control of our actions, and when things go awry we move from virtual to active control. Even in active control, however, my control extends only so far: it extends only to the limits of the self, to the limits of my capacities to act in a timely fashion. The cop on active control may not be able to stop a crime from happening, just as the safe driver on active control may not be able to stop their car before hitting the child that bolts into the street. We rightly deny that the cop or driver in active control is responsible for failing to stop the criminal or the car because they were not negligent—they were merely human, subject to bad luck, and that is no fault. This is even more true of virtual control because to be human *is* to usually be in virtual control. It is not a moral failing to be in virtual control, and it is unclear to me just what the moral difference is between the cop who fails to stop a crime when in active control and the cop who fails to stop a crime when in virtual control. But there is such a difference, and that difference matters greatly for assessing an agent's responsibility, hence freedom.

The only reason I can imagine for Pettit's reliance on virtual control is to find an actor responsible, hence free, even though the actor is not actively controlling their actions. This strikes me as an excessively moralistic reason to see freedom as responsibility, driven less by a desire to understand how humans can be free even when acting habitually than by a desire to find persons responsible for what they do even though, as creatures usually on virtual control, they are not in active control of their activity. Perhaps the extent of the role of luck in our lives of freedom and responsibility is so great as to extend even into our own natural tendencies toward virtually controlled activity. It is, perhaps, bad luck that we humans spend so much time in virtual control and for that reason are less free, hence less responsible, than Pettit hopes.

A second reason to be skeptical about Pettit's recourse to virtual control is that it may shift our attention away from desirable experiences in which an absence of both active and virtual control is constitutive of our freedom. The experience of improvisation, whether in music, sports, or even conversation is a desirable realization of freedom in the absence of control. Pettit's theory forecloses the possibility that such experiences are experiences of freedom, because they escape both active and virtual control.[11] The jazz musician is not in virtual control or active control when improvising even though the notes played can be understood, upon reflection, to be in accordance with one or another meaning- or order-making set of rules or reasons. The musician is not in active control because our conscious intentional states are often too slow to account for the pace of the music. The musician is not in virtual control because the musician is not on standby, waiting to intervene when his or her fingers do not independently produce the notes that were "supposed" to have been played. An improviser is acting spontaneously, or is not improvising at all.[12] If we can rightly describe the improvisatory actor as free, then freedom sometimes requires us to overcome our tendencies toward control.

Virtual control is a hypothesis, a way of explaining a phenomenon like habit without sacrificing the ascription of freedom to habitual actors. To test this hypothesis would require the difficult job of making clear the ontology of virtual presence in such a way that we could then provide evidence for such a hypothesis. The hypothesis serves the purpose, as already noted, of saving discursive control in the face of the obvious phenomenological fact that we often act habitually, without active discursive control. The hypothesis is unnecessary if, for example, freedom is not internally linked to reason or rationality, to the need for freedom to be more than the mere possibility of having done otherwise. The hypothesis is also unnecessary if one argues that we are not always free, hence not always responsible, but only free and responsible when we have active control over our actions. A mixture of *axiological* and theoretical aims and claims are, unsurprisingly, at work in Pettit's theory of discursive control.

I have spent a significant amount of time on these three questions about Pettit's argument because they set up Arendt's theory of freedom. Pettit surely has answers to these questions, and in my raising them there should be no implication taken that Arendt is right about freedom. My interest here, as in this book as a whole, is largely to examine and identify—but not to dismiss, disprove, debunk, or reject arguments on the basis of—aporias, internal limitations, axiological commitments, and the like, in prominent positions within contemporary political thought.

ARENDT'S THEORY OF FREEDOM AS INITIATING NEWNESS

It is probably inaccurate to attribute a "theory" of freedom to Arendt, although she does offer an analysis of freedom drawn from our intuitions and experiences, asks how it is possible for us to be free, and further specifies a mode of human freedom we can call political freedom as opposed to freedom *as such*.[13] Political freedom in Arendt and Pettit will be discussed in the next chapter, but it is worth noting here that there are strong reasons for denying that Arendt distinguishes between political and non-political freedom. On the one hand, while Arendt does offer a long historical discussion of the will in *The Life of the Mind*, *The Human Condition*, and "What Is Freedom?," the identification of freedom with free will is understood as a pernicious theoretical and political error. On the other hand, Arendt admits that freedom as the capacity to initiate newness can be found throughout human experience—even, she later admits, in the experience of willing—and thus it is worth making, at least for explanatory purposes, a distinction between freedom as such and political freedom.

There is a freedom in action but there is also a freedom in fabrication, in thinking, and in judgment. Perhaps only labor, among the human activities, contains no moment of freedom, although this overstates the way in which necessity conditions laboring. There are not different kinds of freedom in Arendt's work, just the same freedom variously visible or invisible to the self and others. The freedom in these activities is the *freedom of initiating the new*.

Arendt's clearest definition of freedom is "the freedom to call something into being which did not exist before, which was not given, not even as an object of cognition or imagination, and which therefore, strictly speaking, could not be known" (Arendt 1993, 151; see also Arendt 1998, 177–178). This freedom exists only in action, for "Men *are* free—as distinguished from their possessing the gift for freedom—as long as they act, neither before nor after; for to *be* free and to act are the same" (Arendt 1993, 151). The context of Arendt's claim shows that by "action" Arendt does not mean only political action as a specific activity within the *vita activa* as described in *The Human Condition*. For although Arendt claims our acquaintance with freedom has its origin in "intercourse with others" rather than "intercourse with ourselves," we know that on her view of thinking, this mental activity is perhaps more of an activity than any other (Arendt 1993, 148; see also Arendt 1998, 325; 1978a). Moreover, Arendt readily admits that there is a moment of freedom in the creative arts, although that freedom does not appear to others (Arendt 1993, 154). More broadly, Arendt's insistence that freedom exists only in action is set against three rival views of freedom. The first is the "inner freedom" of the Stoic who, freeing himself from desires that lead him to suffer, isolating himself from the world, and reconciling himself to only desire what is in his power, may "feel" free but is deluding himself (Arendt 1993, 146–147). Freedom is not found in a retreat into the self. Freedom is also not reducible to two of the conditions necessary for freedom: liberation from necessity or tyranny or oppression, and the free status of the citizen, the sheer capacity to move about freely (Arendt 1993, 148; 1998, 31; 1965, 140–141).[14] While one cannot be free without liberation from necessity and freedom of movement, such fundaments of freedom do not make one free. Finally, Arendt is challenging the identification of freedom with free will, and more specifically, the understanding of freedom in terms of self-sovereignty and autonomy. Freedom as sovereignty and autonomy is Arendt's central target, and as we will see in the next chapter, Arendt's endorsement of isonomy—a condition in which one neither rules nor is ruled—is for her the form of political organization most conducive to freedom.[15] But even the activity of willing must spring from freedom as initiating the new, even if this leads to the paradoxical result of unfreedom. At any rate, "action" in the statement quoted here refers not only to political action but to human activity in general.

If we take Arendt's "definition" of freedom as calling the new into being together with her claim that we are free only when we act, we can paraphrase Arendtian freedom as "action that calls something new into being."[16] Whether through words or deeds, freedom is action that—to rely on Arendt's Augustinian influence—*initiates* something new.[17] Hence, my shorthand for Arendtian freedom is "freedom as initiating the new."

Not only must a free act initiate something new in the sense that what is initiated could not have been foreseen, thought, or even imagined; a free act must also transcend or exceed the will, that is, a free act must not be *commanded* by the will: "Action insofar as it is free is neither under the guidance of the intellect nor under the dictate of the will—although it needs both for the execution of any particular goal" (Arendt 1993, 152). This claim is central to Arendt's account of freedom, but it is far from clear. In order to understand Arendt's theory of freedom, we must reconstruct the claim that an act is free insofar as it transcends intellect, will, and judgment.

From what we have seen so far, freedom must meet two conditions: (1) a free action must initiate something new, that is, it must be "creative" in a broad sense of the term; and (2) a free action must not be guided or dictated, which, as we will see, means that an act is free only insofar as it is neither controlled by others nor by the self.

First, we need to sort out how an action that *requires* intellect (that is, a set of beliefs), judgment (the application of those beliefs to a particular situation), and will (the impetus to carry out a specific action) can be free only to the extent that it is not *determined* by intellect, judgment, and will. Arendt is not claiming that a free action has no relation to intellect, judgment, and will; on the contrary, what Arendt abbreviates as "motives and aims" are crucial components of any action: various ends, beliefs, desires, and so on. To this extent Arendt agrees with a Davidsonian account of action. It is unclear how one could even speak of action, as opposed to behavior, without beliefs, desires, judgments, and goals (Arendt 1993, 151). However, Arendt describes motives and aims—the work of the intellect, judgment, and will—as "determining factors" of actions (Arendt 1993, 151). Action must transcend these determining factors in order to be free. But how can it do that, especially since what is initiated must be new even from the perspective of the actor? Like Henri Bergson's symphony that was not possible before being actual, whatever a free action brings into being cannot pre-exist its emergence. Thus, even the actor will be surprised by their action—if that action is free. These qualifications only make matters more obscure, for now it seems as if freedom is a blind flailing about.[18]

One can make some sense of Arendt's claims by noting that something genuinely new would be, by definition, unavailable to cognition or imagination. This is precisely Bergson's claim about the symphony: if the symphony already exists in a state of possibility (whether in Aristotelian potentiality or simply in the imagination of the composer), then the symphony is not new; it simply awaits its performance or reification (Bergson 1992, 21; Arendt 1978b, 15). Arendt's claim about newness shares this Bergsonian conclusion and has an air of ineffability only because we are captivated by a picture of newness or invention or creativity drawn from *homo faber*, from the sphere of fabrication.[19] To the extent that there is freedom in fabrication, in making things—and this includes the artwork—the newness is not "in" the thing made but in the moment of "inspiration" in which even the artist first has a glimpse of what they will then make. There may also be freedom in the process of fabrication itself insofar as it is not entirely determined by a blueprint. For Arendt, "the point here is not whether the creative artist is free in the process of creation"—the artist *is* free there—"but that the creative process is not displayed in public and not destined to appear in the world. Hence the element of freedom, certainly present in the creative arts, remains hidden; it is not the free creative process which finally appears and matters for the world, but the work of art itself, the end product of the process" (Arendt 1993, 153; see also Arendt 1998, 168–169). The picture of newness drawn from *homo faber* requires a thing: an invention, say, or a painting. On Arendt's account, the newness of an artwork cannot be in the thing but only in some moment within the creative process prior to fabrication. One reason the performing arts play such an important role for Arendt in her thinking about action is that in performance newness appears in the performance itself rather than in the hidden process of fabrication and inspiration.

Yet, there is more in Arendt's claim than a logical point about the meaning and implications of newness. For one could also draw the conclusion that, phenomenologically, any action is new and thus free insofar as the agent is a unique entity operating in a unique time and space. Or one might make an inference from indeterminacy in the physical universe to newness. While the former approach might hold some appeal for Arendt, it is clear from her division of human activities into labor, work, and action, that not all human activities are free. Labor, for example, produces nothing new, on Arendt's account: it is endless repetition. So, Arendt clearly does not mean that the newness of an action, hence its freedom, is guaranteed by an account of the causality of the physical universe as indeterminate. Nor does she think that newness is a permanent fact of human action regardless of the state of the physical universe. Some activities, like eating and defecating, do not initiate newness and, hence, are not free. How, then, to determine whether an action is free or not?

I noted earlier that there are two conditions of free action in Arendt: (1) that the act initiate something new; and (2) that the act is not controlled, either (a) by others or (b) by the self. The first condition refers us to the unrepresentability of the free act, that is, its not being representable in the imagination or by the intellect. Condition 2a is straightforward enough—it is something like the liberal non-interference view—but 2b is not. This latter condition is an application of an argument Arendt takes from Nietzsche about the relationship of the willing subject to itself, and the condition takes us some way toward delineating free from unfree actions.[20]

In Section 19 of *Beyond Good and Evil*, Nietzsche argues that within the act of willing there is a trick played by the willing agent on itself. In every act of willing there is an affect: the affect of the command (Nietzsche 1989, §19). There are also a number of other things going on in every act of willing, an act that is "above all something complicated, something that is a unit only as a word," but with due caution they can be ignored for the moment (Nietzsche 1989, §19). The affect of command can be understood from those moments in which we exercise real self-control: for example, if one resists the temptation for another cigarette or to call an ex-girlfriend. In such moments we often do feel a strong sense of command over ourselves and if we succeed in preventing the behavior then a feeling of victory often accompanies the success of our willing. If there is in all willing an affect of command then there must be something commanded, something that obeys. But as the examples just mentioned reveal, the only thing the will can command is the willing agent: thus, the willing agent is both commander and obeyer: "A man who *wills* commands something within himself that renders obedience, or he believes renders obedience" (Nietzsche 1989, §19).

A trick takes place in willing: the identification of the "I" with the commanding will and the dis-identification of the "I" from the obeying self. When I successfully will something and achieve a victory over myself, I forget or ignore that I have also lost: after all, *I* wanted that cigarette. This is clearest in those thinkers of freedom as autonomy—especially Rousseau and Kant, but in his own way Pettit too—who inevitably posit some sort of "bad" self, a self or will or desire that is to be subordinated for the sake of freedom understood as obeying the "good" self. In Rousseau we find freedom in affirming the "general will," often but not always a general will that stands over and against our own private will. I can be forced to be free only because the I identifies with the general will rather than the private will. In Kant the noumenal, rational willing agent, in order to act morally, must subordinate or shape into a moral form the phenomenal desires and instincts that are expressions of our embodied, animal lives. In each case the "true" self is identified as the commanding willing self through the "synthetic concept 'I'"; but the commanded, obedient self, nonetheless remains (Nietzsche 1989, §19).[21]

For Arendt, Nietzsche's critique shows that "where men wish to be sovereign, as individuals or as organized groups, they must submit to the oppression of the will, be this the individual will with which I force myself, or the 'general will' of an organized group. If men wish to be free, it is precisely sovereignty they must renounce" (Arendt 1993, 164; see also Arendt 1998, 233–236). The reason freedom is incompatible with autonomy, self-sovereignty, political sovereignty, free will, and the like, is that self-command and self-control is necessarily subordination and obedience of the self. How, then, can we understand self-control as freedom if self-control is necessarily subordination of the self? Doesn't this mean that freedom *is*, necessarily if not exclusively, subordination and domination? How does subordination in the name of Reason, the moral law, the common good, the general will, one's avowable interests, and so on, change the fact of subordination, of being dominated? Arendt's Nietzschean answer to these questions is simple: stop falling for the trick of the will, of the synthetic concept "I." Rather than accept the apparently paradoxical consequence that freedom is (also) subordination and domination, Arendt argues that freedom exists only when agents are controlled neither by others nor by the self.[22]

Condition 2b was intended to help answer a question about how to distinguish free acts from un- or non-free acts. The answer now appears to be: a free action is one that is uncontrolled, not only by others but by a commanding, ruling self. To the extent that, on Arendt's account, labor is under the sway of life and its necessities, then laboring is not free. To the extent that fabrication is under the sway of an Idea or blueprint that governs the fabrication process, any freedom in fabrication is either an accidental deviation or improvisation that breaks free from the Idea, or the freedom that comes in the creation of the Idea itself. Certain intellectual capacities, according to Arendt, are not free:

mathematics and logic compel us to accept their conclusions (Arendt 1978a, 59–61). Conversely, political action, thinking, and judgment are all human activities that can be performed freely, that is, they can initiate something new and can be performed without being controlled either by the self or by others.

If one combines this with condition 1, then freedom is an action that is uncontrolled and initiates something new. What, then, is the relation between the two conditions? An agent cannot, if my reconstruction of Arendt is correct, be in control *and* initiate the new for to be in control requires a set of beliefs, desires, aims, and motives that must be represented in the mind before acting. If control requires the representation of something in the mind prior to action, then whatever is represented is not new. Condition 2 is a necessary condition. Condition 2 is not a sufficient condition, however, because an uncontrolled action need not initiate newness.

To see why this is so, we need to recall that for Arendt, men, not Man, inhabit the earth, that is, plurality is a basic condition of human existence. Even in our mental activities, Arendt claims, there is a reflexivity that introduces a plurality into the self: "Mental activities themselves all testify by their reflexive nature to a duality inherent in consciousness; the mental agent cannot be active except by acting, implicitly or explicitly, back on itself. . . . Every *cogitare*, no matter what its object, is also a *cogito me cogitare*, every volition a *volo me velle*, and even judgment is possible, as Montesquieu once remarked, only through a '*retour secret sur moi-même*'" (Arendt 1978a, 74–75). The plurality of human existence is on display more obviously in our social and political lives. Human actions "always fall into an already existing web where their immediate consequences can be felt," a web constituted both by the world individuals have in common as well as the "*inter-est*," the intangible world of speech and deeds that lies between individuals born into a common shared world that will survive their death (Arendt 1998, 182–184). Wherever a person turns, even inward, they will find someone else.

The human condition of plurality conditions freedom in a number of ways. But for freedom as such, the condition of plurality can help us see why an action can be uncontrolled but not initiate newness. If political actions must fall into a web of human relationships, if thinking is a dialogue between the self and itself, if the will is divided, if judgment requires the imaginative representation of the viewpoints of others, then all these actions must be at least minimally intelligible.[23] How intelligible an action must be might vary, but to paraphrase and modify Wallace Stevens: a free action can only resist the intelligence almost successfully. The same condition of minimal intelligibility holds for acting, thinking, willing, and judging. One can strain one's mind to make sense of a square circle or $2 + 2 = 5$, but at the very most such ideas are intelligible only negatively, as impossibilities. Summon up all your energy and try to change the past by willing backward, but as Nietzsche knew, the frustration and resentment will overwhelm and potentially ruin you. Willing backward is unintelligible. I can try to reflectively judge an event, or painting, or policy, without a concept and without taking into account the potential responses of others—but if others are systematically excluded from the judgment then the power and potential truth of the judgment is undermined. In different ways, action, thinking, judging, willing, and so on, require some minimal intelligibility in order to count as a free performance of the activity in question.

Insofar as this is the case, the new that freedom initiates cannot be so unintelligible as to fail to register *as* new, and the specific activity must not fail to register as an action, or a thought, or a will, or a judgment, either to the self or to others. A child banging a piano or splashing paint on paper may produce something akin to Sun Ra or Jackson Pollock, but for Arendtian reasons the difference between Sun Ra and the child is that the former is playing music and the latter is simply playing.[24] Of course, just as in modernism generally, one can rewrite the rules of intelligibility through testing and redefining the limits of the intelligible, but one does so at the risk of becoming unintelligible. A bassist can play in a different key from the rest of the band, or no key at all; play in a wildly different time signature; and can possibly make this intelligible if they are good enough. But in the hands of most people, it will be unintelligible noise. Similarly, an orator can act or speak in uncontrolled, spontaneous ways, emitting words and parataxic speeches, gesticulating wildly, and so on, and if they are a good enough speaker, a compelling enough actor, then perhaps they will be understood. But in most cases the speaker's sanity will be questioned. A new action, to be free, must be uncontrolled but intelligible. If a condition of all human activity is its intelligibility, then we can now say there are three conditions an action must meet to be free: (1) the action must initiate something new; (2) the action must be (a) free from the control of others, and (b) free from the control of the self; and (3) the action must be minimally intelligible to at least some others. Condition 3 shows us why condition 2 is not sufficient for freedom. One can act without control and not initiate the new because what one initiates when one acts in an uncontrolled way is unintelligible. One can also satisfy condition 3 without satisfying 1 and 2. An action is free, then, if it intelligibly initiates newness and is not controlled by the self or others.

The argument so far has been largely abstract, but there is an intuitive plausibility to Arendt's theory of freedom. If, for Pettit, freedom as responsibility finds intuitive support in the links between ascriptions of freedom and responsibility in our ordinary lives, it is also no doubt the case that one connotation of freedom in our ordinary lives is absence of control, at least by others. An agent is free, for example, when there is nobody around forcing them to do something, or when they can take their pick of any number of options, or when their mother yells at their brother and stops him from being bossy. Arendt goes further than liberal non-interference because she also argues that we are not free when we control our selves, that is, when either collective or individual sovereignty reigns.

The intuitive plausibility of this seemingly radical idea is easier to see by returning to the example of the athlete and the jazz musician, paradigms of spontaneous, improvised, but nonetheless intelligible, free activity. Ordinary conversations too, at their best, often take on similar aspects of intelligible spontaneity. When we are deeply involved in conversations with others, we often speak and respond spontaneously in a number of ways. A conversation in which each idea was thought before spoken, or each word deliberately chosen before uttered—that is, an entirely controlled conversation—would not only be incredibly awkward, it would also lack many of the usual aspects of conversation. There is a mystery about how, as I am writing now, or when I am speaking extemporaneously, I can so obviously not think through everything I am about to write or say, and yet, what appears on the computer screen or comes out of my mouth usually (hopefully) makes a great deal of sense. I am clearly not in control in any conscious way. Moreover, a controlled conversation would undermine a vitally important aspect of conversation: that in speaking with others something new often comes into being *between* us. Philosophy, if it sometimes takes the form of dialogue and conversation, depends on the possibility that new ideas will emerge in the course of conversation. But everyday conversations—about whether to marry; what career to choose; how to design a syllabus for a new course; what to make of health care plans—often provoke new ideas, interpretations, or desires, without any conscious plan or intention on the part of the speakers. The "aha" moments of conversation are moments where we feel, much like the musician or artist or athlete, inspired, as if we are passive mediums for the new. It is not inaccurate or a strain upon ordinary language to describe these experiences as experiences of freedom. This freedom is only possible in the absence of control.

Standard advice to a struggling basketball player is "let the game come to you." In a good conversation speakers are free to speak but also free for the new. One can understand condition 2b as follows: freedom as initiating newness requires openness and responsiveness to oneself and/or to others. In order to be responsive to others, I must relinquish control.

These experiences of freedom show that freedom as initiating newness is grounded in everyday experience. The new that is initiated in freedom need not be anything great or excellent or even, as it were, absolutely new. A guitarist may be a mediocre musician, yet have moments of freedom, moments of playing something intelligible never thought of or heard before, at least by them. The insights that emerge in a conversation may not revolutionize political philosophy or one's life, but they may still be genuinely new insights. These moments of freedom often feel like the disclosures of a new world or a new self or a new person, or more precisely, of perceptions of this world otherwise than it has been perceived before. The initiation of the new is a moment of freedom because what emerges is not fully determined by what came before. Although limited by the need to be intelligible, initiating the new is not determined by the limits of the intelligible, or by anything else. The intelligible is not fully determined, not static, and not fully determining. Modernism depends upon the relative stability, and permanent possibility of the change of, the limits of the intelligible. So does significant change in our own lives.

If this reconstruction of Arendtian freedom is right, then we should ask why we value freedom. Arendt's answer emerges as a response to two difficulties human beings face, one a consequence of mortality, the other of the development of Western culture. The "existential problem" is nothing other than how to answer the challenge posed by the chorus in Sophocles' *Oedipus at Colonus*: "Not to be born is best of all / when life is there, the second best / to go hence where you came, / with the best speed you may" (Sophocles 1991, 1410–1413). One response to this grim counsel is to find ways of making life bearable, and perhaps even lovable and desirable (Arendt 1965, 285). This existential problem is intensified by a second, historically emergent difficulty faced by, at the very least, citizens of western societies: the rise of the social, world- and earth-alienation, and the consequent dangers to our individuality and self. The danger is condensed in Arendt's transformation of the traditional question "why is there something rather than nothing?" into this question: "Why is there anybody at all and not rather nobody?" (Arendt 2005, 204). The danger we moderns face,

Arendt argues, is that the conditions of modernity described and bemoaned by Max Weber and the Frankfurt School—increasing rationalization, bureaucratization, domination, technologization, warfare, unfreedom, and so on and so forth—undermine the possibilities of being an individual, a self. Heidegger claimed that for the most part, the answer to the question "who is Dasein?" is "*das Man*," the One, anyone but oneself in one's singularity and individuality. Arendt contextualizes Heidegger's claim by arguing that the conditions of modernity are such that the ability and desire to enact and/or disclose one's unique self is usually not present. Not only do all human beings face the problem of human finitude—why, after all, is it better to be born and to live than to not have been born or to quickly die?—each modern faces the more specific problem of being a unique individual, of being a self, rather than just being anyone, that is, rather than only doing what *das Man*, what one, does. Freedom also helps to address the problem of world-alienation, but that problem will be discussed in the next chapter.

The value of freedom, for Arendt, is that it is an experience that responds to both the existential and the historical-political problem of de-individualization. Freedom responds to the first problem insofar as the experience of freedom is *pleasurable*. Arendt's evidence for this comes from a number of sources, among them John Adams and Thomas Jefferson, but anyone who has participated in or observed political demonstrations, can see just how fun such activities are, unless violence breaks out (and for some, even or especially then). But the pleasure of freedom exceeds the often carnivalesque fun of political protest. There is ample evidence for the elation felt in creative expression, in initiating newness, in discovering new ideas in conversation, and so on. These experiences often induce the feeling or thought that one would rather not be anywhere else or doing anything else than just being where one is or doing what one is doing. This sense of joy can contest those moments in which the overwhelming futility of human existence is present to mind. Whether such moments can, once and for all, enable an affirmation of human finitude is unclear. But they do provide material for such an affirmation.

How such moments might be affirmed through reflective judgment on those experiences would have played a major role in the unwritten third volume of *The Life of the Mind*: judgment. The great missing piece in Arendt's work is a fully fleshed out theory of judgment—she died before it could be written. But one motivation for such a theory of judgment, Arendt tells us, is that insofar as what Kant called "reflective judgment" can help us make sense of our pleasures and whether we should be pleased by what pleases us; it can also help us make sense of whether we should be pleased by being "natals," that is, finite beings capable of being free (Arendt 1978b, 217). It is safe to assume that Arendt's answer to the question of whether we should be pleased by our being free would have been "yes," although it is not entirely clear how she would have supported that claim. However, from what we do know of Arendt's theory of judgment, the experience of pleasure in freedom would have played a central role in her account.

The existential difficulty that the pleasurable experience of freedom responds to is further complicated in modernity by the loss of the conditions most conducive to and for experiencing freedom. We will return to this problem in the next chapter in conjunction with world-alienation. What should be said here is that if one accepts, to some degree, the Weberian account of rationalization in modernity extended by Adorno and Horkheimer, cautiously appropriated by Habermas, and formulated in very different but nonetheless parallel ways by Foucault and Heidegger, then Arendt's argument that the chances for experiencing freedom—specifically, but not only, political freedom—have diminished significantly, perhaps even catastrophically, has some historical and sociological foundation. Where Arendt differs from the aforementioned thinkers is that she finds in freedom, especially political freedom, the best response to the dangers of modernity (see Villa 1996, 10).

The value of freedom, then, is that the joy of its experience is a potential answer to the existential problem of human finitude as well as the modern problems of world-alienation, the rise of the social, and the withdrawal of the political sphere. Arendt's claims about the value of freedom are certainly unusual. Freedom is not valuable because it is a source of human dignity; nor is it a precondition for the relatively unhampered pursuit of one's own desired ends; nor is it a way in which the human beings can positively participate in a community and work toward social ends. Freedom is valuable, for Arendt, because the human condition in general, and the pressures of modernity in particular, can so easily lead to what Nietzsche called *ressentiment*, that is, frustration and anger at the conditions of human life itself: finitude, the passing of time, suffering, and so on. Modernity has proved a fertile ground for the "politicization" of *ressentiment*. If Arendt is right that *ressentiment* plays such a central role in creating the dangerous politics of modern life, then countering such *ressentiment* is an important political and ethical project. To the extent that freedom is not only an enjoyable experience in itself but also a powerful means of countering *ressentiment*, then freedom also has an instrumental value.

FREEDOM AND CONTROL

Earlier I raised three questions about Pettit's arguments. They concerned the value of freedom, whether there were other connotations of freedom, and the role of virtual control. Arendt has answers to these three questions, answers that diverge significantly from Pettit's. For Arendt, freedom is valuable as a response to our finitude and a culturally pervasive *ressentiment*; freedom is initiating newness; and freedom exists only where all control, whether virtual or actual, whether by others or by the self, is no longer determining action. As is the case throughout this book, I do not "choose sides," not because I don't have a side, but because I don't think we usually can, or ought to, choose sides. This is especially true when considering the problem of freedom.

Pettit and Arendt offer political theorists the two most important non-liberal accounts of freedom in contemporary political theory, and they share an emphasis on the primacy of freedom in politics—as opposed to the primacy of equality, justice, or individual rights—that is rather rare today. But the disagreement between the two over the relationship of freedom to control is so deep, and so difficult to adjudicate, that we learn a great deal from it about the concept of freedom and why it is so hard to give up on either control or non-sovereignty.

The case for freedom as control—whether made by Pettit, Kant, Rousseau, Rawls, or other thinkers of autonomy—is simple: what is the good of a freedom to be wrong, or immoral, or unjust, or needlessly antagonistic, or asocial, and so on? A related problem—returned to in the next chapter—is how we can possibly justify state interference beyond the night-watchman state without denying that some interventions are not violations of an individual's freedom? Further, freedom as control makes sense of our intuitions about, and practices of, responsibility. As we have seen, if freedom were mere underdetermination, that would not give us any reason to hold people responsible, and neither rational nor volitional control is enough to ascribe responsibility. And who, after all, wants to be done with responsibility? The value of freedom may not be clearly articulated by Pettit, nor the value of responsibility, but freedom as control is shown to ground our practices of responsibility in such a way that we can identify and delimit freedom and responsibility in particular cases. If there is a value in being right in our beliefs, in acting responsibly, in desiring worthwhile ends, and so on, then freedom as control enables us to pursue these values.

In contrast, freedom as control is, inevitably, domination of the self, either by friendly others or by the self. Somewhere in an account of freedom as control one will find this domination. In Pettit the watchword for this domination is often "avowable interests." Thus, agents can be coerced in a friendly way if the coercion tracks their avowable interests, but they also cannot be free unless they avoid being an elusive or weak self by taking upon themselves past commitments, unless they act on the basis of reasons, and so on (see Pettit 2001a, 75–77, 82–90, 96). In each case agents are free only insofar as they are controlled by something, be it a friendly other, a personality that maintains and disciplines the self, or good reasons. As we have seen, for Arendt such control is inherently paradoxical and is attractive only insofar as we forget that self-control is inevitably command and domination of the self by the self. How can we accept a freedom that is not freedom, a freedom that is submission as well as command? And how can such freedom possibly serve as an answer to the difficult problems of human finitude and the development of western culture? Being responsible is fine; but what is the good in that? Why is responsibility not just another burden of life, just another reason to detest our finite existence?

Given the centrality of freedom to the practices and languages of responsibility—something which Arendt in no way denies—and further, given the ways in which we account for responsibility in terms of various kinds of control, it is hard to deny that freedom and control certainly play an important role in our everyday moral and political lives (see Austin 1990, 175–204). Yet, it is just as hard to deny that freedom as control and responsibility does and ought to serve a limited, if vitally important, purpose in our lives. If Arendt is right, then freedom as initiating newness is not only an ordinary part of our lives but is also a potentially powerful response to the pressures and dangers that we all confront in our individual and collective lives. There is a real danger to excessive moralization, to the expansion of the sphere of morality, or to the moralization of morality (see Williams 1985; and Cavell 1999, 268–271). The danger is that extremely valuable possibilities and practices are threatened by freedom as control and responsibility. Arendt is a kind of political realist in her protestations against the moralization of politics, even as she is a moralist outside of politics.

Freedom as discursive control or freedom as initiating newness? These do not exhaust the possibilities, but to the extent that the problem of freedom often turns on the relative place of control, it is simply unclear how we could dispense with either freedom as control or as lack of control. Intuitions will not decide the matter; nor will theories or conceptual analysis. Neither physics nor metaphysics will decide the matter, if only because the judgments of either will probably exert no real influence on our practices and everyday conceptual uses of freedom. And yet, neither freedom will really allow for the other. Each will see the other as an obstacle in its way. Each freedom sees in the other freedom either no freedom at all, or a freedom with no value at all. Perhaps political freedom will get us a bit further.

4

PETTIT AND ARENDT ON FREEDOM II

Non-domination and Isonomy

IN THE PREVIOUS CHAPTER we saw how Pettit and Arendt develop distinctive accounts of freedom *as such*. They both rely on intuitions about freedom drawn from phenomenological, theoretical, and axiological considerations. However, Pettit and Arendt are more widely read within political theory for their constructive accounts of *political* freedom. Pettit, on the one hand, argues that republican freedom is *non-domination*. Domination is the power of an agent—individual or collective, public or private—to interfere arbitrarily in one's choices and actions in such a way that the interference does not track the agent's interests.[1] Arendt, on the other hand, argues that political freedom is non-sovereign *self- and world-disclosive action*.

In this chapter I argue that the conflict between Pettit's and Arendt's conclusions about freedom as such shapes and produces a conflict between their accounts of political freedom. Once again the issue is control, but the political consequence of control is a conflict between two ways of conceiving the relationship of freedom to the structure of rule. For Pettit, non-dominating freedom is not only possible under legitimate rule but best protected by a legitimate, rule-of-law democratic regime. In other words, like most republicans, Pettit finds freedom even in state interference so long as that interference tracks the interests of the agent interfered with.

Arendt, however, suggests in a number of places that *isonomy*—which she defines as a structure of "rule" in which one neither rules nor is ruled—is the "regime" most conducive to freedom. If one condition of freedom is neither being in control nor being controlled by others, then it is no surprise that a regime in which one neither rules nor is ruled is best for acting freely.

Both Pettit and Arendt face significant difficulties in their arguments for republican democracy and isonomy. On the one hand, Pettit cannot successfully distinguish his version of republicanism from the dangers he identifies in the "continental" republicanism of Rousseau and Kant: the danger that the state will come to dominate individuals not against, but for the sake of, their freedom. This raises serious questions about the possibility of distinguishing legitimate from illegitimate government interference without reference to a moralized conception of the common good and freedom. On the other hand, Arendtian isonomy faces real difficulties when we think seriously about how to institutionalize a condition of "no-rule." Whatever the value of freedom as disclosive action, without a stable space for political action freedom is only a fleeting experience for a lucky few. Arendt's attempts to think through the institutionalization of the political reveal just how problematic isonomy becomes as a stable structure of "rule."

In this chapter I first outline Pettit's theory of republican freedom before raising some questions—drawn from a couple of examples in his *Republicanism*—that show how Pettit's republicanism actually shares a great deal with a Rousseauian and Kantian republicanism he is rightly wary of. I will then turn to Arendt's description of freedom as self- and world-disclosive action before raising several questions about her under-theorized use of isonomy and the problems isonomy poses for thinking about political institutions.

FREEDOM AS NON-DOMINATION

Freedom as non-domination is defined as the "status of someone who, unlike the slave, is not subject to the arbitrary power of another: that is, someone who is not dominated by anyone else" (Pettit 1997b, 31). An individual dominates another "if and only if they have a certain power over that other, in particular a power of interference on an arbitrary basis" (Pettit 1997b, 52). Interference is arbitrary

> if it is subject to the *arbitrium*, the decision or judgment, of the agent; the agent was in a position to choose it or not choose it, at their pleasure. . . . And, in particular, since interference with others is involved, we imply that it is chosen or rejected without reference to the interests, or the opinions, of those affected. The choice is not forced to track what the interests of those others require according to their own judgments. (Pettit 1997b, 55)[2]

To enjoy freedom as non-domination, then, is to not be subject to another's power of arbitrary interference in your choices. A key feature distinguishing freedom as non-domination from "negative freedom"—that is, freedom as non-interference—is the recognition that one can be dominated even if the dominating agent does *not* interfere in one's choice. One is dominated when one cannot reliably expect non-interference because domination is as much a *capacity* to interfere arbitrarily as it is the actual arbitrary interference itself. If, in order to avoid interference, one has to stay out of the dominator's way, or suck up to them, or simply be thankful for their decency, then one is still dominated. A second crucial feature of freedom as non-domination is that interference that *does* track the agent's interests is *not* dominating (see Pettit 1997b, 63–66). Agents can be interfered with in a non-dominating manner because the interfering agent is acting in accordance with, or in order to further, the agent's avowed interests.

In Chapter 3 we saw that it was unclear what the good of freedom as such is for Pettit. Freedom as non-domination, however, has a clear value: it is a primary or "gateway" good (Pettit 2017, 335). Non-domination "is something that a person has instrumental reasons to want, no matter what else they want: something that promises results that are likely to appeal to them, no matter what they value and pursue" (Pettit 1997b, 90). Insofar as not being dominated protects one's ability to pursue one's goals and allows for interference only when it tracks one's interests, it is a good necessary for the pursuit of other goods, and desirable for that reason. Non-domination is also valuable because of the way in which it grounds something like the "dignity" of each individual. Non-domination protects one's "personhood" so that one cannot be dismissed without reason (Pettit 1997b, 91). The instrumental value of non-domination as a primary good and its intrinsic value as a realization of one's dignity and personhood are status goods. "Status goods" are goods that attach to one's having a status recognized and respected by others. Agents have the status good of freedom as non-domination whether they act or not; whether of one race or another, one religion or another, one gender or another, and so on; and whether their choices and actions are admired or disapproved of by others.

Freedom as possessing a non-dominated status is closely linked to the place of control in Pettit's broader theory of freedom.[3] For what is freedom as non-domination other than the guarantee of control by the agent over his or her choices? Only if the agent is protected against the power of arbitrary interference in their choices can they be said to truly control their actions. Moreover, if freedom is more broadly understood as discursive control and orthonomy, then it is also clear that freedom as non-domination, insofar as it does not exclude interference that tracks my interests, protects or even enhances my orthonomy. For if an agent is to act according to the right—but they occasionally succumb to desires known to be wrong—then the fact that someone can interfere in their choices so long as the interference tracks their avowed interests actually protects their freedom. In short, agents are more orthonomous because of that interference. This is one conclusion to be drawn from the "liquor cabinet" example discussed in Chapter 3 (note 20). Pettit suggests that a republican state, by promoting non-domination, will in fact create the conditions for the individual realization of autonomy or orthonomy, although he does not argue that the state should actively promote that richer ideal (Pettit 1997b, 82; 2012, 48–49). However, Pettit's republican state does not merely promote orthonomy; it seems to *require* the state to intervene in a pro-orthonomy manner that may lead to a mode of domination.

PETTIT: CLOSET ROUSSEAUIAN?

> Republicans do not say, in the modernist manner, that while the law coerces people and thereby reduces their liberty, it compensates for the damage done by preventing more interference than it represents. They hold that the properly constituted law is *constitutive* of liberty in a way that undermines any such talk of compensation. (Pettit 1997b, 35; emphasis added.)

> [B]ut it is freedom that I am giving up for the sake of justice or equality or the love of my fellow men. I should be guilt-stricken, and rightly so, if I were not, in some circumstances, ready to make this sacrifice. But a sacrifice is not an increase in what is being sacrificed, namely freedom, however great the moral need or the compensation for it. *Everything is what it is: liberty is liberty, not equality or fairness or justice or culture, or human happiness or a quiet conscience.* (Berlin 1969, 125; emphasis added.)

Pettit explicitly places republican freedom as non-domination in conversation with Berlin's distinction between negative and positive liberty. Pettit argues that Berlin's negative liberty—freedom as non-interference—leaves an important dimension of unfreedom unacknowledged: the freedom-reducing effects of the *power* to interfere. For the same reasons that Berlin implicitly finds Hobbesian liberty as "non-frustration" of an actually preferred option too weak a conception of freedom, so too Pettit argues that Berlin's negative liberty is too weak. Agents are free, on Hobbes' account of freedom, if they stop desiring the end that they cannot acquire due to the frustrating activities of another. This stoic image of freedom as liberation from unsatisfiable desires is absurd, Pettit's Berlin argues, for agents can then maintain or even increase their freedom by no longer wanting what they are prevented from obtaining. However, the same absurdity results from freedom as non-interference, because if freedom is interfered with only if an interfering agent actually interferes with one's choices, then one is free even when an agent who could interfere opts not to. This would imply that if one simply kowtows to this potential interfering agent and "convinces" them not to interfere, then one is free. This is absurd, because now freedom is in part a matter of subservient, obsequious behavior toward potentially interfering agents (see Pettit 2011). For Pettit, Berlin might very well have been more sympathetic, upon reflection, to freedom as non-domination, but in any case, freedom as non-domination is a distinct view, related to but very different from freedom as non-interference.

For all of Pettit's sympathetic criticism of Berlin, however, it is curious that he never takes on the more obvious Berlinian objection to republican freedom: its apparent refusal to take seriously that "everything is what it is: liberty is liberty." If Pettit's claim is that interference that tracks my interests is not dominating, then we are left trying to imagine how someone in a jail cell is just as free as they were before incarceration. After all, if legal punishment can be non-dominating—as Pettit must think it can—then non-dominating imprisonment is not freedom-reducing. In other words, on Pettit's account, we can ask whether "everything is what it is: liberty is liberty," because, for all we can see, the inmate in prison seems undeniably less free.

Pettit denies that interest-tracking or controlled acts of interference are freedom-reducing. However, Pettit provides little justification for the vitally important republican claim that freedom is *constituted* by a controlled and constitutional legal system that can interfere in my choices without dominating me. In *Republicanism* Pettit relies almost exclusively on the historical authority of Harrington, Locke, and other republican thinkers for the claim that a legitimate law not only carves out a space for freedom, but is necessary, even constitutive, for freedom (Pettit 1997b, 35–41). The claim that the law is *constitutive* of freedom is equally associated with continental republicans, especially Rousseau and Kant. For Rousseau, under legitimate law, citizens can be "forced to be free," and indeed only under a legitimate law can they be morally, as opposed to naturally, free. But Pettit distances himself from the Franco-Germanic republican tradition that represents perhaps the most sensible, if still deeply troubling, theorization of positive liberty. Pettit's main objections to the continental republican tradition include its rejection of a mixed constitution and contestatory citizenry; but Pettit also worries that Rousseau's republicanism reneges on freedom as non-domination insofar as citizens can and often must achieve their independence from each other only by submitting completely to the "public person," the state (Pettit 2012, 12–18; 2013). If coercive law need not be freedom-reducing, but it cannot be freedom-enabling in the Rousseauian sense of freedom as total submission to the state, then what is Pettit's philosophical justification of the freedom-enabling (or at least freedom-indifferent) interference of law?

The answer cannot be that the republican tradition has always seen law and liberty as unopposed, because that plainly begs the question. Republicans might be wrong. The answer also cannot rely on a priori considerations (for example, about natural rights) because Pettit, like many post-Rawlsian political philosophers, relies on the test of reflective equilibrium for justifying freedom as non-domination (see, for example, Pettit 1997b, 99–102). Instances or degrees of freedom, domination, arbitrariness, the common good, and so on, are, for Pettit, even empirically testable and ought to be subject to roughly consequentialist considerations. The answer to the question why doesn't a coercive law reduce my freedom? cannot be, for example, Locke's answer. Pettit places Locke within the republican tradition in part because Locke distinguishes between license and liberty, where the former is doing as one "lists" and the latter is "to dispose, and order" as one lists, "Person, Actions, Possessions" and property "within the allowance of those Laws under which he is" (see Pettit 1997b, 40; and Locke 1988, §57). This distinction rests, however—in both its formulation here and in the earlier formulation of the claim in Section 2 of the *Second Treatise*—on the claim that "Law, in its true Notion, is not so much the Limitation as the direction of a free and intelligent Agent to his *proper* Interest, and prescribes no farther than is for the *general Good of those* under that Law" (Locke 1988, §57; emphasis added). In this passage, as in Locke's discussion of freedom under the law of nature, the point is that individuals have genuine interests and there is a general good that can be distinguished from less genuine or ersatz interests and a private good. This brings Locke, at least in the later formulation, closer to Rousseau than we might at first think. Locke's argument depends on a conception of "proper interests"—and more broadly on a moral realist commitment to the existence of natural rights and natural law—that Pettit doesn't endorse.

Thus, Pettit's claim that a legitimate law can coercively interfere in an agent's choices without reducing the freedom of that agent must be justified without reference (solely) to the claims of earlier republicans, without reference to continental republican versions of the freedom of citizens, and without reference to moralism (see Pettit 2017, 333–335). As I hope to show later in this chapter, the place of control in Pettit's republicanism puts such a justification out of reach. Republican freedom requires the non-dominating interference of law: law is constitutive of republican freedom. But law is necessarily coercive. It necessarily interferes with one's choices, activities, and sometimes physical liberty. All of this, Pettit argues, is not only compatible with liberty but constitutive of it, at least when everything is going right. It is easy to imagine Berlin's response, not to the claim that law is necessary and a democratically legitimized law even better, but to the claim that one is not only no less free but only truly free as a result of a coercive, interfering law.[4] Can Pettit plausibly use the term *freedom* if such freedom at the very least countenances, and at most is constituted by, law's interference? Is everything what it is in Pettit's argument?

PETTIT'S FIRST ANSWER

A first answer is found in *On the People's Terms*, although Pettit is not explicitly dealing there with the question as formulated here. In the chapter "Political Legitimacy," Pettit argues that if state interference is to be non-dominating then state interference must be controlled by the citizenry. However, he claims that this control has limits and requirements that are a feature of the political itself. The requirements are (1) that it is a matter of *historical necessity* that everyone must live in a state; (2) that as a matter of *political necessity* one cannot choose which state to live in even if one has a right to emigrate; (3) that as a matter of *functional necessity* the state must be able to enforce law coercively (Pettit 2012, 160–166). The intuitive idea is simple enough: however contingent the fact of the nation-state form may be, it is now inescapable; however contingent the fact that one is born in the United States, it is very difficult to emigrate; however contingent the fact that coercive law is the means for maintaining social order, one cannot have a state without it.

This argument suggests one broad justification for why the state can interfere in a non-dominating way. The key to the argument is Pettit's claim that the historical, political, and functional necessities referred to are, at least from the perspective of freedom, no more freedom-reducing than the laws of physics (Pettit 2012, 161). Just as one's freedom is not reduced because a desire to fly is interfered with by the laws of gravity, so one's freedom is not reduced because fulfilling a desire to live outside of a nation-state, even one's own nation-state, or beyond the reach of a coercive law, is virtually impossible. In the latter cases freedom is not reduced because these necessities are not imposed by an alien will as a decision that could be otherwise (Pettit 2012, 160–161). As Pettit puts it, the constraints of historical, political, and functional necessity "material-ize on an independent, unwilled basis" (Pettit 2012, 161). It is by analogy with natural necessity that non-natural necessities do not reduce freedom even as they constrain one's choices. Thus, one justification for the claim that the state can interfere without dominating one is that many aspects of modern political life are matters of historical, political, and functional *necessity*. Of course, if the state does impose an alien will on an individual in specific matters, then this justification no longer applies. But we can see how this argument suggests an answer to my question that does not rely on moralism, Rousseauian-Kantian argumentation, or an appeal to earlier proponents of republicanism.

However, Pettit's argument relies on two contentious claims: (1) there are historical, political, and functional necessities; and (2) such necessities are simi-lar enough to natural laws that they are not freedom-reducing.

The first claim is that the nation-state, one's own citizenship in a specific country, and the requirements of the state to enforce coercive law are properly understood as necessities. This seems dubious. Pettit, in a footnote, refers read-ers back to his arguments in *The Common Mind*, surely referring to his holistic individualism. For Pettit, human beings cannot actualize their capacities to think without social relations, and while this is not a matter of trans-world necessity, it is the case that for human beings as they are, social relations are necessary (see Pettit 1996). However, even if human beings are necessarily social beings, that natural species trait is a far cry from the putative necessity of the nation-state, an individual's citizenship, and the force of law.

We should keep in mind that the nation-state as a modern political form is only a few centuries old. Moreover, there are still large areas of the world in which nation-states are only nominally in place and borders are porous, un-controlled, and largely irrelevant. Finally, while the nation-state form itself is only a few centuries old, its global domination is even more recent. The states constituting Italy only unified in 1861. India, the world's most populous state, came into being in 1947, along with its neighbor Pakistan. The point is not that the relatively recent birth of specific nation-states shows an absence of historical necessity; the point is that to say the earth is a "state-bound planet" where one cannot live free from the rule of the state is misleading without significant qualification. Large parts of the world are effectively ungoverned; the nation-state form itself is hardly old enough to be seen as "necessary"; its implementation in the modern world is continuing, not finished; and finally, although I have my deep suspicions, the argument that the nation-state form is and will continue to be undermined by ever-increasing globalization has been on the table for a long time.

To speak of the nation-state in terms of necessity is misleading at best. But even if the world is necessarily state-bound, to make the state form a matter of necessity on a par with the laws of physics is to ignore the important, and consequential, differences between them. We cannot concretely imagine our lives in all of their complexity without the current laws of physics. Science fiction can tell us about other physical worlds and modifications of our earth, but that is fiction, and it relies on the stability of the vast majority of physical laws just to make minimal sense. Even if we are wrong about what the laws of physics are, to argue that we might be wrong that there are laws of physics or at least physical regularities is to raise an unjustified skepticism about science and to refute the most commonsensical, and scientifically justified, explanation of continuity in our experience of the physical world. The power of the idea that gravity does not reduce freedom even though it interferes with the choice to levitate rests on the fact that *all* one can do is *choose* to levitate. Physical laws relevant to human life cannot be broken and thus they are not freedom-reducing, because no genuinely possible action is prevented by the laws.

It is not at all difficult, however, to imagine a world without nation-states or modern political organization because we have historical records and ongoing experiments in living that tell us what that world was, is, or could be. There are a number of steps we can take to reduce the sense of living in a state to an absolute minimum (at least in a reasonably large state). It is easy to imagine a world lacking political organization of any kind without leaving or significantly modifying this world, unlike in science fiction. Such an imagined world may ultimately suggest a necessary human sociality, but that we are social animals does not entail that we are political animals, and that we might be political animals does not mean we are necessitated, even today, to live in states. The fact that we can so easily imagine a world without states, and the further point that we can often approximate living in a stateless world, undermines the analogy of historical to physical necessity. Many of us often can choose to live outside or beyond the state, or our state of birth, or the law, just as the state can choose not to use violence to enforce social order. It is also difficult to be a professional athlete or musician, yet it is nonetheless a real choice. For that reason, Pettit cannot rely on this line of argumentation to answer my question.

Similar arguments apply to the political and functional necessities Pettit refers to. There is little reason to think of the state, our citizenship, and law as historical, political, and functional *necessities*. Further, even if they are in some sense necessities, they cannot imply the same non-freedom-reducing relationship of physical laws to one's choices. The argument for state interference not being freedom-reducing must come from somewhere else.

PETTIT'S SECOND ANSWER

The question I have been asking is whether non-dominating coercive state interference can be understood as freedom-indifferent or even freedom-constituting. Given the undeniable fact that the state and its decisions or policies can interfere with one's choices and even physically restrain or kill one, can we still sensibly describe such cases as ones in which freedom is not reduced or eliminated?[5] I have argued that one potential answer given by Pettit relies on a bad analogy of historical, political, and functional necessity to natural necessity.

However, a second and more explicit answer to my question concerns not the state and its interference as such, but the decisions and policies of a suitably controlled state. In a state democratically controlled by an active, contestatory citizenry, the state is forced to track the avowed or avowable interests of the citizens of that state. To be sure, in the process of making such decisions, there will be winners and losers, given the plurality of interests and reasonable policies in modern societies. Pettit needs to provide an explanation of why political losers should not see themselves as dominated even though the actual decisions of a state do not, apparently, track their avowed interests, and it is at this point that Pettit provides his second answer.

We can frame the issue in terms from the previous chapter: to what extent does freedom as non-domination require the "trick" of the willing subject, in which the willing agent ignores, or represses, that they are both commander and commanded in each act of willing? A political equivalent to this question, familiar to readers of Rousseau (and, in his own way, Kant), is to what extent can citizens be "forced to be free," and does such force require a citizen to identify with the general will rather than with their private will? In other words, to what extent is self-domination, or willful self-delusion, or ideologically produced self-delusion present in freedom as non-domination?[6] If self-domination is not only possible but actually required by republicanism, then the plausibility and desirability of freedom as non-domination is diminished. For why should an agent prefer self-domination to domination by others, or non-domination if it requires self-domination? If the state demands both that some citizens submit to it by denying one of their desires and that those citizens cannot object to such interference because it tracks their avowed interests, then the state is clearly telling citizens what their avowed interests really are. This amounts to a paternalism Pettit otherwise rejects. Moreover, if the state demands that the citizen's own "uncommon" desires must be subordinated to the common good, then how is Pettit's republicanism really any different from the continental republicanism that often requires individuals to submit passively to the state? To repeat the constraints placed on Pettit's answer: it cannot be moralistic (and thus cannot rely on a substantive version of one's "true" or "proper" interests); it cannot invoke the Rousseauian tradition (in which the general will has obvious primacy over the private will because the "sovereign is always right"); and it cannot simply rely on historical sources. The issue at hand makes an important appearance in a quasi-Rousseauian fashion in *Republicanism*. My question is how "quasi" this Rousseauianism is.

In his discussion of political contestation, Pettit acknowledges that not every contestation of a decision or policy can be satisfied. The question, then, is how we can say of those who are contesting a decision that they are not dominated when they lose. Pettit offers some possibilities. The first is that the contestation represents the self-interest of the contesting individual or group, and that the judgment made is that the common interest requires the frustration of that particular party. Consider the appeal by someone convicted of an offence against that conviction or against the sentence; or consider the appeal by a group of local residents against having a road or an airport located in their area (Pettit 1997b, 198). In these cases, Pettit argues, so long as the contesters recognize the legitimacy of the procedures used to come to the decision and the commonness of the interest in question, then although they have lost, "they can look on that disadvantage as a misfortune *on par with a natural accident*" rather than domination by the state (Pettit 1997a, 63, emphasis added; Pettit 1997b, 198).[7]

This response is quasi-Rousseauian because it suggests a line of reasoning similar to that used by Rousseau in *The Social Contract* to explain how an individual can be "forced to be free." For Rousseau, an agent who disagrees with a decision of the general will can be forced to obey the decision, but that use of force does not undermine the agent's freedom. The reason is that the general will is reflective of the common interest, the interest of the citizens as a whole, and insofar as the agent is a citizen, the agent shares that common interest. Thus, to be compelled to obey a decision one disagrees with is really just to be wrong about what the common interest is, but insofar as one is forced only to obey one's own common interest, one is only being forced to be free. Interference in such cases is non-dominating because it tracks one's interests (see Rousseau 1978, 1.7, 2.3, 2.4).[8]

Yet, even if not quite the same, Pettit's republicanism shares an impulse with Rousseau: those whose private, personal interests are undermined by collective decisions can rightly complain only if the collective decision was flawed either procedurally or in its expression of the common interest.[9] If the decision is unflawed in both areas, then by definition at least some of the failed contester's interests are satisfied by the properly followed procedures: thus, the agent is not dominated. The agent is no less free for not having gotten his or her way when decisions reflect common interests and are made through proper procedures. Just as one is not dominated when a hurricane interferes with one's plans to have a picnic at the beach, so one is not dominated when good policy properly chosen and in the common interest happens to affect one negatively. Sometimes, one loses. Of course, we have already seen that the move to "naturalize" politics is deeply problematic.

Implicitly in Rousseau, and explicitly in Kant, the private self or phenomenal self must be dominated by a more rational, "universal," or "general" self: the general will, or the noumenal self. This willing self—just as in Nietzsche's diagnosis—is often identified as the "true" self, whereas the dominated, subjugated private self is ignored or repressed. Something similar happens in Pettit's account.

In the example of the placement of an airport, it may indeed be in the community's interest to have an airport, and an agent may very well agree with this community interest. The question of where the airport is to be placed is, presumably, guided by empirical criteria: available land, sound restrictions, wind currents, and the like. Perhaps there is only one place in town to build the airport and it is next to an agent's house. Now, imagine that the agent—perhaps a few months after agreeing with the decision to build the airport—learns that it is to be placed next to his house. The agent protests and is told that there is no other place to build the airport. Must the agent accept, on the grounds of his already having recognized the common interest in having an airport, the placement of the airport as a non-dominating action by the government? Pettit's answer would surely be yes, and the reason is that although the placement of the airport is unfortunate—like a "natural accident"—it is not dominating if the decision was procedurally fair and substantively correct.

In this version of the airport example, the agent agrees with a decision in the common interest but changes their mind when they realize the personally negative effects of the decision. As Pettit argues, drawing on Brian Barry, the agent has a conflict between their *ex ante* and *ex post* interests (Pettit 2004, 153). Assuming we agree that the agent is negatively affected, then we can ask, why is that undeniable fact not an indication of domination? The answer seems to be: because it is in the common interest, and while the realization of that common interest negatively affects the agent, it still tracks an avowed interest in having an airport. However, does the decision track one's avowed interest in *not living near an airport*? It seems clear that the decision does not track *that* interest at all. There is a conflict between interests within the agent and a potential conflict of interpretations over the dominating character of the government action.

We experience conflicts between our interests quite frequently: "I want to lose weight, but I don't want to exercise." It is tempting to identify the first interest as better, rational, more mature, and so on—because it often is. But we can also imagine cases where it is unclear which of two interests is better or more rational. I order a prix fixe menu and I get a choice of one dessert: cake or ice cream. I certainly can have an interest in eating both, but I cannot order both (let's imagine the restaurant has strict sharing and ordering rules). The airport example is more like the conflict between a "better" and "worse" interest, but in both types of conflicts the same result occurs: where only one of two desires that I have an interest in satisfying can be satisfied, then I am necessarily denying one of my interests. I can tell myself that I made the rational choice, the right choice, the adult choice, the better choice—but I am still necessarily denied one of my interests.

In the airport example, a citizen may have an avowed, shared interest in an airport, and a perhaps unshared avowed interest in not having the airport built nearby. If the government decides to build it nearby, it makes a decision that does not track at least one avowed interest. Granted, the latter interest is not one shared with others, but why prioritize generalizable or common interests? There are arguments for the priority of common over private interests, even republican arguments: those arguments are, however, usually the Rousseauian paternalistic arguments Pettit tends to reject.

When Pettit does address the priority of the common interests over other interests with which they conflict, he argues that the state, "if not forced to track all of the interests and ideas of the person involved," is "at least forced to track the relevant ones" (Pettit 1997b, 55). The relevant interests, Pettit concludes, are "those that are shared in common with others, not those that treat me as exceptional, since the state is meant to serve others as well as me" (Pettit 1997b, 55; see also Pettit 1997a, 73; 2004, 162). However, the question of what interests are relevant in deciding whether a state is dominating an agent cannot be answered by arguing that insofar as the state is meant to serve the public and the public good, only common interests are relevant (see Costa 2007, 299). Pettit's response seems to beg the question: a private interest is often not relevant to the community, therefore interfering with a private interest is not domination so long as one does have a common interest tracked by the state's decision. But we want to know why the state's denying a private interest is not dominating, not why a private interest is irrelevant to the state and to the community. Many, perhaps most, private interests are irrelevant to public life. Why denying private interests and favoring common interests is not domination remains an open question.

A plausible answer might be that rather than compromising freedom, interfering with a private interest *conditions* freedom (Pettit 1997b, 76; 1997a, 62–63). In the airport example, the agent's freedom as a non-dominated citizen is not compromised because the decision to build the airport does track the agent's avowed interests. However, the decision does condition the agent's freedom insofar as it limits the range or ease of their choices (for example, to have a quiet Saturday at home or sell their house at a greater profit). The taxpayer and the prisoner are two examples of individuals who are not dominated, hence not unfree, but nonetheless have their freedom significantly conditioned because the taxpayer may not be able to afford a new car and the prisoner cannot go with his family on vacation (Pettit 1997b, 56n3). But even in these examples the idea that freedom is only being *conditioned* rather than *compromised* implicitly denies the relevance of some interests to the ascription of freedom as non-domination. For if you are not dominated when the airport is built next to your house without your permission or agreement, and if you are not dominated when you are paying taxes or put in jail, then those interests affected by the state's interference must be, in some way, irrelevant to deciding when you are being dominated. But what are the criteria we use to decide which interests count? If the criteria rely on a distinction between public and private interests, then we are back to wanting to know why interfering with private interests is non-dominating so long as the interference is for the sake of a common interest. The converse—where a state interferes with the common interest for the sake of private interests—is one of the paradigms of *imperium*, of unjust domination by the state.[10]

To return to our poor citizen angry at the construction of an airport near their home, the denial that they are being dominated does not seem justified unless we accept that private interests are not relevant to a decision whether or not someone is dominated. This is to inherit, with modifications, the Rousseauian and Kantian tradition of denying or diminishing the claims of a "private" or "phenomenal" self in favor of a superior "public" or "noumenal" self. Nietzsche diagnosed this "trick" of the willing subject and when it comes to collective decision making, the trick is the same: one must identify with something other than just oneself, something common and public. The private self and its interests can then be interfered with in a non-dominating way because such interests are either disavowed as "merely private" or seen as a danger to the polity. Orthonomy as a goal of the self, and the priority of the common good over private interest in public life, are key features of Pettit's arguments, and they are perhaps unwitting heirs to the Rousseauian-Kantian line of republicanism.

This long discussion has assumed that the agent agrees that the airport is in the common interest. But what if the agent never agreed with the decision to build the airport, yet it is nonetheless to be built next to their house? On what grounds could Pettit claim that the agent is not being dominated? The answer must be that it is in the common interest to build the airport, and unfortunately, it can only be built next to the agent's house. The agent disagrees, but is there a *fact* of the matter about what is not in the common interest? How is such a fact discovered? How is that fact justified in terms of evidence and reasons?

Pettit's response is that "the operational test suggested by the tradition is: when it [an interest] is sectional or factional in character. But how to test for what is sectional or factional? The only possible means is by recourse to public discussion in which people may speak for themselves and for the groups to which they belong" (Pettit 1997b, 56). Thus, there is a fact about what is in the common interest and it is revealed through political discussion. To be truly fact-finding, the discussion must allow for widespread contestability, openness to all citizens, and also acceptance of "canons of reasoning," the making of "plausible" arguments, and so on (Pettit 1997b, 188).[11]

These conditions, however, only push the problem of "relevance" back into conditions of reasonable democratic debate: what counts as plausible argument, or pertinent or relevant interests, is itself only partially open to debate. In other words, we move into a deliberative democratic model of republicanism, but as many critics of deliberation have noticed, the possibility of a "tyranny" of reason is, if sometimes overstated, not without plausibility. If what counts as relevant is only partially up for debate, then it seems possible, if not likely, that private interests will be excluded from public deliberation altogether. Rousseau himself sometimes suggests such a position, and constructivist views like those of Rawls and Habermas differ from Rousseau's view perhaps only insofar as they let deliberation itself weed out what is merely private, rather than ban private interests from the start. Whether this is best for discovering the common good is one thing, but why such a fact must be prioritized over the merely private interest is a question still left unanswered.

Moreover, the deliberative democratic view suggests two possibilities, both of which seem at odds with Pettit's position. First, we can imagine the common interest being discovered through finding that everyone *actually* agrees about a particular matter. But then we have not the general will—at least not necessarily—but the will of all, a view of the common good that Pettit disputes (Pettit 1997b, 287). Second, we can imagine the common interest emerging not through actual agreement, but through actual, hypothetical, or reconstructed *rational* agreement. Through the deliberative process individuals can come to see that their differences are the result of limited perspectives and merely private desires and interests. But this once again begs the question, for we want to know why merely individual interests can be interfered with and yet the individual not be dominated, not whether an interest is individual or private. Those goods that all involved in a cooperative enterprise benefit from may be common goods, but many decisions about the common interest necessarily impose on a number of individual's private interests. That is why, perhaps, Pettit argues against an understanding of the common good that sees it as being in each individual's interest (Pettit 1997b, 287). Even if there is a way to justify claims about what is in the common interest, the discovery of a common interest only supports the conclusion that the agent is non-dominated in the airport decision if one claims both that the private interests of the agent must be subordinated to the common interest and that one can be "forced to be free."[12]

I have been arguing that Pettit's example of failed contestation has disturbing Rousseauian overtones. A second, harder case of failed contestation reveals something crucial about the first. The second set of cases Pettit identifies concerns deeply divisive issues such as gay marriage, the rights of indigenous peoples, certain religious beliefs and practices, and so on. In those cases, Pettit argues, we might have to allow for a right to secede, but at the very least there must be robust protections for conscientious objectors (Pettit 1997b, 199–200). The distinction between the first and second set of cases, then, is the "depth" of the questions and conflicts at issue. In the first set we have a criminal who doesn't want to go to jail and a not-in-my-backyard objection to a putative common good; in the second set we have questions of religion, personal conscience, morality, and so on.[13] The question, though, is who decides what is and is not important?

We often rightly rely on our intuitions and our knowledge of history and sociology to aid our decisions about what objections to the common interest matter more than others. There will always be outliers, that is, individuals who value certain things or ideas or practices that few if any others value. But that is precisely the point. If we accept that the individual so attached to home values or quiet mornings that they are willing to contest the airport decision and ask for special protection or the right to secede is an outlier, that idiosyncrasy in no way undermines the claim that such an individual is being dominated, even if the decision to build the airport satisfies the common interest and was procedurally fair. Pettit's argument assumes (1) that we can assess the value of private interests that are not obviously wrong from the outside; (2) that in a conflict between a common and not valuable enough private interest, the common interest must win; (3) that an individual who shares the common interest but has a conflicting private interest must see the subordination of their private interests not as the work of willing agents but as something like a hurricane or earthquake, that is, as natural misfortune. These assumptions are explicit in thinkers such as Rousseau or Kant, and I have been arguing they are present in Pettit's work as well. If so, then the republican ideal of freedom as non-domination needs to address these concerns or clarify the philosophical plausibility of these assumptions.

My hunch is that Robert Talisse is right to argue that Pettit relies heavily on a few extremely telling examples to make freedom as non-domination attractive: the master and the slave, gender inequality, workplace domination, and so on (Talisse 2014). I also agree with Talisse that various counter-examples challenge certain clear instances of freedom removing interference that, on Pettit's account, must be considered to be non-dominating.[14] My goal has been to show that some of Pettit's own examples reveal the difficulties of denying ordinary intuitions and language in order to claim that some forms of interference—even when they clearly restrict or foreclose some of one's choices—are not dominating. Unsurprisingly, the same difficulties beset Rousseauian and Kantian accounts of freedom as autonomy.

The problems republicans like Rousseau, Kant, and indeed Pettit face are an outgrowth, or consequence, of the place of control in their accounts of freedom. Freedom as non-domination, paradoxically, requires control: either by the state over some of its citizens, or by the self over some of its desires and interests. Where the self cannot or will not relinquish its too-private interests for the sake of the common good, the state will coercively ensure that the self follows its common interest. When freedom is understood as autonomy, orthonomy, discursive control, non-domination, and the like, then an obvious question arises: how to account for the fact that states must interfere with citizens in those states for a variety of ends, including the pursuit of the common good? The intuition in the classical liberal response to this problem, as we find in Berlin, is to see actual interference as always a denial or reduction of freedom, and non-interference as a preservation or protection of freedom. The plausible intuition in the republican response is that one is not truly free unless one is free from the *power* of arbitrary interference. Insofar as Pettit makes *that* move, everything remains what it is.

The troubling, and indeed unmanageable, claim Pettit inherits from the republican tradition is that one can be interfered with without being dominated. This requires a crucial assumption: one is not dominated if interference tracks one's avowed interests. The mundane and often disturbing fact is that each human being has many interests, many desires, and many goals. Some of those interests are petty, or self-destructive, or violent, or simply idiosyncratic. Some of those interests might be avowed, and others never uttered aloud or admitted to oneself. Barring some forms of ideological indoctrination, however, they are *all*, nonetheless, interests, desires, and ends of that person. To claim that we are free when one or many of those interests are actively interfered with, simply because the interference tracks at least one of our interests, forces us to deny or devalue those untracked interests—but this is a trick that we might do well to expose.

So, if the centrality of control to an account of freedom raises the problems identified here, why not get rid of the idea of control? As we will now see, that is no solution at all.

ARENDTIAN POLITICAL FREEDOM AS SELF- AND WORLD-DISCLOSURE

Arendt argues that political freedom should be understood as self- and world-disclosure, and I will briefly outline her argument before turning to the problems that account presents for the institutionalization of the space of freedom. Before moving on, however, a terminological distinction relevant to Arendt's work should be clarified. For Arendt, freedom, as we saw in the last chapter, can be found throughout human activity. Not all acts are free, but many different kinds of acts can be described as free. In *The Human Condition* the term *action* is reserved not for human activity as such but for a specific type of political activity distinct from two other types of activity, labor and work. For the purposes of this chapter, I will use the terms *action*, *act*, and *actor*, with a lower-case "a," for human activity as such, and the terms *Action*, *Act*, and *Actor* for the specific type of activity Arendt describes and analyzes in *The Human Condition*.

Arendt argues that freedom generally is the non-sovereign, spontaneous initiation of the new, but Action is found only in the public sphere: Action is political and to Act is to Act freely, that is, to spontaneously initiate the new. The distinctiveness of Action lies in the disclosure of the self that Acts, the revelation of the "who" of the Actor (Arendt 1998, 175–181). Without the disclosure of the self, Action "loses its specific character and becomes one form of achievement among others" (Arendt 1998, 180). Action discloses not only the self but the world as well. Through Action we reveal unrecognized, unacknowledged, or unknown aspects of the world. Self- and world-disclosure, as one would expect from Arendt's non-sovereign account of freedom, is not free from constraints or conditions. On the contrary, a key feature of Arendt's phenomenology of political freedom is that self- and world-disclosure is not only conditioned but *constituted* by the constraints placed on Action in the political sphere (most notably the publicity constraint/condition on Action). In order to briefly examine Arendt's claims, I will focus first on the concept of disclosure and then on a central reason why Arendt focuses so closely on the disclosive characteristic of Action.

Action is discussed primarily in terms of the disclosure of the *self* through word and deed (Arendt 1998, 175–181). The self is performatively produced through speech and deed witnessed by others.[15] What an Actor says and does discloses *who* they are—rather than "what" they are—not by expressing a pre-existing self, but through the retrospective narration of the Actor's words and deeds by others (see Villa 1996, 89–94). Actions reveal what will eventually be, upon the Actor's death, their biography, the story of who they are. This story, though, is available only to others, and in two senses. First, only others can see who the Actor is because the self, for Arendt, is like the Greek *daimon* that only others can see (Arendt 1998, 179). Second, by definition, the Actor's biography can be written only by others insofar as death precludes any Actor's complete control over the story of their life. For both of these reasons, self-disclosure is only possible when the Actor is with others who bear witness to Actions and make sense of them through further speech (hence the publicity condition/constraint).

Action is also *world*-disclosive. As Dana Villa shows, Action is world-disclosive insofar as "political action consists . . . in the way it illuminates the world as appearance; in the way virtuosic action glorifies appearance and makes it into a source of meaning" (Villa 1996, 94). The world, for Arendt, is one of the human conditions—one of the relatively stable conditions of human existence on this earth—and the world (as opposed to another human condition, the earth) consists of the objects created by *homo faber*. Fabricated objects form the relatively durable human artifice that stands between human beings and nature (see Arendt 1998, 7–11). The world is full of objects made by human beings, and that world has the important function of being a stable point of reference for a group of people. Insofar as objects like tables and pencils remain more or less intact across time, they are points of stability in an otherwise changing world (Arendt 1998, 137; 1978a, 50–53). The world of relatively stable things, though, is at first a meaningless world because, however stable and durable, objects are "meant" to be used: like all human objects for use, they are eventually consumed. Worldly objects exist in order to serve as a means to some end (shelter, warmth, transportation, and so on). Thus, the "meaning" of an object is its use, but "utility established as meaning generates meaninglessness" (Arendt 1998, 154). The world of things is durable and stable and a common point of reference for individuals; but it is a meaningless world, a world without significance.

The world becomes meaningful through world-disclosive speech and action. Even artworks, for Arendt, are things whose "living spirit" "can be rescued only when the dead letter comes again into contact with a life willing to resurrect it although this resurrection of the dead shares with all living things that it, too, will die again" (Arendt 1998, 169). Specific interactions with the things of the world can disclose a meaning of those things, although often they do not. Think, for example, of great works of aesthetic criticism. The great critics of art, music, literature, and so forth, are those who reveal the works under discussion in new ways, or reveal those works as debased, inauthentic, original, genius, and so on. What is true of criticism is equally true of political and social criticism and analysis. Platitudinous as it is, whether one "agrees" with Plato or Marx does not change the fact that they managed to transform our ways of thinking about the world by disclosing the world to be other than what we know it, or knew it, to be. A further matter is whether such a disclosure can be affirmed intersubjectively, empirically, or in some other way, as true. But the disclosure itself is prior to the question of truth. Through intense engagement with the things of the world, the great critics in all spheres of life disclose the objects and events of the world *autrement*.

Action in the public sphere can also disclose the world, that is, reveal the world as meaningful in some specific way. The world of things can be made meaningful through the words and deeds that take place between individuals, and this interaction creates an in between or public world that Arendt analogizes to an intangible web overlaying the objective world (Arendt 1998, 182–183). Action differs from disclosive *criticism*, however, in at least three ways. First, Action, as political activity, usually concerns itself with a specific "part" of the world: the world that human beings have in common, that is, the shared world of events, facts, and problems that confront specific human communities. Second, Action is agonistic, to a level far beyond any agon between or among great critics or poets. Insofar as Action must take place in public, with others, what is disclosed through Action is immediately subject to contestation, revision, amendment, or rejection. Third, Action is a democratic activity in a specific sense: the public realm is in principle open to all citizens and in the public realm isonomy, isegoria, isology, and so on, are the norm. All participants are politically equal and all have an equal right to speak. In these ways, Action discloses the multiple and contestable meanings of the world that human beings have in common through words and deeds.

The words and deeds that disclose the world political Actors share are decisively different from the usual modes of speech we find in political theory. Putatively political speech acts include making offers in strategic bargaining, voice-voting, offering reasons for one's opinions, judicial and legislative judgments, and so on. While descriptive in some cases, performative in others, world-disclosive speech and action is unique in that it neither solely describes the world under established criteria (as in constatives), nor solely performs an action in words (as in performatives). Disclosive speech reveals the world, in Wittgensteinian terms, under a certain aspect, so that in light of that revelation other forms of speech can take place and make sense. Disclosive speech and action shows some part of the world to be meaningful in a unique, and perhaps heretofore unrecognized or unknown, manner.[16]

World-disclosive speech is undoubtedly rare in every sphere of human life and politics is no exception. To reveal the world otherwise through speech and deed, to lay it open in a new way, is to speak in a radically transformative way. The great moments of politics that we know of—Martin Luther King Jr.'s "I have a Dream" speech; Abraham Lincoln's Gettysburg Address; Rosa Parks standing up on a bus—often function, as Jacques Rancière would put it, as redistributions of the sensible, reorientations of the ways in which we experience the world. While most political speech is about the world, on Arendt's account, it is not necessarily world-disclosive. The usual ways in which we speak about the objective world presume the meaningfulness of our words and the usual meanings of objects in the world, but they do not always disclose that world. Freedom as world-disclosive Action is the kind of rare, extraordinary occurrence that admirers and critics of Arendt often take her theory of freedom to affirm. Arendt herself claims that the political, for the Greeks, provided a stable, ordinary space within which the extraordinary could become an ordinary occurrence—although it is undoubtedly the case that the extraordinary remained rare (Arendt 1998, 197).

Action specifies freedom and self- and world-disclosive activity in a unique fashion. Action must take place with others in a public space. The reason Action must take place with others is twofold. First, self-disclosure, as noted above, is impossible without others because the self is not a stable entity known to the Actor and expressed through word and deed. The self is itself initiated through speech and deed, disclosed to those who witness the Action and judge the Actor.

Second, Action as world-disclosive requires the presence of others because the *stability* of the meaning disclosed through Action depends on the response of other individuals. While Arendt is not entirely clear about this point, there is no doubt that world-disclosure requires the recognition or assent of others. The reason is that "the only character of the world by which to gauge its reality is its being common to us all, and common sense occupies such a high rank in the hierarchy of political qualities because it is the one sense that fits into reality as a whole our five strictly individual senses and the strictly particular data they perceive" (Arendt 1998, 208). Arendt's point, to repeat, is this: the world consists of a relatively stable and durable set of human-made objects that serve as a common reference point for individuals who each perceive the world from their own particular standpoint. What generally assures us that we share a world is that we see and respond to the same table. The meaningless world of objects can be made meaningful and shared through world-disclosive speech and deed.

How can we know that the meaningfulness of the world disclosed through speech and action is not idiosyncratic, or a hallucination? Only the affirmative responses of others to the world the Actor discloses through Action can provide some guarantee that the meaning of the world revealed is not purely idiosyncratic. We have seen that a condition of Arendtian freedom is minimal intelligibility to others and this same condition reappears here. The meaning of the world disclosed through Action cannot be unintelligible to others if the Action is to count as world-disclosive. Just as the great critics are great in part because they reveal a work of art to us in such a way that we think, "*Of course that's what it means*," the Actor equally relies on the assent of others.

I have tried to briefly make clear—in a way Arendt didn't make clear—what Action as world-disclosive activity meant for Arendt. However, her focus on Action as self- and world-disclosive might seem odd because, even for Arendt, activities other than Action disclose the self and the world. For example, love can reveal the self and art criticism can disclose the meaning of objects. Surely, one can rightly think, what makes Action distinctive cannot be its disclosive power, nor even its freedom, but something more obviously political: for example, its taking place within institutional bodies with authority and power, or in public demonstrations directed against prevailing rules and institutions. Freedom as non-domination, for example, is made possible by a citizen-controlled legitimate state and legal system, and negative freedom requires the interference of a state for the protection of rights and liberties. Positive, negative, and republican freedom are all understood within the context of recognizable modern institutions such as law, the state, the police, the military, private property, and so on. Why, then, does Arendt characterize political Action in terms of disclosiveness? Why is political freedom not oriented toward protecting the possibility of satisfying individual desires? Why doesn't political freedom protect human dignity? Why isn't political freedom a status one ought to have and value?

Arendt emphasizes the disclosive character of political action because the constitutive and dangerous political conditions of modernity are, she claims, *self- and world-alienation*. Self- and world-alienation are preconditions of the political catastrophes of the 20th century. In the *Origins of Totalitarianism* herd and mob mentalities, isolation, then loneliness—"not belonging to the world at all"—are described as the preconditions and products of tyranny and, later, totalitarianism (Arendt 1968). In each case the self, the individual, is lost. A central aim of 20th-century politics, for Arendt, is to destroy the unique individual self through mass propaganda and mob politics, the destruction of the public sphere, and even the destruction of the private sphere. At the end of a lecture course Arendt gave at Berkeley in 1955, she said:

> Yet out of the condition of worldlessness that first appeared in the modern age—which should not be confused with Christian otherworldliness—grew the question of Leibniz, Schelling, and Heidegger: why is there something

rather than nothing? And out of the specific conditions of our contemporary
world, which menace us not only with no-thingness but no-bodyness, may
grow the question, Why is there anybody at all and not rather nobody? These
questions may sound nihilistic, but they are not. On the contrary, they are the
anti-nihilistic questions asked in the objective situation of nihilism where no-
thingness and no-bodyness threaten to destroy the world. (Arendt 2005, 203)

At issue in modernity is nothing less than the "why" of individuality, of the
meaning of individuality, and of a plurality of distinct individuals. At the end
of *On Revolution*, Action—as Arendt understands the lesson of Sophocles in
Oedipus at Colonus—is that which offers an answer to the wisdom of Silenus:
best is never to be born, second best to go quickly (Arendt 1965, 285). Action,
in other words, can "redeem" our finitude, provide our mortal existence with
a reason for affirmation. Self-alienation in its various forms is both the condition and product of modern politics, and Arendt thinks Action can contest
that condition.

And yet, Arendt claims that Marx was wrong to think that self-alienation
is the hallmark of modernity; rather, it is *world*-alienation that is the central
problem of modern life (Arendt 1998, 254). Modern science, capitalism, and
modern philosophy all turn the self away from the world, either by rising to
an Archimedean point, by ignoring or repressing any desire for material satisfaction, or by turning to the self through introspection. Indeed, self- and
world-alienation go hand in hand. For Arendt, as for so many late 19th- and
20th-century thinkers and writers, modernity is characterized by doubt, loneliness, nihilism, political horror, suspicion, loss of tradition, moral and political
decline, and so on. The self becomes an interior, dark, hiding place unknowable by and meaningless to others, and this goes hand in hand with a world
rationalized, controlled, exploited, and potentially destroyed.

Whatever one makes of Arendt's account of modernity, it is the reason
why she focuses so much attention on self- and world-disclosure in Action.
Action is nothing less than a response to the horrifying and politically dangerous forces of modernity. If the conditions for totalitarianism include self- and
world-alienation, then Action provides one means of challenging those forms of
alienation. The specific potential of Action is that unlike great works of art and
their criticism, Action is in principle more democratic, available to anyone who
cares enough about the world to enter the public sphere and speak and act with
others. To bring the self back into the world along with others, and to reveal the

world as a meaningful place fit for human habitation, is to challenge the forces of modernity that led to the horrors of 20th-century fascism and fascisms present or to come. Much has been written on Arendt's phenomenology of Action, so I will stop here. But I hope enough has been said to suggest the importance of Action for Arendt and why she was eager to find a more permanent space for self- and world-disclosive activity in a modern world whose main tendencies are anti-political and world-destructive. As Arendt was well aware, if Action is to do the work she believed it could do, then the question becomes how to institutionalize a space for Action. The problem is great; and unsolvable.

ISONOMY AND THE INSTITUTIONALIZATION OF FREEDOM

Arendt, several times but without much comment, identifies the proper struc-ture of "rule" in the political sphere as *isonomy* (Arendt 1998, 32; 1965, 22–24; 2005, 118). The reference is to Herodotus' *Histories*, specifically to the speech of Otanes concerning the "rule of the many," which has the "best of all names to describe it": isonomy (not "democracy"; see Herodotus 1998, 3.80). Arendt glosses the idea of isonomy as a condition of "no-rule": isonomy "was under-stood as a form of political organization in which the citizens lived together under conditions of no-rule, without a division between ruler and ruled. This notion of no-rule was expressed by the word isonomy, whose outstanding char-acteristic among the forms of government, as the ancients had enumerated them, was that the notion of rule (the '-archy' . . . or the '-cracy' . . .) was entirely absent from it" (Arendt 1965, 22–23). Isonomy, usually translated as "equality," in the sense of equality before the law, is not, Arendt stresses, a natural condi-tion of equality. Rather, isonomy is political equality, an artifice constructed by the polis to put on an equal footing those who are not otherwise equal (Arendt 1965, 23). Isonomy is neither economic equality, nor equality of opportunity, nor merely the equal right of all to vote, nor equality in basic rights. Political equality exists when individuals are artificially equalized, whether the group consists of oligarchs, or the poor, or of a plurality of individuals from differ-ent classes, races, religions, and so forth. Isonomy guarantees not equality of condition but equal "claim to political activity," that is, *isologia*, the equal right to speak (Arendt 2005, 118). Under conditions of isonomy, nobody rules or is ruled: there is no "-archy" or "-cracy," not even the rule of the many that goes by the name of democracy. In democracy, rule still exists. Isonomy is a structure of "rule" in which political agents have equal rights to speak but no individual possesses the right to rule, nor must submit to the rule of others.[17]

Arendt's analysis raises an obvious difficulty: how can we institutionalize isonomy? For to take only one immediate problem, given that political entities like states, or even Arendt's much-admired councils, have to make and *enforce* decisions, what authority to end discussion does the entity as a whole, or individuals within the group, possess?[18] One answer is unanimity, but this seems a recipe for political paralysis given the plurality Arendt not only acknowledges as a fact, but affirms. How to institutionalize the political sphere is a question that, if not always explicitly, Arendt addresses in *On Revolution* and her essay "Civil Disobedience." In both texts Arendt aims to show that an institutionalization of the political sphere is possible and necessary for the redemptive possibilities of political freedom to be more widely and consistently realized. Her suggestions, however, are extremely problematic for a reason that should, at this point, be unsurprising: the place of control in Arendtian freedom.

In *On Revolution* Arendt argues that however successful the American Revolution was in creating a stable political order, it failed to institutionalize the very spaces of freedom—that is, spaces of direct participation in public affairs—that shaped and sustained the success of the revolution (Arendt 1965). This failure has led to a loss of the "revolutionary spirit." The loss of the revolutionary spirit coincided with and was the effect of the success of limited government, the protection of civil liberties, and the economic growth and prosperity that has characterized much of American history (see Arnold 2014). The self-organized spaces of free action—the various compacts, constitutions, townships, and so on—that had existed since the colonization of America by British citizens enabled Americans to solve in practice, but not in theory, the problem of constitutive and constituted power that plagued the French Revolution. The constitutive power of what was to become the United States lay in the mutual promises and collective associations that emerged seemingly everywhere in colonial America, and it was on the basis of those power-generating associations and promises that constitution-making authority could be delegated upward (Arendt 1965, 164–178). The American founders, Arendt continues, were also able to solve the problem of authority and the legitimacy of law by seeing authority as resting in the founding moment itself as it was augmented and extended across time (symptomatically seen in "Constitution worship"; see Arendt 1965, 196–206). But the American founders did not solve, as Thomas Jefferson ruefully recognized, the problem of how to sustain the energies, activities, desires, and experience of and for freedom in an institutionalized form.

Arendt turns to Jefferson's suggestions for a ward system and the spontaneous emergence in revolutions of various council organizations, as an alternative to the nation-state, representative, party-organized political system (see, for example, Jefferson 1984, 1379–1381).[19] This alternative model, Arendt argues, was and is destroyed by the nation-state and the party system, and thus the spaces of freedom for the sake of which the modern revolutions were initiated have failed to find a secure home within the modern nation-state.

The problem, Arendt suggests, is that the councils and wards are not meant to "administer things," to govern welfare states and organize the economic life of society. The point of the ward and council organization is to provide a space for those who desire "public happiness" and "public freedom" to engage in political life, that is, to reveal themselves to others and to disclose the world anew. The ward or council is the isonomic space in which a political freedom that can only exist without control by the self or by others is possible.

However, the difficulty with Arendt's proposal should be obvious, and it is not just the difficulty any alternative to the modern nation-state poses, that is, its implausibility. The problem lies in an implication of freedom as only possible under conditions of no-rule: a political institution the point of which is simply to be free cannot *govern* at all. If to be free is neither to rule nor be ruled, then by definition a political organization that has freedom as its end cannot govern, for it can neither demand a decision be made nor impose a decision. Even if modern nation-states were not primarily devoted to the administration of things, Arendt's suggested institutionalization of freedom is incapable of putting debate to an end and imposing even unanimous decisions upon anyone.

One could try to help Arendt out by drawing a distinction between the political and the administrative akin to the distinction Rousseau draws between the sovereign and the government. On this view, the political body, in Arendt's terms, would debate and discuss and decide but not impose or rule. But even if one could formulate a procedure for decision making that did not undermine freedom, this possible revision of Arendt's idea would not work. Arendt argues that administrative problems are not political problems at all and that experts, not Actors, should administer. Thus, there would be a curious uselessness to the political if, as is the case in modern nation-states, most governing is administrative in character. Indeed, Arendt occasionally recognizes that the real function of her political sphere is to enable those who care about public affairs to happily discuss what is at stake in the world among equals who neither rule nor are ruled.

But if this is all there is to the political, then why institutionalize it? It seems just as obvious that a debating society, or an ad hoc committee, or indeed any collection of individuals can turn themselves into a political community sharing a public space. If the end of the political is freedom in Action—rather than power, justice, legitimate authority, security, or anything else—then why is there a need to institutionalize the political, that is, provide it a place within a constitutionally organized nation-state? One possibility is that only such a constitutionally guaranteed place within a republic can assure the highest levels of the state of their authority, because such authority comes from below. However, Arendt appears to affirm the Roman distinction between power and authority, and at least in the case of the United States, the authority of the state comes not from the people but from the founding act itself and its objective manifestation: the United States Constitution. It is not the consent of the people, on this view, but the resonating and continuing effect of the foundation that is the source of authority for the United States. For similar reasons, guaranteeing a constitutional space for the political does not seem necessary for maintaining the power of the people, for power, on Arendt's account, exists only insofar as people are actually engaging with each other, that is, together in the mode of speech and action. An empty town hall with a legally guaranteed political status is less powerful than a spontaneously organized protest of the shooting of an unarmed African-American teenager by the police. Power is actual or potential, and any advantage the empty town hall has over another space for politics is unclear. One should then ask: if the council or ward system is necessary neither to maintain power, nor to guarantee the authority of the state, nor to make wise decisions about how to administer things, then why integrate the ward system into the constitutional order at all?

Constitutional issues are at the heart of Arendt's other explicit proposal for institutionalizing the political. In the essay "Civil Disobedience," Arendt justifies civil disobedience with reference not to the "dead letter" of the law but on the basis of the *spirit* of American law (Arendt 1972, 99). Civil disobedients "are nothing but the latest form of voluntary association," and "they are thus quite in tune with the oldest traditions of the country" (Arendt 1972, 96). Insofar as the problem civil disobedience poses is how to justify an action that is manifestly and purposely against the law, Arendt argues that "the establishment of civil disobedience among our political institutions" is a solution to the problem. First, Arendt suggests, civil disobedients should be granted the same status as other "special-interest groups" pressuring government officials. The next step is to amend the Constitution to allow for the actual practices of the right of assembly in American politics, a reference to the spontaneous, voluntary, and sometimes law-breaking activities of organized minority movements within the United States (Arendt 1972, 101).

The difficulty with Arendt's first suggestion is that a registered group of individuals working in Washington, D.C., to persuade legislators hardly sounds like civil disobedience anymore but politics as usual. It is unclear how turning civil disobedient groups into more or less permanent fixtures of Washington politics is going to maintain the space of freedom, of spirited association, that attracts Arendt to civil disobedience in the first place. As for the constitutional solution of rewriting or adding to the First Amendment in order to make clear that the right to assemble is more than just a right to *peaceably* gather together to *petition* the *government*, perhaps there is some promise to such an idea. However, providing a legally protected space for civil disobedience hardly seems like the real issue because the reasons so many Americans do not participate in civil disobedient Action surely rarely include "the Constitution doesn't properly protect such activities." The real issue, as Arendt was aware, is that the spirit of Action and the motivation to Act have, for various reasons, ceased to play an important role in contemporary politics. In short, the issue appears to be less a matter of *institutionalizing* than of *reanimating* the spirit of political activity, of a love for freedom, speech, and self- and world-disclosure, and of the world itself.

Whether in the form of the council system or in providing constitutional protection to civil disobedience, Arendt faces a dilemma: the political can be a space of isonomy, and thus a space for recovering the spirit of freedom and challenging the alienating forces of modernity; or the political can be relevant and institutionalized, but at the cost of isonomy and the separation of the political from administration. Arendt seems torn between two competing desires in response to two very important concerns. The first concern is the rise of the social, which is Arendt's version of the Weberian and Frankfurt School analysis of the rise and dominance of instrumental rationality in modernity. Politically, the dominance of instrumental rationality has emerged hand in hand with the rise of the modern nation-state, and unsurprisingly, the modern nation-state is largely instrumental and administrative in character. Arendt sees a stable, isonomic political space as a counter to the institutionalization of instrumental rationality in the modern welfarist nation-state. However, to be a clear alternative to the modern nation-state, Arendt's political sphere needs to have some teeth: it needs to be able to govern. But to accept the burdens of governing would necessarily undermine the political as a space of freedom understood as non-sovereign, spontaneous, disclosive initiation of the new.

The second and related concern is that self- and world-alienation is a cause and effect of the ever-expanding dominance of instrumental rationality since the 17th century. Self- and world-alienation coincides with a retreat into a vaguely felt self, a feeling of futility, the loss of shared concerns, the destruction of a stable common space of appearances, and generally speaking, nihilism. Nihilism, instrumental rationality, the administrative state, self-, world- and indeed earth-alienation: these are the afflictions of modernity, Arendt argues. Like Weber, Adorno and Horkheimer, Benjamin, Heidegger, Foucault and Habermas, Arendt offers a response to the ills of modernity. Unlike those other thinkers, Arendt finds a response to nihilism in political freedom, in the sheer pleasure and love of the world that comes in speaking and acting with one's peers, in disclosing the self and the world through speech and deed. Arendt's interest in maintaining the political sphere in a more stable form is to provide the opportunity for individuals to discover, amid the horrors of modernity, the desire to affirm, and even love, this world. The problem with this reason for institutionalizing the political is akin to what we have already seen: why institutionalize it at all? The basic difficulty is that if a condition of Action is an absence of control by the self and by others, and if the space of freedom must therefore be isonomic, and if governance and decision making are nonetheless elements of the political, then it is unclear how one can institutionalize the political without severely limiting, if not destroying, it.

A key reason for these difficulties is the place of control in Arendtian freedom. Arendtian freedom requires isonomy, but isonomy bans ruling. Many readers of Arendt have recognized that her political sphere is simply unable to cope with the modern requirements of the nation-state, but things are even worse than that. Arendt's politicians are not and cannot be governors, whether they live in classical Athens or 21st-century Germany. Following Habermas' lead, many of Arendt's modern interpreters have dispensed almost entirely with the idea of freedom as self- and world-disclosive action, and have turned instead to Arendt's discussions of judgment and those parts of her work in which she suggests a deliberative democratic model of politics. Freedom becomes the freedom to have a voice in collective decision making, and judgment becomes the preeminent political faculty (see Habermas 1983; Passerin D'Entrèves 1994; Wellmer 2000; 2001; and Benhabib 2003). This response, however, simply ignores the Arendtian hope that Action can counter the nihilism of modernity.

If one construes Arendtian political freedom as primarily a response to nihilism, one saves isonomy and non-sovereign freedom at the cost of "political impotence." The Arendtian political cannot serve as an alternative to the political organization of the modern nation-state if it cannot allow for governance, and thus one can rightly ask why we should any longer describe the Arendtian political as "political." Arendt can define the political in such a way as to distinguish it from government, administration, voting, and the like, but this opens her to the charge of making politics unacceptably pure, hence exclusionary, and insufficient for describing and resolving political problems (see Pitkin 1981; Wolin 1983; and Connolly 2000).[20]

Insofar as a necessary condition of freedom is lack of control and thus an isonomic political sphere, Arendt's political is fated either to political irrelevance as a space to express love of the world through free action, or to self-destruction as an alternative model of political governance.

FREEDOM AND CONTROL

Pettit and Arendt present two of the most powerful alternatives to positive and negative freedom in recent political theory. In spite of several overlapping concerns and inheritances, the two theories of freedom differ significantly on the place of control, either of the self over the self or of the self by others. I have argued in this and the previous chapter that the need for control in freedom leads Pettit to several problematic arguments, specifically for "virtual control" and for a quasi-Rousseauian republicanism that sees state interference as (in the right cases) non-dominating. In contrast, Arendt's attempts to theorize freedom without control lead, on the one hand, to an inability to account for some of our basic intuitions about free action (for example, that it makes one responsible) and, on the other hand, to the undermining of institutionalizing freedom.

Predictably, I have a ready answer for how we should understand the place of control within freedom: freedom is a dense phenomenon. Theodor Adorno, in a long and complex discussion of the negative dialectics of freedom, summarizes the issue succinctly: "Only if one acts as an I, not just reactively, can his action be called free in any sense. And yet, what would be equally free is that which is not tamed by the I as the principle of any determination—that which, as in Kant's moral philosophy, strikes the I as unfree and has indeed been unfree to this day" (Adorno 1973, 222). Freedom refers to our responsibility and autonomy *and* our freedom from constraint, even self-constraint.

The concept of freedom is almost too capacious, as if the unconstrained life freedom promises in reality reflexively expands the boundaries of the concept itself. Freedom is simply so many things, and neither one of those things primarily nor all of those things conjunctively. That is what we learn, or can learn, by thinking about the place of control in freedom. For if both Arendt and Pettit—and Hobbes, Berlin, Locke, and others—offer theories of freedom that, whatever their internal difficulties, appeal to our intuitions about freedom, then the problematic place of control is unlikely to be overcome either in theory or in practice. The concept of freedom also bleeds into so many aspects of our moral and political lives that unlike legitimacy or justice, the problem of freedom cannot be confined. How we understand freedom shapes our concepts and practices of law and punishment, of obligation and authority, of consent and dissent, of responsibility, of rights, of the individual and the collective, and so on. So much of our moral and political lives is shaped by the concept and practice of a freedom that escapes our theorizations of it.

Finally, freedom, more than other political concepts and realities, also plays a more prominent, in some cases dominant, role in contemporary liberal polities than any other political concept. I write this paragraph having just finished a long argument with my wife about the responses to the attack on the offices of the newspaper *Charlie Hebdo* in Paris. The argument turned on the language of "assaults on freedom" or "an attack against free speech." Just by itself, that argument revealed the place of control in thinking about freedom: is free speech compatible with constraints, either external or internal, on certain kinds of speech? The politics of freedom is as or more complex, as or more visible, than any of the politics of legitimacy or justice because in modern western polities, although not there alone, freedom plays a foundational role.

The conflicts within theories of freedom play themselves out, in practice, all the time. In the next chapter we will turn to a concept just as foundational, but often in conflict with freedom: justice.

5

RAWLS AND DERRIDA ON JUSTICE

HEGEL REMARKED THAT "quite generally, the familiar, just because it is familiar, is not cognitively understood" (Hegel 1977, §31). The work of John Rawls is an exception. Few books of political philosophy are as widely read and well understood as *A Theory of Justice* (hereafter *TJ*), *Political Liberalism* (hereafter *PL*), and *Justice as Fairness* (hereafter *JaF*). Whatever difficulties there may be in Rawls' arguments, understanding them is not one of them. An apt example of Hegel's general rule is the work of Jacques Derrida. The difficulty of Derrida's prose—or willful obscurity, as his critics would have it—has led to a number of plausible competing interpretations of his philosophical project as well as a number of outright rejections based, seemingly, on little more than hearsay from contemptuous philosophers. Derrida, like Rawls, has been discussed at length throughout the humanities—with the exception of analytic philosophy. While a few philosophers within or sympathetic to analytic philosophy have engaged Derrida's work on language and/or philosophy generally—John Searle, Stanley Cavell, Richard Rorty, Samuel Wheeler, and Henry Staten come to mind—Derrida's ethical and political writings are almost entirely ignored by contemporary analytic political philosophers. Derrida is acknowledged, if at all, only implicitly in rejections of nihilism, postmodernism, relativism, and other bogeys. For many political philosophers, to the extent that Derrida is familiar, he is for that reason not understood.[1]

This chapter explores Rawls' and Derrida's accounts of the concept and conceptions of justice because when read together Rawls and Derrida expose a

deep difficulty in modern political thought: can we proceed without metaphysics in political theorizing? This question has been asked many times before,
and often answered with a "no." Alasdair MacIntyre argues that "we still, in
spite of the efforts of three centuries of moral philosophy and sociology, lack
any coherent rationally defensible statement of a liberal individualist point of
view," while "on the other hand, the Aristotelian tradition can be restated in a
way that restores intelligibility and rationality to our moral and social attitudes
and commitments" (MacIntyre 1984, 259). For MacIntyre, only a revised classical metaphysics can restore ethical coherence to modernity. William Connolly
argues against the secularist hope for religious and metaphysical neutrality,
arguing that there is no escaping difficult questions of ontology, faith, metaphysics, and religion, whether we are theists or not (see Connolly 1995; 2000;
2005; 2008). Many communitarians claim that justice, rights, freedom, and
the like, only make sense given substantive moral commitments embedded in
specific forms of life, most of which rely on rich ideas about the self, the world,
the divine, and so on. And yet, many liberals, both classical and contemporary,
as well as various other political thinkers, have tried to do without recourse to
metaphysics, ontology, or theology.

Rawls and Derrida navigate this debate in similar ways, albeit from opposite directions: they both try to articulate a "post-metaphysical" conception
of justice by embedding justice in the specific legal and political *history* of the
West. The central innovation in Rawls' view from *TJ* to *PL*, starting with the
essay "Justice as Fairness: Political, Not Metaphysical," is to replace "metaphysical" foundations for justice as fairness with historical "foundations." Rawls, to
recall, argues in that essay that "since justice as fairness is intended solely as a
political conception of justice for a democratic society, it tries to draw solely
upon basic intuitive ideas that are embedded in the political institutions of a
constitutional democratic regime and the public traditions of their interpretation. Justice as fairness is a political conception in part because it starts from
within a certain political tradition" (Rawls 1999a, 390). The ideas that make up
justice as fairness are ideas drawn from a specific historical tradition. Rawls,
in an attempt to dispense with as much of metaphysics as possible, turns to a
tradition: his own.

Derrida, somewhat ironically given his reputation as a "post-structural" or
"post-modern" philosopher, does not dispense with what appears to be metaphysics, nor could he, given his philosophical views. Drawing upon a Kantian lineage, Derrida argues that justice—the *concept* of justice, in Rawlsian

terms—is *unconditional* and thus exceeds any phenomenal, *conditioned*, attempt to institutionalize justice on the basis of a *conception* of justice. Justice must be given, but it will never finally be given. Derrida argues that justice must be rendered in *law*, specifically, the law as it has developed in the western tradition. Derrida, like Rawls, turns to a specifically western history of constitutionalism, democracy, and international law in order to make sense of justice.

Rawls relies on history to escape metaphysics and Derrida turns to history to make effective a quasi-metaphysical Idea. In both cases, I argue, history *cannot* justify the normative validity and applicability of justice, and we are left with a compelling problem without an obvious answer: we can neither dispense with metaphysics nor, for familiar Rawlsian reasons, use it to ground politics and law in modern liberal democracies. We have, in short, an aporia that comes to light most clearly when we bring Rawls and Derrida together. This chapter, like the previous two, is aporetic cross-tradition theorizing in action, and I hope that it gives you a further, and better, sense of what we stand to gain by working in my preferred cross-tradition mode.

RAWLS FROM *TJ* TO *PL*

Leif Wenar helpfully summarizes the many negative responses to *PL* but argues that Rawls' work from *TJ* to *The Law of Peoples* actually reveals a coherent and unified theory relating justice and legitimacy (Wenar 2004, 265–267). The move from *TJ* to *PL*, according to Rawls, was spurred by a concern for the *stability* of justice as fairness under modern conditions of reasonable pluralism. The problem of stability is the subject of the third part of *TJ*, but in *TJ*, stability is secured, first, through a psychology of moral development that leads to a sense of justice in normal people. Second, Rawls argues for a congruence between justice and goodness such that acting on a sense of justice is part of an individual's good, thereby showing that individuals have a reason to act justly (Rawls 1971, especially §§85–86).

In *PL*, however, Rawls admits that justice as fairness will not be stable because "although the distinction between a political conception of justice and a comprehensive philosophical doctrine is not discussed in *Theory*, once the question is raised, it is clear, I think, that the text regards justice as fairness and utilitarianism as comprehensive, or partially comprehensive, doctrines" (Rawls 1996, xviii). The problem is that under modern conditions of moral pluralism within liberal democracies, a (perhaps partial) comprehensive account of justice as fairness cannot and will not attract enough support. There is simply too much metaphysical baggage in any comprehensive view to attract widespread acceptance given the fact of reasonable pluralism. Thus, Rawls seeks to justify a political conception of justice as fairness capable of receiving support as a freestanding moral doctrine from the vast majority of citizens despite their individual commitments to one or another comprehensive doctrine.

This is all well and good, but as some critics point out, something is lost in the move from *TJ* to *PL*. First, Rawls moves away from questions about the *normative validity* of justice as fairness. Habermas, in a sympathetic but critical review of *PL*, argues that Rawls undermines the *acceptability*, that is, the rational justifiability, of justice as fairness because of his concern with the eventual *acceptance* of justice within an actual political society (Habermas 1995, 121–122; see also Barry 1995, 890). Insofar as *PL* strives for neutrality—but not skepticism—vis-à-vis reasonable comprehensive doctrines, the validity of the political conception of justice as a free-standing moral doctrine is left hanging. We are to accept justice as fairness in *PL* not because it is true—we must remain neutral on its truth—but first, because it is at least one rationally acceptable, reasonable liberal conception that embodies the intuitive ideas and practices of constitutional democracy, and second, because it can be accepted by citizens holding different comprehensive doctrines. For Habermas, the second condition is the problem. Rawls, for the sake of stability, undermines normative validity. In order to gain acceptance, justice as fairness must deny its claim to truth, hence undermine the normative import of its being chosen in the original position. Whatever the problems of *TJ*, Rawls did attempt to show that justice as fairness was a normatively valid conception of justice even for those who would, outside of the original position, reject it. The high standard of universal normative validity, however, is hard to reach given the fact of reasonable pluralism, and Rawls largely rejects it in *PL*: it is part of his move from metaphysics to politics.[2]

Second, Rawls realizes, if obscurely, that justice as fairness in *TJ* requires the Kantian interpretation for its stability. Brian Barry's caustic criticism of *PL* rightly shows that Rawls is mistaken in thinking that justice as fairness, in *TJ*, comes even close to satisfying Rawls' own definition of even a partially comprehensive doctrine (Barry 1995, 876–880). However, as Barry also shows, the *stability* of justice as fairness in *TJ* does require the Kantian interpretation of justice as fairness, hence it is at least a partially comprehensive view (Barry 1995, 887). Recall that the argument for stability requires an account of moral psychology and moral learning that takes up much of the first half of Part 3 of *TJ* (§§69–75). The moral psychology and theory of moral learning Rawls defends lends itself to—perhaps it presupposes—a Kantian interpretation of morality, freedom, and justice. The Kantian interpretation of justice as fairness relies on claims about human freedom, indeed human nature, such that "acting from these principles [the principles of justice] persons express their nature as free and equal rational beings subject to the general conditions of human life" (Rawls 1971, 253). The stability of justice as fairness requires substantial ideas about the moral agent, moral psychology, moral development, freedom, equality, human nature, and so on. For Barry, *PL* is such a bad book because it constitutes an even worse response to the worst part of *TJ*: the last chapter, in which Rawls tries to assure the stability of justice as fairness by showing its congruence with each individual's good. But for *PL*, the need to dispense with the Kantian interpretation of justice as fairness is paramount because of its metaphysical commitments.

Third, beyond the Kantian interpretation and its metaphysical baggage, in *TJ* the theory of justice is a part of the theory of rational choice (Rawls 1971, 16), itself a theory laden with a number of contestable assumptions about human agency and rationality. On this view the choice of the principles of justice depends on an abstract model of human agency and rationality that is susceptible to philosophical challenge. Rawls rejects the earlier construal of justice as fairness as part of the theory of rational choice by suggesting that "only as a result of philosophy, or a subject in which the rational has a large place (as in economics or social decision theory), would anyone think it necessary to derive the reasonable from the rational, moved by the thought that only the latter was intelligible" (Rawls 1996, 52). While Rawls does not, as some critics claim, think of *actual* human beings in terms of the agent in rational choice theory, the very idea that a theory of justice is part of rational choice theory opens justice as fairness to a range of philosophical criticisms about the nature of rationality as well as the justification for thinking of justice in terms of rational choice in the first place. Moreover, as Rawls later acknowledges, it is neither necessary to rely on the rational to ground the reasonable nor even within the spirit of justice as fairness in *TJ*. Rational choice theory only creates more philosophical difficulties, and unnecessary ones at that.

Finally, in *TJ*, justice as fairness is seemingly of universal scope. Given the assumptions of rational choice, the account and importance of primary goods, basic facts about human nature, society, economy, and so on, it is reasonably clear that Rawls' argument in *TJ* is meant to hold for anyone who runs the original position thought experiment. So long as justice as fairness *is* the rational choice, then rational agents would choose it solely because it is rational. In *PL*, and especially in *The Law of Peoples*, justice as fairness, and liberalism more broadly, are not justified as universally valid nor are they to be imposed on non-liberal peoples (Rawls 1999b). In the real world of modern liberal democracies, the odds are against individuals accepting the premises, much less the conclusions, of the original position. Justice as fairness is for those cultures that inherit a specific tradition, and principles of justice chosen in the original position represent ideas already present and largely accepted in a political culture.

While not a complete comprehensive view, justice as fairness in *TJ* does require significant agreement on difficult questions about human nature, politics, economics, rationality, and morality. Rawls misspoke, strictly speaking, in claiming that justice as fairness is a comprehensive moral view, because justice as fairness leaves most religious, moral, and philosophical questions unasked, much less answered. However, justice as fairness in *TJ* does require commitments to a number of contestable philosophical claims. Thus, Rawls "politicizes" justice as fairness by grounding it in the political tradition of constitutional democracy rather than the western metaphysical tradition.

Justice as Fairness and History

Rawls' appeal to the public political culture for the intuitive ideas that inform justice as fairness is connected with his description of the four roles of political philosophy (Rawls 1999a, 305–307; 2001, 1–5). Tellingly, in all four the philosopher is placed within a historical context, facing a pressing political need, and aiming to help the philosopher's political culture. The first role of political philosophy is to find *agreement* beneath significant and potentially dangerous *disagreement*; the second role is to *orient* the ideas of citizens toward the meaning, aims, and purposes of the political culture; the third role is to *reconcile* individuals to the social and political world they find themselves in, that is, to overcome an always possible rage, resentment, and envy; the fourth role is "realistically utopian," to *discover* the practically possible ideal institutions, laws, goals, and purpose of a reasonably decent, just regime. These four roles of political philosophy involve abstract thought and general normative questions, but they are surprisingly concrete. They are the roles of political philosophy conceived as sorting through, ordering, modifying and justifying an existing polity to itself while working to solve its most intractable problems.

Given the importance of a public political culture and the nature of political philosophy, it is unsurprising that the original position is described as a *model*, a "device of representation" (Rawls 1999a, 400; see also Rawls 1996, 24; 2001, 17). The original position, in *TJ*, was also a model; but *TJ* modeled "rational persons concerned to advance their interests" (Rawls 1971, 118). These rational persons were also moral persons, hence were, among other things, equal, had a sense of justice, and had a conception of their good. The veil of ignorance was meant to rule out morally irrelevant knowledge so that rational, moral persons would be able to decide on principles of justice. The individuals in this original position represented rational, moral persons: in other words, any and all human beings.

In the later work, the original position doesn't model human beings in their rational and moral capacities *as such*, and the veil of ignorance is not intended to screen out all morally irrelevant information. The original position after *PL* is meant to model and represent within it the fundamental ideas of constitutional liberal democracies.

The central idea of justice as fairness is the conception of political society itself: "the most fundamental idea in this conception of justice is the idea of society as a fair system of social cooperation over time from one generation to the next" (Rawls 2001, 5). Rawls footnotes *TJ*'s definition of society at this point, but it is clear that there are major differences between the earlier Hart-inspired conception of society and the definition in *PL* and *JaF* (Rawls 1971, 4; see also Hart 1955, 185). In *TJ* the definition of society is normatively neutral: the term *fair* doesn't appear (Rawls 1971, 4). Society, defined neutrally in terms of rules of cooperation for individuals seeking their own good, requires principles to determine which rules are to be followed and how to distribute goods. *Any* society is a rule-bound cooperative venture, and so forth; but a *just*, hence *fair*, society is one that has chosen the two principles of justice. A fair society is *chosen* in the original position in *TJ*, and we are to imagine individuals choosing justice as fairness over both utilitarianism and perfectionism as well as other principles, including those we think are unjust principles when we are outside the original position (for example, "to each according to their caste/race/gender/class"). Given Rawls' argument, we have to actually see whether principles based on caste would be rejected in the original position, for even if our intuitions tell us such principles are unjust, it is possible that our intuitions are wrong.

One way of emphasizing the change in Rawls' ideas is to note that in the revised edition of *TJ*, published after the shift toward political liberalism, Rawls twice employs the "fair system of cooperation" definition of society, although he also retains the neutral definition. For example, in the revised edition we find, in Section 17, "And so the more advantaged are entitled to whatever they can acquire in accordance with the rules of a fair system of cooperation" (Rawls 1999c, 89). In the original version of *TJ* we find no mention of fair systems of cooperation (Rawls 1971, 104), just a "scheme of cooperation." The idea of society *as* a fair system of cooperation is a distinctively late Rawlsian idea.

In the later definition of society, fairness is *built into* the definition. Social cooperation has three characteristics: (1) it is structured by public rules, (2) the terms of cooperation are fair, and (3) the goal of cooperation is the better securing of the rational good of each individual. In *TJ*, characteristics 1 and 3 were already present in the definition of society, but characteristic 2 was not. That social cooperation *must* be fair *in order to be* cooperation is not—cannot be?—a conclusion discovered by conceptual analysis; it is surely an interpretation drawn from the public political culture (Rawls 2001, 6). This has two important consequences for Rawls' later work. First, it stands as further proof that Rawls is not seeking to justify justice as fairness to any and all, because the conception of society is already normatively loaded. Second, and for this reason, the burden of justifying the normative validity of (justice as) fairness shifts to the justification of the normative validity of a historical, hence contingent, culture's laws, institutions, ideas, and so on, to those who live in that society. This latter point is crucial for my argument. In *TJ* justice as fairness is justified because suitably described rational and moral persons would choose the two principles of justice on the basis of rational and reasonable considerations. These considerations were relevant to any and all rational moral persons behind the veil of ignorance. Justice as fairness ought to be, rationally must be, chosen, but that is something we *discover* only in the original position.

In *PL* and *JaF*, however, choosing an unfair system of cooperation is not an option because "we *start* with the organizing idea of society as a fair system of cooperation between free and equal persons. Immediately the question arises as to how the fair terms of cooperation are specified" (Rawls 2001, 14; emphasis added). Representatives in the original position are not, one must assume, even given principles of cooperation—say, principles based on a racial caste system—which would then be rejected as unfair. In *PL* and *JaF*, it is not only that moral realist and theological conceptions of fairness are precluded from the start because of the conditions of reasonable pluralism and the burdens of judgment; unfair systems of cooperation are precluded as well. But why?

The reason is that not only do the burdens of judgment and reasonable pluralism—historical features of modern liberal regimes—condition the basis of public justification for justice as fairness (it cannot be justified from within or as a comprehensive moral doctrine), but also fairness itself is an *inheritance* of that history. For liberals living in modern constitutional democracies, unfairness is not an option to be considered and rejected. While Rawls' two principles of justice might not be chosen in the original position, only a fair set of principles will be offered for choice. This constraint places the burden of specifying the fair principles of justice on historical interpretation.

Similar considerations apply for two further fundamental ideas of justice as fairness represented in the original position: free and equal citizenship and a well-ordered society. Individuals in the original position in *PL* and *JaF* represent citizens of modern constitutional democracies. These citizens have two moral powers—a capacity for a sense of justice and a capacity for a conception of the good—and each citizen is free and equal. Freedom and equality of the citizen as represented in the original position are not metaphysical ideas; rather, they are specifications of the concepts of freedom and equality inherited from the tradition of political liberalism (Rawls 2001, 19). Similarly, there is a broad concept of a well-ordered society in which there is an acknowledged public conception of justice—largely if not completely realized—and made up of citizens holding an effective sense of justice (Rawls 2001, 9). This concept, however, is specified into a conception that fits political liberalism, and thus a liberal well-ordered society must also find its basis in the public political culture of constitutional democracy.

The original position represents a historically specific conception of the freedom and equality of citizens as well as a well-ordered society. First, the original position "models what we regard—here and now—as fair conditions under which the representatives of *citizens*, viewed solely as free and equal persons, are to agree to the fair terms of cooperation whereby the basic structure is to be regulated" (Rawls 2001, 17). Second, the original position "models what we regard—here and now—as acceptable restrictions on the basis of which the parties, situated in fair conditions, may properly put forward certain principles of political justice and reject others" (Rawls 2001, 17). The ideas of "society as a fair system of cooperation," "free and equal persons," "acceptable restrictions on the basis of political principles," and so forth, are not ideas inherited from moral philosophy or known through reason alone. Rather, they are ideas found in the public political culture of constitutional democracies. These ideas are then represented in the original position insofar as representatives are situated equally with respect to each other, and understood as free with respect to their values, goods, life-plans, and so on. Just as with the definition of society as a "fair system of cooperation," so the ideas of freedom, equality, publicity, well-orderedness, and the like, must come from the public political culture and be represented in the original position. This means, again, that the original position does not, and cannot, normatively justify the fundamental ideas of and in political liberalism even though ideas such as "free and equal personhood" are normative ideas (Rawls 2001, 24). To the extent that representatives of citizens are choosing principles of justice, the description of the original position precludes unfreedom, inequality, disorder, non-publicity, and so on, from even being considered, much less chosen.

These latter possibilities are excluded because ideas in the public political culture become part of the *description*, the *architecture*, of the original position. The parties themselves and how they are situated with respect to each other, the conditions placed upon choice by reasonable pluralism and the burdens of judgment, what kinds of reasons can be given, and all other formal features of the original position model ideas in the public culture (Rawls 2001, 85). To be sure, in *TJ* the formal features of the original position also precluded the possibility of certain principles being chosen, but that was largely a consequence of the veil of ignorance. It was irrational to choose perfectionism, or certain kinds of utilitarianism because one didn't know one's actual place in the society. The veil of ignorance was intended to screen out morally irrelevant information so that the choice of principles would be normatively justified. The original position in *TJ* was designed so as to make a choice of principles of justice possible, morally significant, and rationally justified. The veil of ignorance was designed to lead to the most rational and reasonable conception of justice. These conditions relied not on the historical facts of constitutional democracy, but on general sociological and economic facts as well as ideas drawn from moral philosophy.

In the later work the veil of ignorance performs similar functions but with one key exception in the knowledge of the representatives: they know that reasonably favorable conditions of constitutional democracy obtain (Rawls 2001, 87). This, however, is no ordinary piece of knowledge, akin to the general facts about society, moderate scarcity, and human psychology that we find in *TJ*. This new bit of knowledge provides further evidence—given that we set up the original position, Rawls claims, in a way that "best suits our aims in developing a political conception of justice"—that the parties are really choosing only between principles of justice conceivable within the term of constitutional liberal democracies. Given the historical constraints placed on choice in the original position, some principles are not even up for discussion. This is a significant restriction on the choice of principles, although not one inconsistent with the basic idea of the original position in *TJ*. For the original position as a device faces a fundamental objection: insofar as we are free to describe the original position to suit our aims, then we are, in a sense, always rigging the result. In other words, we get the result we desire every time by modifying our description of the original position so that it guarantees our desired conclusion. If utilitarianism seems to result from a description of the original position, then we can always change the description of the person who chooses. In the later work the restrictions on choice are greater because, rather than choosing conceptions of equality and freedom over inequality and unfreedom, in *PL* and *JaF* citizens can and will choose only some conception of equal freedom. Utilitarianism is a serious option only in some forms, and even those forms are plausible only because they accept many of the basic ideas of justice as fairness, albeit utilitarian conceptions of freedom and equality are different. The major difference between *TJ* and the later work is, again, that constraints on choice in *PL* and *JaF* are drawn from the public political culture rather than morality as such.

Rawls claims that the parties in the original position "in effect try to fashion a certain kind of social world; they regard the social world not as given by history, but, at least in part, as up to them" (Rawls 2001, 118). My claim, however, is that Rawls' "in part" is too modest: the social world representatives in the original position try to fashion is *almost entirely* the social world given to them by history, but that world purified of its deep, and persisting, injustices.[3] Representatives in the original position do not normatively justify most of the world they fashion because they take for granted the fundamental values of that world. They cannot but choose constitutional democracy.

History and Normativity

So far I have tried to make two points. First, I have laid out uncontroversial, well-known reasons why Rawls turns to a political conception of justice. Second, and for these reasons, I have suggested that Rawls *must* shift the normative justification for the fundamental ideas of justice as fairness from moral philosophy and the decision procedure of the original position to the *actual* history of constitutional democracy.

Can history provide a normative justification for freedom, equality, and society as a fair system of cooperation? In other words, are the ideas, institutions, and practices of constitutional democracy normatively valid? This question forces two more. First, can we agree about which are the fundamental ideas of the historical tradition in which justice as fairness is embedded? Second, even if we presume that Rawls is right about the public political culture, is the *existence* of that tradition enough to normatively justify its values and ideas, even to those of us born into the tradition? In short: does Rawls give citizens of modern constitutional democracies *normative* reasons to accept the validity of fundamental normative ideas in the historical traditions these citizens belong to?

First: what *are* the central ideas, institutions, practices, values, and interpretations in the public political culture of western constitutional democracies? Given the pluralism that Rawls not only recognizes but affirms, there are bound to be a number of conflicting views in and of the public culture. George Klosko argued that polling data at the time he was writing showed that many of the ideas Rawls claims to be part of the public culture of the United States are not present in the minds of U.S. citizens (Klosko 1993). Klosko concludes that Rawls is caught in a dilemma in which he can either give up his more substantive views and align his thinking more closely with ideas in the public culture, or give up that alignment and retain the more substantive views (Klosko 1993, 355). So, a first problem with the appeal to the public political culture is that the *actual* ideas held by *actual* members of that culture are often at odds with Rawls' interpretation of the culture.[4]

Second, any interpretation of the political history of constitutional democracy must acknowledge, and account for, competing interpretations, a point I explored in the first chapter. To take but one well-worn example from American political thought, liberalism and republicanism can both explain key features of American history, specifically in the revolutionary period. On the one hand, Louis Hartz famously argued that the "dogmatic liberalism of a liberal way of life . . . is the secret root from which have sprung many of the most puzzling of American cultural phenomena" (Hartz 1991, 9). Bernard Bailyn, on the other hand, just as famously argued that radical 17th-century English thought in conjunction with various Republican ideas, English common law, and Puritan theology were definitive of the revolutionary period (Bailyn 1992, especially chaps. 2 and 3; see also Wood 1998). For Rawls, these debates cannot be merely academic: they support or undermine his argument. Whether a liberal or republican interpretation is more historically accurate is of some consequence for political liberalism. Rawls rejects republicanism insofar as it is a partially comprehensive moral doctrine (Rawls 1996, 205–206). But if republican conceptions of freedom, equality, a well-ordered society, and the like, are part of the public political culture, then Rawls can hardly reject them so easily. On the basis of Rawls' own argument, one can emphasize republican features of the political culture and then challenge political liberalism on the basis that it imposes ideas less central to the public culture.

The interpretive problem is intensified by the moral ambiguity—to put it mildly—of the last four centuries of western history. Widespread violence, racism, sexism, genocide, war, and other harms, have marked the laws, the practices, and the values of western constitutional democracy. Rawls is aware of this history, but he never addresses this objection, or even the facts, in any detail. From within a Rawlsian perspective, however, a response to this history is fairly clear: the injustices of slavery, for example, were clearly against the spirit of western liberalism. The failure of liberal democrats to realize the liberal society they aspired to build does not undermine liberalism as such.

There is a powerful counter-argument to this Rawlsian line. If the public tradition of liberalism begins in the late 17th century, then for the vast majority of liberalism's existence, its theorists and later its statesmen have often violated their own principles. At some point, someone who lies consistently, even if not always, is rightly taken to be a liar. To return again to just the United States: on a *generous* reading, only since the late 1960s has there been true formal equality before the law; slavery was an institution within liberal democracies until the middle of the 19th century; women were not given the right to vote until the 20th century; unionization of workers was actively and violently resisted, and still is; extensive income inequality exists and is increasing; and let's not ignore the mass genocide and expropriation of the land of indigenous peoples from the 17th century on. We have too much testimony to the violence and injustice of actual liberal democracies not to wonder whether these injustices are, in spite of liberal values and ideas, intrinsic to liberalism. To the extent that Rawls' argument embeds justice as fairness in the actual public culture and history of democracy, the injustices of that history require greater explanation and, presumably, a theodicy.

A final reason to be suspicious of Rawls' appeal to history and the public political culture is the difficulty of interpretation more generally and historical interpretation in particular. Given basic hermeneutic problems of "fusing horizons," discovering the intentions of speech acts, and the crucial role of narrative structure in historiography, identifying just what are the key ideas of a public culture, and the meaning of those ideas, is a fraught enterprise (Gadamer 1998; see also Skinner 1969; and White 1978; 1987). This does not mean that interpretation cannot or should not be done; far from it. However, we should keep in mind—as we saw in the first chapter—one particular thing that is at stake in political liberalism, which is also a theory of political legitimacy: the use of state violence. Rawls must answer the question: Given the contestable nature of historical interpretation, how can you legitimize state violence by appealing to, if not directly, the public political culture? For in the last instance, Rawls' response to the potential object of state violence must be "the public political culture is your public political culture, the ideas I have identified are part of that culture, you would have agreed to the principles of justice in the original position, fair cooperation requires the possibility of coercion, therefore . . . " If, however, the ideas Rawls identifies are *not* part of the public political culture, or are only contestably so, then the case for state legitimacy and state violence is weakened. Again, these questions about historical facts and interpretation are hardly "academic" for political liberalism.

Let's assume, though, that Rawls is right, and that the original position does represent ideas found in the public political culture. A further problem is that Rawls does not, and cannot, normatively justify the historical ideas that are the fundamental ideas of justice as fairness without either (1) relying on a comprehensive, hence metaphysical, moral doctrine (as he does in *TJ*), or (2) elaborating a philosophy of history that, like Hegel and Kant, invests history with metaphysical significance. Rawls, rejects the first possibility and although he rarely deals with the philosophy of history, the burdens of such a philosophy are too much for a *political* conception of justice as fairness. If a philosophy of history is unavailable to Rawls, then the normative ideas of the public political culture of western constitutional democracies cannot be normatively justified from within Rawls' argument. Yet, these ideas play a central organizing role in the argument for justice as fairness insofar as they are represented in the formal structure of the original position. This is a significant problem for Rawls' arguments, for the conclusions reached in a hypothetical original position would no longer have normative authority until western liberal culture itself was normatively justified.

The central problem is that being a citizen of a particular culture with particular normative ideas is no reason for the citizen to accept the normative validity of those ideas. Being born American, or French, or British is a morally irrelevant contingency in the same way race, class, gender, sexuality, and the like, are supposed to be morally irrelevant. Yet, Rawls' original position can no longer screen out the morally irrelevant facts of citizenship because those facts are represented and modeled in the formal structure of the original position. These normatively irrelevant contingencies infect the original position and undermine its normative power. Even a political conception of justice as fairness needs, but cannot accept, the aid of metaphysics.

This objection to Rawls can only get going if, first, the conceptions of freedom, equality, society, and so forth, in the public political culture cannot be normatively justified from within Rawls' theory, and if, second, a person's specific citizenship is a morally irrelevant fact about that person.

That ideas in the public political culture *can* be normatively justified is not the issue. The issue is whether, from within his argument for a political conception of justice, Rawls can justify the normative validity of the culture's normative conceptions. I don't see how he can. First, the original position does not, and cannot, justify conceptions of freedom, equality, and the like. The original position "is introduced in order to work out which traditional conceptions of justice, or which variant of one of those conceptions, specifies the appropriate principles for realizing liberty and equality once society is viewed as a fair system of cooperation between free and equal citizens" (Rawls 1996, 22). There is no doubt that free and equal citizenship and society as a fair system of cooperation are *presupposed* by representatives in the original position, for their job is to specify principles of justice which will realize freedom, equality, and fairness. These latter ideas are taken from the public political culture and interpreted in light of that culture. The original position cannot normatively justify its own presuppositions.

Second, freedom and equality of the person are political conceptions, not metaphysical, and the political conception of the person "is worked up from the way citizens are regarded in the public political culture of a democratic society, in its basic political texts (constitutions and declarations of human rights), and in the historical tradition of the interpretation of those texts" (Rawls 2001, 19). Now, if Rawls is really to avoid metaphysics, then claims about rights in, for example, the Declaration of Independence, must be understood and employed solely as ideas in the culture, not as philosophically grounded. Thus, we cannot normatively justify freedom and equality from within Rawls' argument without imposing a comprehensive doctrine on those who may not hold that doctrine.

Third—and this takes me to the question of citizenship—normative ideas of the public political culture cannot be normatively justified from within different reasonable comprehensive doctrines. This is an important point because one might think Rawls can turn to sources from within different comprehensive doctrines, each of which can support the views of freedom, equality, fairness, and so on, albeit for different reasons. Recall that for Rawls, the liberal principle of legitimacy is that "our exercise of political power is fully proper only when it is exercised in accordance with a constitution the essentials of which all citizens as free and equal may reasonably be expected to endorse in the light of principles and ideals acceptable to their common human reason" (Rawls 1996, 137). Thus, the freestanding view of political liberalism is to be endorsed by all or nearly all citizens, but the relation between an individual's non-political values and the political are left to an individual's own conscience and reason (Rawls 1996, 140). Moreover, each citizen judges the political conception from the perspective of their comprehensive view and avoids compromising their own values by finding reasons for the political conception coherent with their comprehensive doctrines (Rawls 1996, 150, 171). Given that we do not all have to affirm the political conception of justice for the same reasons, then we might assume that each reasonable comprehensive doctrine can affirm political liberalism and its fundamental ideas of freedom, equality, fairness, and the like, independently of the original position, such that they can be justifiably represented in the original position. If this is right, then the normative facts of a political culture can be normatively justified.

The problem with this solution can be shown by a simple example. Imagine that Citizen A holds a reasonable comprehensive doctrine including the religious duty to realize God's will on Earth, which requires a theocratic state. Assuming that Citizen A is born into a liberal democratic culture and the comprehensive doctrine is reasonable—that is, that Citizen A recognizes that others may disagree with the view and that it would be unfair to impose it on others using state power—then in the original position a representative of Citizen A might adopt the two principles of justice, given that the representative would not know what doctrine Citizen A actually held. Independently, Citizen A might even endorse the liberal conceptions of freedom and related concepts for reasons internal to the comprehensive doctrine. Citizen A's doctrine is reasonable in part because under conditions of reasonable pluralism the doctrine holds that one should not use political power to impose one's ideas even if one has that power (Rawls 1996, 61).

Now, imagine that Citizen A is not born into a liberal democratic culture, but into a culture the ideas of which are entirely the ideas of Citizen A's comprehensive doctrine, there is no reasonable pluralism, and thus there are no burdens of judgment. In this culture, principles of justice might still be chosen in the original position if necessary, but absent the circumstances of liberal democracy there is no need to find a distinctly political conception of justice. There may also be no need to independently endorse liberal conceptions of citizenship, freedom, equality, and the like, given that in this culture such conceptions may not exist. Even if these ideas do exist—even if they are the same ideas—there is no need for a political conception and justification of the ideas. In short, there is no need for Citizen A to draw on a public political culture in order to articulate a political conception of justice.

If this latter sketch is plausible—and it draws in a few lines the idea of a homogeneous religious and theocratic society, surely something that is not unthinkable or even unprecedented—then it suggests that one's citizenship, the contingencies of one's birth, play a significant role in whether one even *needs* to draw on the ideas of a public political culture in a theory of justice. In the first scenario Citizen A had to make sense of himself or herself and his or her doctrine in light of a liberal political culture; in the second scenario, Citizen A did not. Even though the comprehensive doctrine remains absolutely the same in both societies, only in the first do the ideas of freedom, equality, and the like, stand in need of normative justification. In the second society the ideas don't even exist. In the first society Citizen A's doctrine is reasonable because it does not claim that political power should be used to impose the doctrine on those who don't accept it; in the second society it is entirely plausible that political power will justifiably enforce the doctrine, not on non-believers but on those who fail to satisfy the view's requirements. Sin will not be politically judged and punished in the first society; it will justifiably be judged and punished in the second. In one society Citizen A is a citizen of liberal democracy with its associated circumstances; in the other he or she is a citizen of a theocracy. In one society Citizen A must be a liberal and his or her view must be reasonable; in the other he or she need not.

Where and when we are born is entirely out of our control, and just as we do not choose our race, religion, gender, and many other characteristics, so we do not choose, at birth, our citizenship. The ideas of one's political culture are just that: the ideas of one's political culture. Placed in another culture, a citizen would inherit different ideas. Rawls himself acknowledges this very point in his lectures on Hegel, a statement worth quoting in full:

> If citizens of a constitutional democracy are to recognize one another as free and equal, basic institutions must educate them to this conception of themselves, as well as exhibit and encourage this ideal of political justice publicly.

This task of education is part of the role of a political conception. In this role, such a conception is part of the public political culture: its first principles are embodied in the institutions of the basic structure and appealed to in their interpretation. Acquaintance with and participation in that public culture is one way citizens learn that conception of themselves, *a conception which, if left to their own reflections, they would most likely never form, much less accept and desire to realize.* (Rawls 2000, 367, emphasis added.)

The mere fact of inheritance gives no authority, no normative validity, to my culture's ideas. Holders of comprehensive doctrines need only to find reasons for a political conception of justice, and thus justify justice as fairness, if the holders of those doctrines live in liberal democracies. If they do not, then they need not justify any aspect of liberal democracy; in fact, they might be strongly opposed to liberal democracy. This seems obvious.

The implication of this obvious point is that a citizen of a liberal democracy who understands citizenship as contingent and thus the political ideas of the culture as in need of independent normative justification *can* turn to a comprehensive doctrine for support. But the citizen need only imagine having been born somewhere else, into another culture, to realize that whatever support for the ideas of political liberalism the doctrine *could* give *need* be given *only* because of the contingencies of birth. Just as anyone can place themselves in a hypothetical original position, anyone can place themselves in a real or hypothetical non-liberal culture and see that the ideas of one's culture are not normatively valid simply because of membership in the culture.[5] If the choice is between validating those ideas or facing rejection from the culture, then this is hardly a position from which to assess the normative validity of the ideas.

The veil of ignorance is employed in the original position so that morally irrelevant contingencies do not play a role in the choice and justification of principles of justice. Citizenship is such a contingency and *the ideas of one's public political culture are too.* However, the original position in Rawls' later work presupposes a specific citizenship and the ideas of a specific political culture. The veil of ignorance veils *citizens*, not moral persons as such, and thus it cannot, but ought to, eliminate the contingency of citizenship. This implies that whatever principles of justice are chosen in the original position are chosen against a background of ideas that are not normatively justified, nor would even need to be justified but for the contingent fact of birth and citizenship. A citizen can always, and easily, imagine themselves born otherwise, and quickly conclude that the ideas of the culture have no normative validity until they are justified. For this reason Rawls' argument cannot succeed: that is, it relies on the validity of normative facts for which it cannot possibly provide any normative justification without employing metaphysics. Rawls needs, but cannot turn to, metaphysics. With the metaphysical interpretation of justice as fairness in *TJ* having been left behind in order to seek a solely political conception of justice embedded in history, it turns out that only a metaphysics of history can possibly justify political liberalism.

Suffice it to say that political liberalism would be in trouble if it requires a metaphysics of history. In his brief discussion of Hegel's philosophy of history, Rawls outlines, but neither endorses nor criticizes, Hegel's view that history has a final meaning and goal, part of which includes (more or less) liberal political institutions (Rawls 2000, 369–371). However, even if Rawls the philosopher endorses some Hegelian version of history, Rawls the political theorist cannot. Take just the key Hegelian idea that "Reason is the law of the world" and that Reason "is its own exclusive presupposition and absolutely final purpose, and itself works out this purpose from potentiality into actuality, from inward source to outward appearance, not only in the natural but also in the spiritual universe, in world history" (Hegel 1997, 11). Surely this idea can have no place in justifying a political conception of justice as fairness. Nor could Rawls rely on those Kantian texts in which a philosophy of history is sketched. Take "Idea for a Universal History with a Cosmopolitan Intent," for example, and remember that one promising aspect of such an essay is the term *Idea*, which in Kantian thought means that the Idea is only to regulate our thinking toward a certain end rather than describe or conceptually determine an empirical object (Kant 1998, A643/B670–A647/B675). In this essay Kant argues that seemingly contingent and unconnected historical events can actually be seen to manifest some underlying order. This order is, as an Idea, not itself something we can know, but we can, Kant argues, discover a "guiding thread" for understanding human history, an Idea that can regulate our knowledge of history (Kant 1983, 30). This guiding thread starts with a teleological conception of nature, moves through an analysis of Reason in light of teleology, and then suggests that the goal of human history is, akin to but different from Hegel's view, to create liberal political institutions under which human reason can fully develop and flourish. The problem, however, is the same: Kant relies on deeply contestable ideas about reason, nature, human nature, and so on, in order to suggest the meaning and goal of history.

Given the difficulty of imagining how Rawls could possibly endorse, within political liberalism, a philosophy of history that would normatively justify the ideas of a liberal culture, and given that Rawls cannot turn to other metaphysical grounds of support, I conclude that Rawls cannot succeed in escaping from metaphysics and into history. Derrida, as we will now see, has the same problem in reverse: how to get from a quasi-metaphysical conception into history. I will argue that he cannot succeed either.

DERRIDA

If Rawls tries to justify a political conception of justice as fairness by appealing to history, Derrida's task is to show how an "Idea of justice" can be *enforced* in the historically conditioned institution of law as it has developed in the West. The problem is that the Idea of justice—"Idea" taken here in a modified Kantian sense—cannot ever be realized in the world of courts, procedures, administrative rulings, and so on. And yet, Derrida wants to argue, justice *must* be realized, enforced, and it must be realized in and through law.[6] Law, for Derrida, employs force in the name of, and for the sake of, a justice it can never (fully) realize.[7] Complicating matters even more, Derrida argues that positive law is neither legitimate nor illegitimate because it can never be fully founded (Derrida 2002, 241–242). The legitimacy of the force of law, therefore, is never finally secured against all criticism or "deconstruction." Thus, a justice that can never be realized in law nonetheless *must* be realized in a law the force of which is never legitimate: "But it turns out that law claims to exercise itself in the name of justice and that justice demands for itself that it be established in the name of a law that must be put to work [*mis en oeuvre*] (constituted and applied by force 'enforced')" (Derrida 2002, 251).[8] My question is simple: what privilege does law have such that justice *itself* demands [*exige*] that it be enforced through law? The question is even more urgent because it is clear that the law Derrida has in mind is not law *as such*, but law as a historically developed and developing *western* institution.

Derrida faces a problem similar to Rawls': even with a "metaphysical" conception of justice, Derrida cannot show why a historically contingent, a-legitimate, law must be the privileged, indeed sole, means for effecting justice. Rawls cannot normatively justify justice as fairness by appealing to a specific, contingent history; Derrida cannot show why an Idea of justice must be enforced through a contingent institution within a contingent history.

The Idea of Justice

Discussions of what Aristotle called "particular," rather than "universal," justice assume that the adverbial and adjectival terms *justly* and *just* are primary, and they conceptualize justice on the basis of those terms (Aristotle 1976,

1130a18–1131a22). Justice concerns the "how" of our actions, laws, or governments, and since "what is just is equal; as is universally accepted even without the support of argument," justice is primarily about fairness (Aristotle 1976, 1130b32–1131–a22). The real issue for Aristotle is not what justice is, but how to achieve it: in virtue of what is a distribution or a penalty fair? H.L.A. Hart, two millennia later, makes largely the same point about justice being fairness, strongly influencing Rawls in the process. For Hart, while a law may be good because it is just, a law cannot be just because good (Hart 1961, 154). A law is just or unjust in virtue of the fairness with which it is applied; an action is just or unjust in virtue of how it is performed; and a person is just or unjust in virtue of their dispositions toward acting justly or unjustly.

Derrida appears to reject the primacy of what I will call *adverbial justice* because he neither assumes, as Aristotle does, that we all know what justice is, nor does he, like Plato's Socrates, try to move from particular instances or definitions of justice to a universal concept of justice. Derrida offers two related, but distinct, accounts of justice. First, justice is a specific kind of *experience* rather than a way of acting or being; and second, justice is an *Idea*—in a modified Kantian sense—rather than a concept. Given the departure from the tradition that this move represents, it is important to see the limitations of the traditional concept of justice and the intuitive grounds for Derrida's departure.[9] Rather than start with those limitations and the intuitions underlying Derrida's "theory" of justice, I will present his claims and show the reasoning supporting them, interspersing the limitations of adverbial justice and the intuitions guiding Derrida's argument when appropriate.

We can understand "justice as experience" by looking at Derrida's argument for "justice as Idea." Although Derrida insists that we should not "assimilate too quickly" the Idea of justice to a "regulative Idea in the Kantian sense," this precaution is easily followed and the Kantian undertones prove useful for understanding what Derrida is up to (Derrida 2002, 254–255).[10] An Idea, for Kant, is a concept of Reason employed to regulate our cognition without adding to it, because an Idea cannot have an empirical object fall under it (Kant 1998, A310/B366–A332/B389). In theoretical reason, the Idea of the unconditioned directs us to seek in a series of appearances their "ultimate," unconditioned ground, even though the unconditioned ground of appearances can never be empirically experienced, hence cognized. In practical philosophy, the requirements of the moral law enable us to "know" that Ideas such as an immortal soul, freedom, and God objectively exist even though we cannot know anything else about these "objects" other than the fact that they must exist (Kant 1996, 5:134–5:142).

If we accept a Kantian distinction between phenomena and noumena, then it is fairly clear why we cannot know anything about the soul and its immortality, God, or freedom. Simply analyzing the concepts of the soul, God, and freedom shows that the conditions of possible experience exclude such "objects" from any kind of empirical perception. So, how can Derrida argue that justice is an Idea in at least an analogous sense to a Kantian Idea?

Derrida implicitly "analyzes" the concept of justice throughout "Force of Law," and we can gather some of its parts:

1. It is unthematizable (237);
2. it is not an object (237);
3. it is not deconstructible (because deconstruction is justice) (243);
4. it is aporetic;
5. it is *called* for, demanded (244);
6. it is incalculable (244);
7. it is an experience of the impossible (244);
8. it is an address, and an address is always singular (245);
9. it is infinite (248);
10. because it is irreducible (254);
11. because it is owed to the singular other (254);
12. it must be realized now, urgently (255);
13. it has no horizon of expectation (256);
14. it does have an *à-venir*, a future that is not a future present (256);
15. it commands calculation (257).

Some of these elements of justice presuppose that it is an Idea, but the key elements are 4 and 7 (to be discussed in detail later), 8 through 11, and 13. Much turns on 11, so we should begin there.

The claim that justice is owed to a singular other is a spade-turning moment in Derrida's argument, a moment based on an entire conception of ethics and ontology. That justice is owed to an other is surely uncontroversial, for if not to an other, then to whom? It might be controversial that, as Derrida puts it in *The Gift of Death*, "*tout autre est tout autre*," that is, every other is totally, absolutely, other (Derrida 1995). Derrida's argument that each other is absolutely other is drawn in part from Søren Kierkegaard and, even more directly, from Emmanuel Levinas. It is beyond the scope of this chapter to detail the dense phenomenological descriptions and philosophical arguments made for the singularity of the other by Levinas, as well as Derrida's important critique of Levinas in "Violence and Metaphysics" and continued engagement with Levinasian texts and themes.[11]

But the intuition or "experience" that leads to the recognition of the other's singularity is not strange at all, and is common to a number of philosophers, not to mention novelists, painters, poets, and other artists. An other is singular because it is absolutely irreplaceable and unrepeatable in its spatio-temporal existence. For this reason our necessarily general concepts and categories cannot fully capture, fully cognize, an other. While limiting singularity to human beings (or to God) is a mistake, the singularity of the human other proves to be a compelling example, one explicitly or implicitly at work in a number of philosophical contexts. For example, Kant's claim that each human being is a *person* because, as a rational being, it is an objective end-in-itself with absolute value, and thus must be treated as an object of reverence, hints at the singularity of the other, it's being irreducible to any of its conditioned wants, needs, or characteristics (Kant 1964, 4:428). Surely the problem of "other minds" begins with a sense that the other, any and every other, might be a mystery to, unknowable by, me (see Wittgenstein 1958, 178–180; Austin 1979, 76–116; and Cavell 1969, 238–266). In a different vein—but working with a related intuition—the problem of the sense and reference of a proper name has been of immense interest to a number of philosophers, in part because a proper name is supposed to name what is utterly individual, the lump of animate material that is a person (see Kripke 1981; Derrida 1988; Searle 1958; and Strawson 1959). Examples abound, but the basic intuition is straightforward and surely indisputable: every person is, from a certain perspective, singular, utterly unique. That we often overlook this uniqueness is something that has been and can be accounted for in a number of ways, often by reference to pragmatic needs and ends. But we can, without too much difficulty, push ourselves to a "recognition" of singularity, although it is likely that most of the time our experience of singularity is thrust upon us.

If justice is a matter of fairness, but justice is owed to a singular other, then a problem emerges: how can we determine what we owe to a *singular* other? This is a serious question because a singular other is irreducible to any determination of it. In practice, the singularity of the other entails that any attempt to determine what we owe to a singular other must not rely on any specific determinations, conceptualizations, or "thematizations." If the other, for example, is conceptualized as a thief and we want to penalize that thief fairly, then the justice we give is not given to a singular other but to a thief, a specific determination of the singular other. To take an example from distributive justice, if we want to determine a fair, just distribution of primary goods, then we have to conceptualize the receivers of those goods in specific ways, regardless of whether primary goods are understood as what "a rational man wants whatever else he wants" (Rawls 1971, 92) or as "things needed and required by persons in light of the political conception of persons" (Rawls 2001, 58). We can only be fair in our distribution of primary goods, whatever that distribution turns out to be, by determining a singular other as a "rational person" or a "free and equal citizen." Finally, if we seek to make suitably general rules or laws for any society, fairness demands that we identify various singular others under categories such as homeowner, parent, soldier, taxpayer, citizen, and so on. We think the rule of law is fair when it treats equals equally and unequals unequally, yet from a Derridean perspective, the fairness of law requires us to unjustly determine the singular other. At this point the dilemma is clear. If justice is owed to the singular other, but the traditional adverbial conception of justice as fairness requires us to determine the other, then either justice is *not* fairness or it is *not possible* to *give* justice to the singular other.[12]

Derrida nowhere denies that justice is fairness, nor does he suggest an alternative definition. He does, however, deny that it is possible to (fully) give justice to the singular other. It is easy to conclude, given Derrida's argument, that there is something "wrong" with the adverbial conception of justice, and more specifically with the rule of law, given that it can only fail to give justice. Nothing could be further from the truth. Recall that justice itself *demands* that law enforce it, and we have no choice but to give justice to the other through the usual means: the decisions of authoritative judges in official courts relying on statutory and common law as well as judicial norms. Derrida's argument is not an argument for "imperfect procedural justice," or for that matter, for pure procedural justice. The problem is not lack of knowledge, imperfect human understanding, limited time to make decisions, and so on (Derrida 2002, 255–256). Even absolute knowledge and unlimited time could not render justice to the other. The reason that justice remains forever unrealizable by law is not empirical but a priori.

Law, for Derrida, is a domain of reasons, calculations, comparisons, justifications, institutions, and so on. Law requires that judges give reasons for their decisions lest a decision be rightly considered invalid (Derrida 2002, 251–252, 257). Derrida does not argue that judges, to be just, must dispense with reasons, arguments, precedents, and so on; to the contrary, an unjustified decision is, almost by definition, unjust. A legal system without rules fairly applied by judges who justify their decisions through rational argumentation and a reliance on existing law and precedent would be, for Derrida, an unjust legal system.

However, the rules, laws, canons of reasoning, and so on, that are necessary features of a legitimate legal system foreclose the possibility of giving justice to a singular other, for reasons we have seen. Rationality requires that we make determinations, deductions, inductions, abductions, and the like, and thus rationality *must* ignore or repress the singularity of the other.[13] We cannot do otherwise if we are to remain rational. But just for that reason, the singularity of the other, hence justice, escapes. Justice is distinct, separated as if by an abyss, from law.

Justice is an Idea, a concept of reason that regulates our cognition but that has no empirical object falling under it. Justice regulates our thinking about law, responsibility, ethics, what we owe to others, how decisions should be made, and the like; but nothing in the empirical world can *be* just. There is no present justice, no action that can properly be called just, no decision of which we can say correctly, "it was just." Insofar as justice is an Idea that can never be realized in the phenomenal world, we cannot *properly* use the terms *just* or *justly* to describe a person, penalty, decision, action, or distribution of goods. The adverbial conception of justice, on Derrida's argument, is undermined by the fact that justice is an Idea, and it is an Idea, in part, because justice is owed to a singular other.[14]

Rather than a property of actions, persons, decisions, distributions, and so forth, justice is a paradoxical *experience*. The experience is paradoxical because it is an experience of aporia. For Derrida:

> As its name indicates, an experience is a traversal, something that traverses and travels towards a destination for which it finds a passage. The experience finds its way, its passage, it is possible. Yet, in this sense there cannot be a full experience of aporia, that is, something that does not allow passage. Aporia is a nonpath. From this point of view, justice would be the experience of what we are unable to experience.

He then adds:

> But I believe that there is no justice without this experience, however impossible it may be, of aporia. Justice is an experience of the impossible: a will, a desire, a demand for justice the structure of which would not be an experience of aporia, would have no chance to be what it is—namely, a just *call* for justice. (Derrida 2002, 244)

What is this (non)experience "like"?

Derrida identifies three aporias of justice that are different realizations of "one aporetic potential that infinitely distributes itself" (Derrida 2002, 250).[15]

The first aporia is experienced by a judge deciding a case. The judge must act on the basis of two irreconcilable imperatives. First, the judge must decide a case in accordance with rules and on the basis of sound reasoning and principles. Second, any *decision* the judge makes must free itself from the mere technical application of rules. The first imperative needs no explanation. The second imperative follows from Derrida's claim that a decision is *properly* a decision only if the judge is free and responsible for the decision, which entails that the judge does not merely follow a rule or principle (Derrida 2002, 251). If the judge merely applies a rule to a case, or feels compelled to apply a rule to a case, then the judge does not truly *decide* anything, for the "decision" is compelled by the rule and the judge is a "calculating machine" (Derrida 2002, 252). Derrida's point is that "each case is other, each decision is different and requires an absolutely unique interpretation which no coded rule can or ought to guarantee absolutely" (Derrida 2002, 251). Derrida, importantly, claims that a rule both *cannot* and *ought not* to absolutely guarantee a decision. A rule *cannot* guarantee a decision because of the singularity of the other and of each case; a rule *ought not* to guarantee a decision because this would undermine ethical *responsibility*. Ethical responsibility is only possible if one *freely* responds to the singularity of the other, where this means refusing to reduce the other to an instance of a concept and a case to an instance of a rule. Responsibility is the central ethical concept in Derrida's work, and it plays a major role in "Force of Law." As we know, law itself, however fair, cannot render justice because it cannot respond to the singularity of the other. Law is necessarily general. If the judge lets the law decide then the judge is refusing to properly decide the case, hence take responsibility for the decision. In such a case, not only will the law fail to render justice, as it must, but the judge will refuse to even accept responsibility for or to the singular other for the injustice done to the singular other. This refusal of responsibility is a second injustice done to the other, and a more "primordial" one at that. If law must fail in its rendering of justice, the judge's decision to refuse responsibility is not a destined, structural failure: it is a choice. The decision of the judge who lets the law decide is a refusal of responsibility and a denial of an ethical relation, to the other.

The judge experiences a paradoxical "must": in order to act justly the judge must refer to rules, reasons, and principles; and the judge must bracket, or set aside, rules, reasons, and principles. Derrida insists, though, that this is not merely the "oscillation" between contradictory imperatives. Rather, justice demands that we, as it were *at the same time*, freely, properly, decide without rules while taking account of reasons and rules (Derrida 2002, 252). In other words, the experience of justice is not merely the going back and forth between rules and reasons on the one hand and the free, rule-less decision on the other. We have to square the circle. We have to do the impossible. And this we cannot do. Thus, a second aporia of justice requires us to undergo the "test and ordeal of the undecidable," of the impossible experience of doing the impossible (Derrida 2002, 253). This test, Derrida claims, must *haunt* every attempt to render justice. The haunting of the undecidable undermines any reassurance that we have actually rendered justice. In order to be responsible we must let the undecidability of the relation between, and the requirements of, justice and law haunt us so that we never fool ourselves into believing that we are just, or that our decision is just, or that justice has been fully delivered.

If justice can never be realized then it is always "to come." However, justice cannot wait (Derrida 2002, 255). This is the third aporia of justice: insofar as justice is an Idea, it is always to come, but justice must be realized now. Thus, a just decision would "rend time and defy dialectics," that is, the instant of just decision would necessarily be of another temporal order than the past-present, present-present, and future-present (Derrida 2002, 255).[16] Once again, the experience of justice is an experience of impossibility and it is an experience that must be undergone lest just actions and decisions turn into mere applications of rules for which no judge or actor can take responsibility. Justice, as an Idea, cannot be realized, but it can be "experienced." More precisely, what can be experienced is the impossibility of a justice that nonetheless must be realized. Without this experience, a decision or action can never be just. Thus, even if justice has no chance of being realized, judges and actors must undergo the aporetic, impossible experience of justice so that justice might have a chance to be realized.

The aporetic experience of justice is conceptually linked to the argument that justice is an Idea. Justice, like any Idea, regulates our ethical, legal, and political thought, actions, and institutions; and justice demands that it be realized, however impossibly, in law. For these reasons, we can never say of any action, decision, person, or institution that they are "just" or that they have acted, or are acting, or will act justly. Adverbial justice is impossible. All we can and must do is respond responsibly to justice's impossible demand to realize it.

I have refrained from criticizing Derrida up to this point, but within the admittedly extravagant rhetoric of Derrida's text lies a rather straightforward argument. Insofar as justice is owed to a singular other, it cannot be realized in any existent institutions or practices or any instance of these institutions or practices. However, the Idea of justice requires us to realize justice in existing institutions and practices. In order to remain faithful in our attempts to realize justice, we must undergo and be haunted by the experience of the ethical double-bind placed upon us to render justice to the singular other through a law and a reason that denies singularity. While this argument certainly contains a number of potentially controversial premises, it is not implausible. The arguments in support of the premises themselves are to be found in Derrida's other writings, as well as in the sources Derrida is critically appropriating (especially Kierkegaard, Levinas, and Walter Benjamin).[17] It is beyond the scope of this chapter to fully defend Derrida's ethical position, but I would suggest that it can be understood as a significantly modified, somewhat extreme, but nonetheless recognizable, Kantian position in moral philosophy.[18]

Most important for my purposes, though, is that "Force of Law" invokes what can reasonably, if not entirely accurately, be described as a "metaphysical," or "quasi-metaphysical," conception of justice. It is certainly *not* a political conception of justice. Derridean justice clearly relies on a number of deeply contestable claims in the area of decision theory, philosophy of language, moral theory, political theory, legal theory, and so on. Whatever the merits of and support for Derrida's arguments, they are not "tolerant" vis-à-vis a plurality of different, perhaps irreconcilable, comprehensive moral doctrines. Derrida argues that this quasi-metaphysical conception of justice demands realization in law. But which law? And why law?

From the Idea of Justice to the Fact of Law

Derridean justice is owed to a singular other, and the impossibility of actually rendering that justice is why Derrida conceives of justice as a (regulative) Idea and an aporetic experience. Part of the aporetic experience of justice is responsiveness to justice's demand that it be effective, hence *enforced* in law—even though justice cannot be realized in law. One of the main themes of Derrida's "Force of Law" is, unsurprisingly, the conceptual and practical entwinement of force and law: law is necessarily forceful. The concept of *force*, however, is not reducible to "coercion," that is, the use of (threats of) physical violence to compel or punish behavior (Derrida 2002, 241). For example, law is founded in a "law-making" performative speech-act, the force of which is illocutionary (Benjamin 1978, 283–287; Derrida 2002, 241–242; 1986; see also Honig 1991). Legal judgments and decisions have both an illocutionary force ("I sentence you"; "I pronounce you man and wife") and a perlocutionary force, insofar as we expect legal statements to change the behavior of others, at least indirectly. Force is a rich concept for Derrida, and one that has played a role in his work from the very beginning. Derrida's use of the term *force* is undeniably complex. And yet, what is supposed to make law different from other employments of force is that law can *legitimately* employ force. However, law, Derrida argues, is instituted by a performative speech act the force of which is itself not legitimized, hence it can be neither (fully) legitimate nor illegitimate. If law is distinctive in its claim to use force legitimately—hence potentially justly—but law cannot legitimately employ force, then why *must* justice be realized in law?

Recall that the issue here is that justice needs to be enforced. The fact that force is intrinsic to law does not itself provide a reason to enforce justice through law. Force is intrinsic to any number of human institutions if we take *force* to mean the linguistic and physical ability to transform states of affairs, behavior, people, and so on. There is force in family relations because parents typically have authority over their children. Of course, paternal authority *is* a model of political authority, albeit one that has been rightly rejected (by Locke, among many others). Parental authority—while often legally recognized and limited by laws—is different from legal authority, but still forceful. It seems fair to say that in the capacious sense of *force* employed by Derrida, any and all authorities will use force: force is intrinsic to authority. Law is or has an authority, hence it employs force, but it is only one kind of authority. So, the fact that force is intrinsic to law cannot be the reason why justice *must* be enforced in and through law.

Perhaps law is required for the enforcement of justice because law is a system of *rules*, and it is precisely the aporetic experience of, as it were, rule-fullness and rule-lessness that is key to the experience of justice. While law is a system of rules, not all systems of rules are law. Games and universities also contain rules, as well as means for enforcing the rules, but that hardly makes the rules, penalties, and umpires in games and universities legal. It is possible that a teacher or principal may be granted a legal authority to preside over a student or classroom, but that legal authority is delegated by the law, by someone or some office *in* authority (see Flathman 1980). The fact that legal systems are systems of rules (albeit not only that) does not give law any special status.

Another possibility is that law requires not only authoritative decisions on the basis of rules; legal decisions also require rational *justification*. As we saw earlier in this chapter, Derrida claims that a legal decision is unjust if it is free of the rational support provided in part by justifiable interpretations of rules and facts using standard canons of legal reasoning. Unlike parents, whose authority often requires no immediate rational justification to those who are under that authority, and unlike rules of games, where rules are usually perfectly clear and only the facts are in question, we demand of legal decisions that they be rationally justified. Derrida is quick to point out that a legal decision, no matter how rationally justified, cannot be just for that reason. However, a decision cannot be just without rational justification either. Yet here too, rational justification is not enough to distinguish law from, for example, morality. Whether one is a realist, non-cognitivist, relativist, or constructivist, a prominent assumption in moral inquiry as well as in moral life is that moral judgments appear to demand rational justification. The non-cognitivist may deny that moral judgments can be given rational justification, and the relativist may claim that justification is relative to one's moral community, but both positions must accept that, phenomenologically, moral reasoning is a part of moral life. The demand for rational justification does not distinguish law from morality. On Derrida's account, law is not legitimate; nor is it unique in employing force, being a system of rules, or requiring rational justification for its decisions and actions. So, why law? Why must justice be enforced in and through law?

The best remaining possibility is that there is an internal conceptual link between law and justice.[19] Derrida, however, does not and cannot make such an argument. The argument for an internal conceptual link between law and justice is foreclosed because, unlike Derrida's readings of hospitality, forgiveness, the gift, and so on, there is no specific, phenomenal, conditioned, recognizable activity made (im)possible by justice. For example, Derrida makes an argument structurally similar to that in the "Force of Law" in his work on forgiveness. To truly, properly, unconditionally forgive, we must forgive the unforgiveable:

> In order to approach now the very concept of forgiveness, logic and common sense agree for once with the paradox: it is necessary, it seems to me, to begin from the fact that, yes, there is the unforgiveable. Is this not, in truth, the only thing to forgive? The only thing that calls for forgiveness? If one is only prepared to forgive what appears forgivable, what the church calls "venial sin," then the very idea of forgiveness would disappear. (Derrida 2001a, 32, see also 32–34)

The logic here is aporetic, just as in "Force of Law," but with an important difference. The impossible act of forgiving the unforgiveable is the only true forgiveness because any conditional forgiveness that forgives what is forgivable does not *truly, properly*, forgive (Derrida 2001a, 44–45). Forgiveness is what it properly is only when the unforgiveable is forgiven; but we cannot, by definition, forgive the unforgiveable, hence we have an aporia. Derrida's argument, similar to that in the "Force of Law" in so many ways, differs from it because it rests on the phenomenological fact that we do forgive, every day, even if improperly. We also see people not forgive, every day. The same goes for hospitality, and giving gifts: we see people treat others hospitably, and give gifts, all of the time. When we are told that "true" forgiving must forgive the unforgiveable and "true" hospitality must be hospitable to the inhospitable, we can see what Derrida is getting at. Derrida's arguments in these texts show how a specific, recognizable phenomenal action is made possible, and impossible, by an unconditional Idea of the same practice. There is an internal link between unconditional and conditional forgiveness, hospitality, giving, and the like.

On Derrida's account of justice, the phenomenal, improper rendering of justice would appear to be the "just" legal decision. But legal decisions, as such, are not obviously an "impure" or "improper" or "conditional" version of justice, if only because many legal decisions, as well as laws and legal systems, are manifestly *unjust*: there is nothing just about them *at all*. To make a legal decision is not *necessarily* to render a conditional form of justice if the decision is obviously wrong and unjust. Some legal decisions are "unjust" in the sense that they fail to full render justice for Derridean reasons, but other legal decisions fail all reasonable criteria for being just. But does it make any sense to say that a phenomenal act of forgiveness is obviously not forgiveness? If you hurt my feelings and I say "I forgive you," is there a sense in which we could imagine that speech act as not only impure forgiveness, but not forgiveness at all? One possibility is that I don't "mean it." But as Austin rightly claimed, "accuracy and morality alike are on the side of the plain saying that *our word is our bond*" (Austin 1975, 10). Our intentions, our failure to "mean it," don't make "I forgive you" any less an act of forgiveness (even though it might be given in "bad faith"). We have a good sense of what forgiveness is and we have a language in which to forgive. Conditional forgiveness is still recognizably forgiveness, even if improper, or conditioned. A legal decision, however, is not necessarily conditional, or impure, justice at all. Moreover, it seems intuitively clear that we can act justly or unjustly without any law being at issue.

A significant difference between Derrida's account of justice and his work on forgiveness and related concepts is that justice is *adjectival* and *adverbial*. Justice is not, like forgiving, itself an action; we ascribe justness to laws, decisions, people, and other actions of very different kinds. Traditionally, philosophers often tried to gather what these different ascriptions of justice had in common in order to define justice as such or, as Plato did, they just went ahead and defined justice (Plato 1968, 433a–436a). But justice is not itself an action: it is a way of acting. For these reasons Derrida cannot argue that there is an internal conceptual link between justice and law such that legal acts are conditioned or improper or phenomenal "versions" of a pure, impossible justice. If justice is to be heterogeneous to law while inescapably tied to it, another reason for the inescapability is required.

That reason is surely the long western historical tradition of thinking law and justice together. Julius Stone argued for a Judaic, rather than Greek, origin to the claim that justice is intimately connected to law (Stone 1965, 18–31); but Michael Gagarin and Paul Woodruff provide evidence, both etymological and historical, that justice and law were equally connected in early Greek thought (Miller 2007, 7–33). They argue that Anaximander's famous fragment on justice (*dike*) and retribution (*tisis*) and Heraclitus' fragment identifying justice with strife (*eris*) both figure Greek practices of dispute settlement (Miller 2007, 13).[20] Aristotle's arguments about universal, particular, and political justice conceive justice as, at least in part, a certain conformity to law. Unsurprisingly, Thomas Aquinas largely follows Aristotle in thinking justice and law together, even if justice is not reducible to law (for example, Aquinas 2002, IIaIIae 57, IIaIIae 58 art. 5). Hobbes, challenging Aristotle and scholasticism generally, makes covenants the basis of justice, and effective justice dependent on covenants backed by coercive power, that is, sovereignty and, presumably, civil law (Hobbes 1997, chaps. 15 and 26). One could go on, complicating the story in a number of ways by including, for example, the Paulinian claim in Romans 13:10 that "love is fulfilling of the law," and Kropotkin's anarchist claim that law is useless and hurtful, a barrier to just social relations (Kropotkin 2002, 212). But whether as a matter of political history or theoretical reflection, law and justice have more often than not been thought together in the history of the west, even if the conceptions and practices of justice exceed legal theory and institutions.

The philosophical problems Derrida faces in showing an aporetic internal connection between the infinite Idea of justice and the conditioned practices of law, are, to my knowledge, never addressed. Instead, Derrida affirms, without argument, the "*fortunate* perfectibility" and "undeniable progress" of international law and institutions (Derrida 1994, 83; emphasis added). We should take the word "fortunate" seriously. Even though the failures of international law and institutions are so widespread and disappointing that they constitute one of the "ten plagues" of the "new world order," they are, for Derrida, "empirical" failures, not failures of law as such. The failings of international law include, for example, the dominance of some nation-states within international institutions. But the *limits* of international law are twofold. First, international law and its institutions are limited by their dependence on "certain European philosophical concepts," as well as "a concept of State or national sovereignty whose genealogical closure is more and more evident, not only in a theoretico-juridical or speculative fashion, but concretely, practically, and practically quotidian" (Derrida 1994, 83). This "most radical" limit is connected to a second limit: the failing just mentioned, the failure of international law to remain free from domination by some nation-states. And yet, "these facts do not suffice to disqualify international institutions. Justice demands, on the contrary, that one pay tribute to certain of those who are working within them in the direction of the perfectibility and emancipation of institutions that must never be renounced" (Derrida 1994, 84). Derrida's insistence that justice demands law, a better law, a more just law, is consistent throughout his work. Although Derrida never justifies the claim that justice demands its enforcement through law, it is Derrida's fidelity to the progress and perfectibility of law—that is, to the historicity and specific history of western law—that serves to ground the connection between justice and law.

Peter Fenves argues that "from his earliest writings onward Derrida has wondered about this appeal to history as a way out of a 'meta-philosophical' aporia. Wondering about history precludes celebrating it as the solution to every—or any—philosophical problem" (Fenves 2001, 271). Derrida, Fenves shows, criticizes appeals to both originary and teleological histories: there is no originary, or final, meaning to history, for the very possibility of history is, for Derrida, the endangerment of meaning, its possible impossibility. If Fenves' argument about Derrida's earliest writings applies equally to the later works—and at least on this issue Derrida still denies that history has a pure origin or determined telos—then there is nothing about the history of law in the west that can possibly serve as a foundation or ground or fundament for the claim that justice demands its enforcement in, and only in, law (Derrida 2005, 141–159).

However perfectible and progressive, law and its institutions are, on Derrida's own argument, nothing other than contingent, indeed fortunate, concepts and practices of western history. Law cannot claim any moral legitimacy of its own, and history cannot endow law with legitimacy any more than can consent. There is no reason that justice must be enforced in law. Justice is an Idea; law is a fact. Nothing in Derrida's work shows us how we can, or why we must, go from the Idea of justice to the fact of law.

THE MORAL OF THE STORY

Rawls' attempt to escape metaphysics by appealing to history fails because history, as a set of contingent facts, cannot do what Rawls wants it to do: provide normative reasons for why citizens of modern liberal democracies must affirm or accept the legitimacy of the political-moral ideas they contingently inherit. Derrida's turn to a quasi-metaphysical Idea of justice cannot show how and why the contingent practices and institutions of law in the west are the privileged institution for justice's enforcement.

More generally, Rawls and Derrida reveal a deep difficulty of and in political thought today: we cannot dispense with metaphysics, nor can we rely on it. It is not that philosophers and theorists today do not, as a matter of fact, rely on metaphysics, or dispense with metaphysics. I hope to have suggested that neither option is truly "live" for us today. What we want from a theory of justice is some rational account of, and sometimes a case for accepting, normative beliefs, desires, and goals, as well as certain political and legal institutions. The sheer fact that we inherit from a tradition some set of beliefs, desires, goals, and institutions is not enough. I hope my criticism of Rawls and Derrida has shown that. But direct appeals to one or another metaphysics, ontology, ontotheology, theology, faith, and so on, also ring hollow: except to the believer. And yet, whatever the failures of the politics of secularism, it is true that in a secular, post-metaphysical age, we cannot reasonably and rationally maintain a self-reflexive relationship to our most fundamental beliefs without, to some degree, undermining the validity of those beliefs. In other words, reasonable and rational belief requires us to doubt, at least minimally, that our beliefs are correct. Metaphysics, under these conditions, cannot fully be believed, and thus it cannot do the work it might or used to do: providing reasons for what we find normatively important, valuable, and/or correct.

Just as with the legitimacy of state violence, or the role of control in freedom, here too we theorists can only muddle through, drawing on as many traditions as we can to inch forward, if possible, toward a deeper understanding of dense political phenomena.

CONCLUSION

In Defense of Aporetic Cross-tradition Theorizing

Bob Weir, a guitarist with the Grateful Dead, described himself and his band-mates as so pathologically anti-authoritarian that no member of the band would suffer being told how to play their part in a song. I'm afflicted with a less extreme form of that pathology and have little desire to tell anyone how they ought to do political theory. While there is much to be said in favor of cross-tradition political theory—including what is taking place in "comparative political theory" and in interdisciplinary work—cross-tradition theorizing is but one option for political theorists. To the extent that many political theorists already work with texts and ideas from literature, art history and aesthetics, political economy, sociology, the physical sciences, gender studies, queer theory, critical theory of race, and so on, cross-tradition theorizing is already taking place. What is not taking place to the extent possible and desirable is the specific cross-tradition theorizing that moves between the analytic and continental traditions. In this concluding chapter I want to argue for three further claims that deepen and expand the arguments for aporetic cross-tradition theorizing that I made in the Introduction.

CLAIM 1: APORETIC CROSS-TRADITION THEORIZING IS MORE VIABLE THAN SYNTHETIC CROSS-TRADITION THEORIZING.

Focusing on the density of political phenomena doesn't rule out the possibility of synthesis as one mode of cross-tradition theorizing, which is why political realism and Cavellian consent afforded an opportunity to "test" the synthetic mode. Political realists, as we saw in Chapter One, are working in an analytic mode but drawing upon theoretical resources and assumptions more commonly found in the continental tradition. A tendency of much continental political theory is to give up on asking what are the necessary and sufficient conditions for state legitimacy and to focus on the dissensual, conflictual, and agonistic characteristics of modern polities. Conversely, analytic philosophers engaged in formulating theories of legitimacy, justice, equality, and the like, largely ignore conflict, dissensus, antagonism, historical context, and so on, tending to justify state legitimacy on the basis of moral considerations and ideal theory. Whether realists ultimately succeed in providing a political theory of legitimacy that is both anti-moralist and responsive to political conflict and contingency is an open question, but the synthetic impulse is surely worth pursuing even though it doesn't seem promising to me. We should still attempt to find out if synthetic cross-tradition theorizing works, but I am not optimistic.

Cavell explicitly responds to the analytic-continental split, and his sensitivity to literariness, to the work of Nietzsche and Emerson and Heidegger, to Freud and to film, enables his surprising engagements with canonical works of and ideas in political theory. It is not quite right to call Cavell a "synthesizer" of the traditions, but he is attracted to various features of both traditions and has no scruples about bringing ideas from one of the traditions to bear on the concerns of the other.

I argued in the first two chapters that the synthetic mode, practiced differently by political realists and Cavell, does not solve the problem of state violence. State violence escapes the synthetic impulse because of the density of the phenomenon. There is something rotten (*Morsches*) in the state, and the rot is a consequence of state violence. You can stuff a corpse, bury it, ignore it, deify it, burn it or whatever you want, but death is in the state, in one form or another. And that fact, like death itself, cannot be, ought not to be, mastered, but understood. Yet, death resists the understanding, no matter how many concepts and theories and traditions we add together. We must do our best to understand the violence of the state, but my bet is that no amount of synthesis will silence our worries about state violence, for some of the reasons canvassed in the Introduction. The same is true of aporetic theorizing, but aporetic theorists are committed only to further, deeper understanding.

I am skeptical about the prospects of the synthetic mode because if there is an ur-difference between analytic and continental political theorizing, it lies in the "picture," the vision each tradition presupposes in its attempts to theorize politics. The "difference in picture" hypothesis is my provisional explanation for the dim prospects of the synthetic mode. One way of identifying the distinct pictures of analytic and continental theorizing is captured in a suggestion of Cavell's. Paraphrasing and extending his point: the analytic myth, resurrecting an Enlightenment dream, is to figure the philosopher as having read nothing, always beginning afresh; whereas the continental myth figures the philosopher as needing to read everything before saying a single word (see Cavell 1988, 15). At stake in these myths is not only the extent to which the history of philosophy matters in philosophy. In fact, political philosophers in the analytic tradition are far more willing to engage the history of philosophy than philosophers in other subfields—or so it seems to me. More deeply, and consequentially, the two myths suggest a different relationship between the theorist and the theorized. In the analytic myth, the human mind is up to the challenge, unaided or in conjunction with a few other minds, of cutting through the underbrush, of cancelling the noise, and of bringing order and clarity to the problems the world poses to and for us. J. M Coetzee's novel *Elizabeth Costello* opens this way:

> There is first of all the problem of the opening, namely, how to get us from where we are, which is, as yet, nowhere, to the far bank. It is a simple bridging problem, a problem of knocking together a bridge. People solve such problems every day. They solve them, and having solved them push on. (Coetzee 2004, 1)

If this is another, surely unintended but accurate, version of the analytic myth, the accuracy is in part a consequence of the fact that where we begin in theorizing is, as yet, *nowhere*. Where we are, on the analytic myth, isn't as important as the problem at hand, the problem to solve: we need a bridge.

Having to start *somewhere*, just *here*, on *this* side of *a* river, having taken *a* path, but not the only possible path, to this point in time and space, is central to the continental myth. The problem is not, or not only, building the bridge and moving on, but understanding why we have, here and now, just this problem, which is a matter of understanding how we arrived here and now, with just these tools at hand. Only when we understand where we are can we begin to think about where we are going. But understanding where we are is the work of a lifetime. The bridge never gets built.

If these myths are useful then they suggest a deep incompatibility between analytic and continental theorizing, what Paulina Ochoa Espejo and Tom Donahue identify as the difference between "problem-pressing" and "problem-solving." The former demonstrates the extreme complexity of a problem; the latter tries to get the work done (Donahue and Ochoa 2016). Both "styles" of theorizing have their merits and faults, but they cannot co-exist peacefully. Their presuppositions and goals are so at odds that they cannot be synthesized. It is difficult to be committed to the idea that a given problem is always harder than it seems and be committed to the idea that the problem can be solved, for every solution will inevitably be seen as resting on an oversimplification. This dialectic is unlikely to admit of any *Aufhebung*. If that is right, then the synthetic mode is unlikely to succeed. We have here another instance of two intellectual needs that cannot be reconciled: the need to solve problems raised by dense political phenomena, and the need to do justice to the density of the phenomena.

In the comparative mode of Chapters 3, 4, and 5, I really tried my hand at aporetic cross-tradition theorizing, and if the arguments were persuasive then we should have learned something new about Pettit, Arendt, Rawls, and Derrida, and about freedom and justice. Or, if not something new, then at least old ideas seen in a new light. While not as grim a subject as violence, freedom and justice are no less resistant to our theorizing and rather than take sides or synthesize, I simply let the difficulty remain because the difficulty is, as it were, the "truth" of freedom and justice.

We are and ought to remain in a crevasse between traditions, stuck with difficulties both political and theoretical that we cannot overcome. Yet, we ought to struggle for purchase wherever we can in the hopes of at least gaining a better view of our situation. This may be a dispiriting picture of the political philosophical project, but these are despairing times, and if one response to despair is to seek theoretical reconciliation of evils and failings and contradictions—what Nietzsche called "metaphysical solace"—a perfectly sensible response is to refuse all solace and, with good cheer I would add, seek in failure and disappointment a different kind of reward. Aporetic cross-tradition political theory renews a tendency, found in both traditions, to seek insight through diminishment of expectations and knowledge through fragmented and incomplete theorization. This is a tendency of high modernism, captured as much in the preface to Wittgenstein's *Philosophical Investigations* as in Beckett's "Ever tried. Ever failed. No matter. Try Again. Fail again. Fail better."

It is a platitude, but of course true, that failure can teach us a great deal. Aporetic cross-tradition theorizing teaches us something important about politics, especially when we try to understand freedom, legitimacy, violence, justice, equality, community, and so on. What we learn is that political phenomena are dense, resistant to the theorist's grip. Aporetic theorizing is not the only route to this knowledge, but there is a rhetorical advantage to aporetic cross-tradition theorizing: we are more likely to convince a diverse group of readers that the aporias we identify are really there and that the knowledge we have gained is genuine. We are less likely to so if we presuppose, in Adorno's terms, "non-identity" and a "negative dialectics"—not that a masterful dialectician like Adorno would *ever* presuppose negative dialectics rather than demonstrate it. I will return to this rhetorical claim in a moment. The main point is this: if aporetic cross-tradition theorizing doesn't increase our political knowledge, or at least our political theoretical knowledge, then it is not worth doing.

I have only claimed, without any argument or evidence, that we learn something important and new from aporetic cross-tradition theorizing, not just about political theory but about politics. Let me suggest a possible "application" to understanding contemporary politics on the basis of one of the aporias we have seen in this book.

Example: The Case for Reparations

Take the relationship of justice to history dealt with in Chapter 5. In 2014, Ta-Nehisi Coates published a widely discussed article in *The Atlantic* titled "The Case for Reparations." The bulk of the article recounts the obscene injustices black people have faced in the United States for centuries, in order to make the case for reparations virtually unassailable. The facts show that the crime is real, the injustice overwhelming, and the consequences ongoing, and the consistent failure of white Americans to accept these facts and instead to see reparations as a "hare-brained scheme" is "fear masquerading as laughter" (Coates 2014). Fear, that is, of the truth of American history, of the great crimes upon which (white) American wealth has been accumulated and of the violence that created and recreates America. Justice does indeed demand reparations. However, if the truth of the historical facts of white supremacy and black subordination and domination are evidence in the case for reparations, these facts are "emplotted" in a familiar type of American story, a story that shows the inescapable intertwining of history and metaphysics in a call for justice.

For Coates, "reparations—by which I mean the full acceptance of our collective biography and its consequences—is the price we must pay to see ourselves squarely." He immediately draws a comparison with a recovering alcoholic who may never get over alcoholism but is at least no longer living a lie. The recovery from disease begins with admitting the disease, and so America's recovery from injustice equally begins with the confession of guilt. The tropes of confession, spiritual disease, guilt, and the like, continue:

> What is needed is an airing of family secrets, a settling with old ghosts. What is needed is a healing of the American psyche and the banishment of white guilt. What I'm talking about is more than recompense for past injustices— more than a handout, a payoff, hush money, or a reluctant bribe. What I'm talking about is a national reckoning that would lead to spiritual renewal. . . . Reparations would mean a revolution of the American consciousness, a reconciling of our self-image as the great democratizer with the facts of our history.

Toward the end of the article Coates admits that perhaps no number can even be found to quantify the injustice done to black people in America, but he adds that

> wrestling publicly with these questions matters as much as—if not more than—the specific answers that might be produced. An America that asks what it owes its most vulnerable citizens is improved and humane. An America that looks away is ignoring not just the sins of the past but the sins of the present and the certain sins of the future. More important than any single check cut to any African American, the payment of reparations would represent America's maturation out of the childhood myth of its innocence into a wisdom worthy of its founders.

These passages repeat one of the oldest themes in American literature, dating to the Puritan jeremiads of the early 17th century: America is in a state of spiritual failure, despair, or decline, usually caused by some aspect of material life, typically the pursuit of wealth.[1] If anything unites Cotton Mather, Walt Whitman, James Baldwin, Hannah Arendt, William F. Buckley, David Brooks, and Coates, it is the tendency to see America's national failings as in part, but most importantly, spiritual, as sin. This is true even when the author is not religious at all and even when economic and legal justice is also called for.

Coates collects a horrifying set of facts detailing the very *material* economic exploitation and bodily terrorization of black people but makes the case for reparations largely in *spiritual* terms, as a form of national confession that is prelude to national redemption. Why? Part of the answer is surely the disappointing political reality that makes enacting a reparations scheme so unlikely as to verge on the impossible, but there is more than just disappointment at work here. Why, after the realistic acceptance of the unlikelihood of material justice being rendered, is there recourse to a deeper, more meaningful and more important spiritual justice that might still be possible? One answer is that there is an American tradition, from John Winthrop's speech aboard the *Arabella* to Coates' article, of seeing a just American society not only, or really at all, in terms of economic or legal justice, but as the realization of a spiritual justice, the truly Godly nation-state. What *counts* as justice, as real justice, is, unsurprisingly, given what we saw in Chapter 5, grounded in a particular historical tradition.

The historical tradition Coates inherits, however, is contestable, one-sided, and even ideological (in the Marxist sense) insofar as it subordinates economic justice to a putatively deeper and more important spiritual justice, whether in the first instance or as a consequence of recognizing the limits of political reality. Coates, intentionally or not, continues an American tradition that, given what Rawls calls the circumstances of justice, cannot justify to all citizens a claim to the justness of reparations. If the justice of reparations finds its justification in *a* history, it cannot convince any American who rejects that history. The same goes for Rawlsian political justice and for Derridean justice, both of which turn to contingent historical institutions and traditions to ground normative claims about justice.

The jeremiadic form, though, gains its persuasive power from its metaphysical, spiritual, underpinnings: a Protestant conception of the wickedness of worldliness, the corrupting power of the flesh, original sin, and in contrast to that, the higher spiritual life to which individuals, and America as a nation, are called. It is not any history that justifies reparations but a *redemptive* history, a story of original sin redeemed through self- and national transformation. Coates' sudden turn to spiritual redemption as the true meaning and purpose of reparations is a striking repetition of a trope deeply embedded in an American tradition. This move pushes his case for reparations away from material harm, and even history, to the deeper injustice in need of rectification: the spiritual failings of the American democratic experiment and the collective guilt of white people. The charge of spiritual failure is metaphysical, and thus the justice called for by Coates requires a metaphysics, not just a history, to be persuasive. But I am no more persuaded, nor do I have rational reason to be, by the idea that America has failed spiritually than I am by the idea that each of us is a body inhabited by a spirit that may or may not need redemption. Nor am I persuaded that, read post-metaphysically, the history of the American jeremiad in American culture provides any normative grounding for claims to justice. And yet, justice demands reparations, not only for black people in America but also for various oppressed peoples around the world. But on what grounds?

If the aporetic conclusion of Chapter 5 is correct, then we shouldn't be surprised that a persuasive case for reparations relies unstably on history and metaphysics. Many of us cannot accept metaphysical claims about individual or national souls standing in need of redemption, and yet without metaphysical premises, arguments for reparations appear far less rationally obligatory. Many of us cannot accept the always perspectival histories of our polities on the basis of which the justice of reparations is asserted, even if we agree with the claimants. What hangs in the balance is justice, and as Derrida reminds us, justice doesn't wait. But how, then, are we to make the case for reparations given the circumstances of justice, the burdens of judgment, and the inability of history to substitute for comprehensive doctrines? I have no idea. But we have a better understanding of the situation by coming to see the problem of rendering justice in these aporetic terms, and that is why aporetic cross-tradition theorizing contributes to political knowledge rather than skeptically undermining it.

To return to the myths above, we should read everything and yet not be dominated by our reading. We should understand where we are here and now and still build bridges. No doubt we will often be dominated by our reading and our bridges will fail. But "fail better" is the motto of aporetic cross-tradition theorizing.

CLAIM 2: CROSS-TRADITION THEORIZING CHALLENGES BOTH SPECIALIZATION AND INTRA-TRADITION CLOISTERING, WHICH CAN BROADEN, DIVERSIFY, PLURALIZE, AND ENLIVEN POLITICAL THEORETICAL DEBATE.

It is my impression, supported by some of the statistics on citation patterns briefly mentioned in the Introduction, that political theorists from one tradition don't read theorists in the other tradition. Even if this is wrong and they do read each other, they are not acknowledging and engaging the other tradition in print. Theorists usually talk to their own. There are understandable sociological reasons for this mutual shunning, including training in graduate school, specialization, professional incentives, personal interest, and so on. There are other reasons for all of us to limit what we read and respond to, including the precariousness of many academic jobs and the constraints on time we all face. But my hunch is that what brought many of us to professional political theory was a deep interest in understanding and entering an ongoing conversation about political, and political theoretical, problems. To the extent that we remain stuck within our traditions, that conversation is limited, and in my experience, quickly becomes repetitive and stultifying. If we want to talk to as many people as possible, it is necessary to be fluent enough in the different languages of political theory that readers will find our work, at the very least, readable and intelligible. Cross-tradition theorizing requires this kind of minimal fluency and perhaps more, and it can and should be written so as to increase the range of people able to critically respond to the work.

Ten years ago I had no idea I would, or could, write this book. My earlier work led me to new texts and conceptual worlds because of the theoretical problems I was confronting. Understanding these new worlds wasn't easy. The charge of obscurity, or difficulty, or nonsensicality leveled at continental philosophy by many analytic philosophers is sometimes true, sometimes a red herring, sometimes a projection or transference of the same fact of obscurity. There is nothing clear and obvious and commonsensical about the language of analytic philosophy, including a great deal of analytic political philosophy. Much of that philosophy is as technical, allusive, and intertextual as any of the writing in continental philosophy, although in both traditions, thankfully, there are exceptions to the general rule. The point is this, and it is not self-congratulatory: it is not easy to enter a different tradition of thought and to try to understand and judge it on its own terms. It is work. But it can be done. It is a further task to then see how one tradition of thought reframes and reveals aspects of another tradition. This is less difficult then the first task, but it too takes time.

The reward of this work has been—beyond the sense that I understand more, and more deeply, the diverse intellectual worlds of political theory—increasing confidence in addressing a wider audience, speaking and writing in terms that exclude fewer readers than in my earlier work. That confidence might be self-delusion; you are the judge of that. Political theorists stand to gain a great deal by deepening and broadening their audience beyond the cloistered world of any one tradition. This is not, to be sure, an argument for my preferred mode of cross-tradition theorizing, but it is an argument for that theorizing in general.

CLAIM 3: APORETIC CROSS-TRADITION THEORIZING CAN REALIZE A WORTHY SCHOLARLY ETHIC OF RESPONSIVENESS AND OPENNESS.

Responsiveness and openness do not coincide with the intellectual virtues of open-mindedness and the willingness to engage arguments. These latter virtues are necessary, especially in a moment when they are often neglected or rejected in academic settings, but they are not sufficient for responsiveness and openness. Responsiveness and openness are ideas adopted from Cora Diamond's "The Difficulty of Reality and the Difficulty of Philosophy," and before arguing that aporetic cross-tradition theorizing realizes these virtues, we should be clear about what they are.

Diamond identifies a phenomenon that I, and I assume many others, have experienced often enough, if intermittently. In reference to a poem by Ted Hughes, she writes:

> What Hughes gives us is a case of what I want to call the difficulty of reality . . . experiences in which we take something in reality to be resistant to our thinking it, or possibly to be painful in its inexplicability, difficult in that way, or perhaps awesome and astonishing in its inexplicability. *We take things so.* And the things we take so may simply not, to others, present the kind of difficulty—of being hard or impossible or agonizing to get one's mind around. (Diamond 2003, 2)

Diamond's interest is largely in understanding how experiences of inexplicability and astonishment are deflected, especially by philosophy, into arguments that deflate that air of wonder and mystery. My interest, however, is the situation in which what one person takes to be astonishing and inexplicable is, to someone else, so obvious, that her or his interest in the issue never arises, or quickly disappears.

This radical difference in two ways of seeing the same facts may also help to explain the divide in political theory, because the divide can be traced to competing senses, in response to the same facts, of importance, inexplicability, incomprehension, and so on. In these cases, what appears to be of paramount importance and difficulty to one theorist is, to another, not important and difficult at all. This is a different myth of the analytic and the continental, or another version of the same myth discussed before.

Take, as one example, what I understand to be the real ethical and political impulse of Rawls' *A Theory of Justice*, based on something Rawls is best described as *seeing*. The reason the basic structure of society is the primary subject of justice is that

> its effects are so profound and present from the start. The *intuitive* notion here is that this structure contains various social positions and that men *born into* different positions have difference expectations of life determined, in part, by the political system as well as by economic and social circumstances. In this way the institutions of society favor certain starting places over others. *These are especially deep inequalities.* Not only are they pervasive, but they affect

men's initial chances in life; *yet* they cannot be possibly justified by an appeal to the notions of merit or desert. It is these inequalities, presumably inevitable in the basic structure of any society, to which the principles of social justice must in the first instance apply. (Rawls 1971, 7, emphasis added.)

The emphasized words reveal what is really troubling Rawls: our lives are over-determined by factors over which we have no control because we are born into powerful social structures and often challenging circumstances. But if we have no control over these determining facts, then our fate, as it were, cannot be said to be fully deserved or merited, as if the ancient notion of Fate returns in modern society with an often less violent, but still destructive, vengeance. Rawls' project is to discover the principles that will rectify or at least mitigate the social, economic, and political conditions of our birth so that we can finally achieve a society in which Fate, at least sociopolitical Fate, no longer plays as much of a determining role in our lives.

Rawls doesn't use the language of Fate. However, seeing Rawls' project as a response to the astonishing fact that something like Fate plays such a powerful role in modern life even though notions like Fate are pre-modern enabled me to appreciate, to a much greater degree, Rawls' work. This passage only resonated with me in this way after several years of reading and teaching *A Theory of Justice*, and subsequently I have been far more charitable to Rawls' work than I might otherwise have been. Prior to this appreciation for what was bugging Rawls, I thought of his project as what happens to political philosophy in the administered society: the theoretical attempt to explain how to efficiently and fairly administer things, to justify the best form of a bureaucratic, technocratic, liberal democratic society that itself is unquestioned despite its significant problems. This project was not all that interesting to me, nor to a number of political theorists. Reading Rawls, for many theorists, is a professional necessity, in the same way a restaurant needs to put salmon and chicken breast on the menu. But upon realizing, or imputing to Rawls, his real motivation, several hundred pages of often tedious prose and argument became, at the very least, responsive to a deep and real problem. Whatever one makes of the response, the problem was genuine, as deep as Rawls thought it was, another moment in the dialectic of enlightenment.

I might have been primed for being struck by Rawls' project as a response to a specific interpretation of what it is to be born because of my interest in Arendt, specifically in her concept of natality. Natality is central to Arendt's work, but it is almost always named, associated with the power of beginning, and then left behind. Natality is not even a concept but one of the human conditions: that we are born, just as much as the fact that we die, is for Arendt key to understanding what it is to be human. Given the relative neglect of natality in the history of western philosophy, Arendt's focus on the fact of birth is a "difficulty of reality" for Arendt. Many followers of Rawls might find Arendt's repeated, unexplained but normatively and descriptively foundational insistence on the fact of natality to be just as opaque or uninteresting to them as a concern with distributing primary goods is to those who find little interest in Rawls' writing. Yet, by implicitly putting Rawls and Arendt together, I was able to overcome my failure to see the "difficulty of reality" possessing Rawls and to see one reason why an admirer of Rawls would be perplexed by Arendt—and how I might get a Rawlsian to see Arendt's difficulty as real.

The admirable intellectual ethic of responsiveness and openness that concerns me is a responsiveness to the "difficulty of reality" that preoccupies a writer—presuming, what is not always the case, that a text responds to a difficulty of reality at all. Most of us write in response to all sorts of problems, many of them not inexplicable or astonishing or awesome. However, at least part of the reason other traditions of thought, or writers within that tradition, seem so distant from our own is that we make no attempt to understand what difficulty of reality they are confronting. Perhaps we cannot understand that difficulty even if we try, but many of us don't try. What it takes to understand Arendt's difficulty is nothing less than the willingness to accept for many a page that a dramatic break in the tradition of thought and social life took place around the middle of the 19th century; that this break played a role in the horrors of the 20th century; and that the only way to overcome the self-destructive tendencies of modernity shaped by the break is to retrieve and reinterpret neglected possibilities of western history and philosophy. One neglected possibility is to begin with the fact of natality. That is a lot to accept simply to get to that final point. If one doesn't accept, preliminarily, those premises, or sensibilities, or historicizations, then much of Arendt's work will be uninteresting, unreadable, or worse.

An intellectual ethic of responsiveness and openness is at its heart an ethics of reading that includes hermeneutic charity, but the latter notion is too restricted. Hermeneutic charity assumes that the author of the text, or a speaker, is rational, self-consistent, intelligent, perhaps serious (rather than ironic), and so on. This is necessary for an ethics of responsiveness, but not sufficient, because assuming that an author is self-consistent and rational doesn't require us also to assume that the author has any point, or problem, worth discussing. To be open to another person's "difficulty," to attempt to understand why someone would so much as be bothered or interested in the problem they are interested in, is not an act of charity but, to use a suspicious term, an act of *communion*. The term *communion* captures the sense in which to understand someone's difficulty is to *participate* in it *with* them, not as one person and not only as me "in their shoes," but together, apart. Insofar as difficulties have an affective component, it is not enough to merely understand the difficulty; it must also be felt. My image of responsiveness is not of two becoming one, but of two together standing in awe of the same thing. The process that leads to two standing together in awe of the same thing is, for the reader, a process of seeing the difficulty as a difficulty, which often requires "translating" another writer's problem or question into terms—like Fate—that open the reader to a writer's difficulty of reality. That is what transformed my interest in Rawls. In seeing Rawls as someone dealing with the unfair consequences of a modern form of Fate, I was able to see why someone would spend 500 pages trying to undo the work of Fate, or at least make it tolerable. This interpretive key is not a projection into Rawls' text, nor is it without textual support; but it is surely true that few if any readers of Rawls standardly see his project in these terms. That's fine. The point is that the interest and urgency of Rawls' work only intensified after my seeing what he was doing in terms that made his difficulty seem real and pressing, not just to him, but to me.

If this makes sense, then aporetic cross-tradition theorizing can be seen as both presupposing an ethic of responsiveness and deepening and developing that ethic. I have not defended this ethic at all because it seems to me obviously, and importantly, part of the ethics of scholarship. Responsiveness doesn't preclude judgment, but it does preclude prejudice and demands that we reflect on our prejudices when encountering new work. The virtues of openness and responsiveness seem to me so old-fashioned, and yet so right, that it is hard to imagine why they are often doubted, in practice if not in theory. Doubted, not unrealized. I often fail to realize this virtue, but I have never doubted it. Yet, to paraphrase Emerson, responsiveness is a virtue not most in request today, and if that is right, then scholarship will suffer from scholars' aversion to this fundamental virtue. Aporetic cross-tradition theorizing embodies openness and responsiveness, and insofar as it does, it is a valuable and ethical form of scholarship.

My hope is that this defense of aporetic cross-tradition theorizing, both in the Introduction and here, succeeds at convincing you of at least the viability and desirability of reading across the divide. I also hope that the individual chapters reveal something worth learning when we engage in aporetic cross-tradition theorizing. If neither hope has been fulfilled, then I will fail better next time.

NOTES

1. As Peter Gordon has argued in an extremely detailed and lucid history of Davos, while many in attendance were aware of the significance of the event, it was not quite understood to be a "parting of the ways" in Friedman's sense. At the time, the dispute was often seen as a "generational" conflict and linked to the sense of "crisis" in Weimar Germany, but even that reading is not necessarily exhaustive of what took place at Davos. Gordon argues quite persuasively that the history of Davos as it has been told since 1929 has been shaped by a variety of concerns, not all of them philosophical (or invested in a division between continental and analytic philosophers). See Gordon 2010.

2. See Carnap 1959, 69–73. A useful account of the place of logic in analytic-continental debates can be found in D'Agostini 2001.

3. See Ryle 1929. That things are somewhat different now in this regard is indisputable. In political thought specifically, some philosophers have simply transcended the divide, for example John Rawls and Jürgen Habermas. Others in political theory have simply ignored the division. Richard Flathman comes to mind, and some post-Habermasian critical theorists have followed Habermas' own (controversial) appropriation of both traditions. Paul Patton has put Gilles Deleuze and Jacques Derrida into conversation with Rawls and other liberals. See Patton 2007 and 2010. Finally, largely because of the work of Rawls and Habermas, Michael Sandel and Charles Taylor and Michael Walzer, many continental theorists engage in debates about "deliberative democracy" and communitarianism, and the like. But these are uninteresting exceptions to the rule, given the virtually unparalleled global significance of philosophers like Rawls and Habermas.

4. See, for more examples, Akehurst 2008; Buckle 2004; Campbell 2001; Dascal 2001; Levy 2003; Rockmore 2004; Staiti 2013; and Simons 2001. Two very different accounts (both in length and argument) of the history of analytic philosophy can be found in, on the one hand, the two volumes of Soames 2003 and, on the other, many of the essays, but especially the last one, in Rorty 1982. Defining "continental philosophy" is a more contentious matter because, as Richard Campbell rightly acknowledges, analytic philosophers are far more likely to self-identify as analytic. It is hard to imagine Derrida, or Foucault,

or Heidegger, or political theorists like William Connolly, Bonnie Honig, Chantal Mouffe, Ernesto Laclau, and others self-identifying as "continental." See Campbell 2001, 342.

5. Hans-Johann Glock comes closest in his *What Is Analytic Philosophy?* However, his concern is not to examine the different methods, concepts, inheritances, and problems that divide analytic and continental philosophers, nor why they emerged. Rather, he defends analytic philosophy against the charge that it is apolitical and conservative, rather than engaged and progressive as the continental philosophical tradition putatively is. See Glock 2008, 179–203.

6. This story is well documented and historically examined. Two justifications of political theory and philosophy against behaviorism, from within the mid-century debate, are Magid 1955 and Wolin 1969. On those debates see Barber 2006. A history of the place of Straussianism and theory more generally in the pages of the *American Political Science Review* during the behavioral revolution can be found in Kettler 2006. A contemporary report of a conference held at Northwestern University focusing on the political theory "question" and attended by, among others, Sheldon Wolin and David Easton can be found in Eckstein 1956. Representative discussions from outside the United States include Berlin 1999, 143–172. For a brief overview of the quite different situation in the history of European political science, see Berg-Schlosser 2006.

7. This tense relation between political *science* and (American-style) liberalism is a recurring theme in histories of the discipline. See Smith 1997 and Farr 1988, 1177. Needless to say, the debate continues. See, on the one hand, Kaufman-Osborn 2010, Gunnell 2010, and DiSalvo 2013; and on the other, Grant 2005.

8. These procedures include, among others, close reading of canonical texts; theoretically grounded exegeses and criticisms of contemporary politics; accounts of the nature of political theory and the knowledge it provides; the creation of theoretical concepts; and engagement with texts, ideas, and problems in adjacent disciplines (including sociology, geography, history, anthropology, literary criticism, and so on). On the importance and effect of Wolin in political theory, see William Connolly's introduction to Botwinick and Connolly 2001.

9. A full text search on jstor.org for articles and reviews mentioning "Foucault" in *Philosophy and Public Affairs* (*PPA*)—spanning 1971–2013—gave *four* results. A search for such articles in *Ethics* gave nine results over virtually the same time period. For comparison, a search for "Foucault" in *Political Theory* (*PT*) articles over roughly the same time period returned 188 results. Searching for "Rawls" in *PT* articles yielded 322 results; in *PPA*, 276. Given that *PPA* in that time published around 600 articles, that is almost 50% of articles with a mention of Rawls, compared to 322 out of around 1150 articles in *PT*, or a little under 30%. Further searches for citations and references reveal mostly similar results. There may be many explanations for this fact. For example, citation practices in analytic and in continental philosophy more generally are often very different and this may affect the number of appearances of search terms in journals. And to be sure, *PPA* was in its early days a place for Rawls-friendly philosophers to publish. Still, the evidence from journal searches points more directly toward either mutual ignorance or mutual indifference between analytic and continental theorists.

10. Informative histories of analytic political and moral philosophy can be found in the chapter by Jonathan Wolff in Beaney 2013; in Soames 2003a and 2003b; and in Bevir and Blakley 2010.

11. However, as Mark Bevir and Jason Blakely argue, ethics and indeed political philosophy was not as moribund and, when still practiced, monolithically emotivist, as histories of analytic philosophy tend to conclude (Bevir and Blakely 2010).

12. Deleuze, for example, writes that philosophy must begin with a "necessary modesty," with the philosopher "modestly denying what everybody is supposed to recognize" (Deleuze 1994, 130). Compare this with Saul Kripke in *Naming and Necessity*: "Of course, some philosophers think that something's having intuitive content is very inconclusive evidence in favor of it. I think it is very heavy evidence in favor of anything, myself. I really don't know, in a way, what more conclusive evidence one can have about anything, ultimately speaking" (Kripke 1981, 42).

13. As noted previously, Flathman is a good example of a theorist who could not care less about the divide, as evidenced here.

14. Habermas and those inspired by him (for example, Seyla Benhabib) would seem to be an obvious choice for a book like this, given their cross-tradition work. However, I do not find in Habermas' political philosophy much that distinguishes him, in broad outline and goal (although not in detail), from analytic philosophers. There are important differences between Rawls and Habermas, for example, but they are family squabbles. Habermas is taken seriously by analytic political philosophers, even when he is criticized; the same cannot be said for Habermas' intellectual fathers in the Frankfurt school: Theodor Adorno, Walter Benjamin, and Max Horkheimer; and for Habermas' opponents on the Continent: Foucault and Derrida especially. A chapter on Habermas and the early Frankfurt school, if I could write it, would put Habermas squarely on the analytic side of things. Habermas is a powerful philosopher, but his political philosophy does not, I would argue, represent much of a break from the liberal tradition of analytic philosophy, even if the path he takes to his political philosophy winds through continental forests.

15. The most important criticisms of this reading of Derrida, at least, are found in Gasché 1994, 3–13; as well as Gasché 1986; and Norris 1989.

16. For more on this issue see Donahue and Ochoa Espejo 2016.

CHAPTER 1

1. The two best overviews are Galston 2010; and Rossi and Sleat 2014.

2. Whether the realist really can keep moralism, or at least ethical thought (in Williams' sense of ethics), distinct from political theory is an issue in the realist literature. Those who dispute the possibility include Bavister-Gould 2013 and Erman and Möller 2015. For responses to these types of criticisms, specifically Erman and Möller, see Jubb and Rossi 2015.

3. Geuss, Honig, and Mouffe are clearly not interested in replacing a moralist with a realist theory of legitimacy. See Geuss 2005; 2008; 2010; Honig 1993; 2009, 12–39; and Mouffe 2005.

4. This absence is captured nowhere more clearly than in Williams' essay "From Freedom to Liberty": "Since liberty is freedom as a political value, no complaint is a complaint in liberty if it would apply to any political system or any state whatsoever" (Williams 2005, 85). This is manifestly false if we recall the centrality of practices of state violence to any real state, for it implies that imprisonment or the death penalty are not infringements upon individual liberty. Only a Kantian or Rousseauian could really make such a claim, and Williams rightly finds such theorists objectionable. It is not manifestly false if we are thinking, as Williams is in this essay, about losing a political battle (for example, over redistributing wealth). Curiously, when Williams does directly discuss legal punishment, it is clear that he is rightly skeptical of the possibility of *justifying* legal punishment, either in terms of deterrence or retribution; but he doesn't connect these ideas with his account of political legitimacy. Williams is sympathetic to the retributive theory of punishment, but does not seem to think that such a theory justifies punishment; it only tells us a significant part of the point and purpose of punishment. See Williams 1997, 99–102.

5. See Scheuerman 2013.

6. For definitions of violence see Arendt 1969; Bufacchi 2009; Coady 2008; and Wolff 1969.

7. Since the publication of Nozick's essay "Coercion," the dominant framework for thinking about coercion is the conditional threat (or offer) rather than physical force. I am using the term *coercion* in the broader, everyday (and also Hobbesian, Kantian, and Millian) sense of forceful restraint and compulsion, be it physical or as threat. To the extent that Nozick provides a reason for ruling out violence as a form of coercion, it is to avoid confusions generated by specific examples of violence that occur "suddenly," without warning or threat or possible repetition (Nozick's example is of a group of drunks beating up a random person; see Nozick 1969, 444).

8. These are minimal conditions of *full* human agency, and thus they exclude certain groups of humans (most obviously children and, perhaps, those with various psychological or physical disabilities) and include all "normal" adults. These conditions also exclude, without denying the possibility of, non-human agency, both animal agency and what Jane Bennett calls the "agency of things" (Bennett 2010).

9. An agent may be able to move a finger intentionally in some imagined scenario of significant restraint, and if all actions are primitive bodily movements, then there is some agency here (Davidson 2001, 59). So perhaps there is, short of death, no complete destruction of human agency imaginable. But the usefulness of this point, if it is correct, is unclear to me.

10. See Sleat 2007; 2010; and Hall 2015.

11. A debate over the extent of this "acceptability" condition can be found in Sleat 2010 and Hall 2015. The issue turns on whether a justification of state legitimacy must be acceptable to all those subject to the state's power or only to citizens of a state. For a different realist account of legitimacy invoking the criterion of acceptability, see Horton 2010; and 2012.

12. These issues return in Chapter 5.

13. On this issue see Sreedhar 2008.

CHAPTER 2

1. For instance, see Hammer 2002, 119–148; Mulhall 1997; Shusterman 1997; Owen 1999; Norris 2002; 2006; von Rautenfeld 2004; and Wolfe 1994. Of particular benefit are Mulhall's and von Rautenfeld's examinations of whether and how Cavell's criticisms of Rawls' *Theory of Justice* apply as well to his *Political Liberalism*.

2. See Stroud 1980; Rorty 1982; Williams 1996; Bearn 1998; Hammer 2002, 142–174; and de Vries 2006. This is not to say that there have not been critical readings of Cavell on other political issues. For example, see Norris 2006, 164–185.

3. Hanna Pitkin has, in response to Wittgenstein (but in a book drawing heavily on Cavell), already pointed out many of the problems with fully analogizing linguistic and political communities. Although I focus on different aspects of that dis-analogy and draw different consequences from it, similar arguments, and others that support my argument here, can be found in Pitkin 1972, 193–218.

4. The best places to see the philosophical analysis of the transcendental status of community are, obviously, in *The Claim of Reason*, especially Part One, but also in "Must We Mean What We Say?" (especially pp. 12–21) and "The Availability of the Later Wittgenstein," both in Cavell 1969.

5. Cavell expands the question as he does in part because he has already reiterated the contract theorist's point that consent to a contract implies some advantage to be gained from the contract; and also because he has "de-transcendentalized" the contract, insofar as in actual societies, where injustices are to be found, the question of the social contract is not "what are the advantages of citizenship *in general* (as opposed to living in a state of nature or some other non-political state)?"; rather the question is "what is the advantage of being a citizen of *this* polity?" See Cavell 1999, 23–24.

6. Aristotle 1992, 1288b10–1289a26.

7. Cavell "defines" the conversation of justice in, among other places, *Cities of Words* (Cavel 2004, 172–173).

8. For further elaborations of these ideas, see among other places, Cavell 1999, 395–403.

9. The most pertinent texts (beyond most of *The Claim of Reason*, especially Part Four) are "Emerson" and "Mill" in *Cities of Words* (Cavell 2004); "Emerson, Coleridge, Kant" in *In Quest of the Ordinary* (Cavell 1988); "The Avoidance of Love" in *Must We Mean What We Say?* (Cavel 1969); and nearly all the texts on remarriage comedies and melodramas.

CHAPTER 3

1. This despite Pettit's occasional dismissals of Arendt's work. For example, Pettit claims that Arendt (along with Sandel) is an inheritor of, or identifies with, the Rousseauian republican tradition (Pettit 2012, 12). This claim is simply false, as there are few thinkers as vociferously and continuously opposed to Rousseau's thought as Arendt. See Arendt 1965, 68–110.

2. For the sake of brevity I will use the phrase "freedom as responsibility" from henceforth, which should be taken to mean freedom as "being fit to be held responsible."

3. To the extent that Arendt chooses one of these options, it is the underdetermination path.

4. Unless one understands ownership and underdetermination in solely causal terms, that is, that the owner of an action is the causal agent responsible for the action, and physical underdetermination leaves room for the causal agency of the agent. Pettit's skepticism toward this line of thinking is on display in Pettit 2007a, 242.

5. Pettit's account of discourse is, generally speaking, congruent with accounts of deliberation we find in Habermas. See Pettit 2001b.

6. Pettit does not address what seems like a real danger of this view: that by losing oneself, as it were, an agent has a "get out of jail free" card. To respond to a past action with "that wasn't me," or to fail to follow through on a promise by excusing one's own weakness of will, seems, intuitively, to suggest either genuine moral incompetence or a genuine disadvantage to freedom. For why, after all, isn't an elusive or weak self, however unfree, not something to be sought, at least at times?

7. Sharon Krause rightly argues that we ought to have a pluralist account of freedom in which various definitions of freedom—non-interference, non-domination, non-oppression, non-sovereign world- and self-disclosure—are all taken to mark complex relations between and among individuals, groups, and institutions. However, I would also argue that insofar as the definition of freedom is itself a real political problem—one that affects public policy; economic theory and policy; discourses of race, gender, sexuality, and so on—then even a pluralist account of freedom may be forced to strategically emphasize some freedoms over others. See Krause 2012.

8. A fuller sense of what this means will become apparent in my discussion of Arendt's theorizing.

9. At the limit—and that limit is high modernism—the connection between an improvised performance and the patterns, rules, conventions, and so on that make a practice intelligible is stretched and sometimes broken. This is where freedom as pure improvisation can, in Nietzsche's words, become a form of exile, unbearable, a "Siberia" (Nietzsche 1974, §295).

10. In a later formulation of this point, Pettit modifies the terms a bit:

> A controller for a type of effect E—call it C—will be virtual under the following conditions. The effect E is normally occasioned not by C, but by some other factor, N (for normal). But in any case where N fails to produce E, then C steps into the breach and takes over the productive role. When C steps in like this, it actively controls for the appearance of E. But insofar as it is there as a standby cause, ready to intervene on a need-to-act basis, it controls for the appearance of C even when it is not actively in charge. It is a virtual controller of the effect in question. It rides herd on the normal mechanism of production, ready to compensate for failures in the process or to readjust the process so that it no longer fails. (Pettit 2007a, 226)

While still problematic, this language is a bit clearer.

11. While we may "blame" Magic Johnson for turning the ball over on a fast break, or the saxophonist for hitting a "wrong" note during "Impressions," the important point

is that "doing the wrong thing" is as essential to the practice of spontaneous activity as "pulling it off." Risk is inherent in spontaneous activity, and that is the "price" of such freedom, a price that is often high but in many contexts is worth paying for the possibility of experiencing one type of extremely pleasurable and valuable freedom. There is still an open question about how, since sometimes we should, morally assess "bad" improvisatory activity. But it matters a great deal whether the bad pass is thrown by Johnson or Charles Oakley, the note played by Coltrane or a thirteen–year–old musical neophyte. That these issues matter is one way in which the issues here align with Williams' concerns in *Moral Luck* about assessing Gauguin (Williams 1981).

12. Pettit's views on these matters could be interestingly compared to Heidegger's descriptions of the breakdown of the ready-to-hand, which can eventually bring about the theoretical, observational, subject-looking-at-object relation to the present-at-hand. See Heidegger 1962, §§13; 15–16. As Hubert Dreyfus puts it, "Heidegger leaves open a place for traditional intentionality at the point where there is a breakdown [i.e., of our involved, everyday, non-consciously intentional dealings with the world]. For example, if the doorknob sticks, we find ourselves deliberately *trying* to turn the doorknob, *desiring* that it turn, *expecting* the door to open, etc. (This, of course, does not imply that we were trying, desiring, expecting, etc. all along.) With disturbance, a new way of Daseining comes into being" (Dreyfus 1991, 70). The Heideggerian idea Dreyfus is glossing is that when we have a breakdown in our habitual, involved activities, we orient ourselves toward the world in a different way. But this doesn't mean that we were always oriented toward the world in that way nor that we were always virtually oriented toward the world in that way.

13. Seyla Benhabib's claim that Arendt engages in "phenomenological essentialism" is pretty close to correct, although this implies, not without some justification, that Arendt sees the human conditions as well as the meaning of certain modes of activity as fixed (Benhabib 2003, 123). I would suggest that Arendt reveals her anti-essentialism in those moments where her faithfulness to the phenomena she describes conflicts with her normative commitments. I discuss this issue in the context of *On Revolution* in Arnold 2014.

14. Hanna Pitkin critically analyzes Arendt's distinction between liberty and freedom, arguing that although she is right to distinguish the two, careful attention to etymology and ordinary usage reveals and explains the limits of Arendt's distinction both as conceptual analysis and as placing her reader in the best position to independently— one might say freely—engage her ideas. See Pitkin 1988.

15. A reading of Arendt that tries to find some place for sovereignty in Arendt's conception of freedom is Martel 2008; see also Arnold 2012.

16. The use of the verb "to call" in Arendt's definition may suggest a purely verbal account of free action in which the new that appears through action is akin to a baptism or originary naming. It is true that Arendt understands most political action as taking place in speech, but using the verb "to call" is probably a quirk of Arendt's non-native English.

17. Arendt relies heavily on Augustine's claim in *City of God* that man was created by God to be a beginner, and that man's specific creative capacity is *initium* rather than *principium*. See, among many places, Arendt 1978b, 108.

18. In the cited passages Arendt turns to the concept of a "principle" as well as *virtú*—drawing on Montesquieu and Machiavelli—to help make sense, presumably, of how free action transcends intellect, judgment, and will (Arendt 1993, 152–153). Examples of principles include honor, glory, and courage. Principles are not goals or aims of actions, for even if an actor sets out to be glorious, or honored, or excellent, these goals are, necessarily, out of their control. What honor, glory, and excellence share is that they are judgments made about the action of the actor by others. An actor cannot be honored, excellent, virtuous, or glorious without others. Similarly, an actor cannot express virtuosity in action without others. A virtuoso is a performer, and one cannot perform without others. Yo-Yo Ma sitting alone in his practice room playing a cello may be many things, but he is not, at the time, a virtuoso. That we want to call him one even when he is alone in his room is a product of our having heard him perform with others.

Principles and virtuosity share, in addition to their intrinsic reliance on the presence of others, what Michael Oakeshott would call an "adverbial" character. Both principles and *virtús* (and not virtues, to use Richard Flathman's distinction between virtues and *virtús*; Flathman 1998, 3–16) are predicated of actions, specifically of the "how" of actions, of the specific way or ways in which an action was performed. Here too, adverbial descriptions of an action are not in the control of the actor. A musician can strive to play a particularly difficult passage of a sonata with virtuosic ease, but whether it is a virtuoso performance is not up to them (or if up to them, only insofar as they can be a third-person spectator of their own actions).

19. Dana Villa's *Arendt and Heidegger*—to my mind the best book on Arendt—is extremely useful in making sense of this idea. See Villa 1996, chaps. 3–4.

20. Arendt discusses the following passage from Nietzsche in *The Life of the Mind*, but it is clear to me that it plays a role in her earlier criticisms of the identification of freedom with the freedom of the will. See Arendt 1978b, 160–163. Although he doesn't mention Nietzsche at all, Berlin makes the exact same point in "Two Concepts of Liberty." See Berlin 1969, 132–133.

21. Compare Pettit on the different but analogous example of authorizing someone else to enforce your will upon yourself (in the example, giving someone a key to your liquor cabinet to prevent you from drinking): "The arrangement in place with the key is a means, we might say, whereby you impose your own longer term will on yourself, not a means whereby I impose my will on you. . . . The lesson of the example is that the interference that I or any others practice in a choice of yours will not impose an alien will, and not therefore invade your freedom of choice, to the extent that my discretion in exercising interference is subject to your control" (Pettit 2012, 57). Substitute "one's own stable or authoritative will" for "the will of another" in this example and the point becomes clear: the individual in this example may, after all, *really* want a drink. That desire may not be the desire the self affirms as a desirable desire, but it is nonetheless a desire of the self. The self is undeniably subordinating a part of itself in such an example, and thus it is unclear how Pettit might resolve the conceptual difficulties of a freedom that requires subordination (at least some of the time).

22. Arendt's resistance to theories of freedom that suppress the uncontrollable, non-sovereign aspects of free action is pervasive in her work. See, for example, her discussion of Hegel in Arendt 1965, 45–52; and her, to my mind extremely ambivalent and ironic, reading of Heidegger in Arendt 1978b, 172–194.

23. The idea of intelligibility as a condition of newness is not the same as, but is congruent with part of Patchen Markell's provocative argument about how to understand Arendt's account of ruling and beginning. I share with Markell the idea that whether an action initiates newness depends a great deal on how that action is received and responded to by others (Markell 2006, 10). I disagree with Markell's claim that newness is actualized in responsiveness because it leaves unanswered the obvious question, Why would anyone respond to *this* action in *this* way, so as to actualize its newness? Surely there is something in the "how" and the "what" of action—its "style" or "form" as well as its "content"—that provokes the responsiveness Markell identifies. Undoubtedly, historical context and traditions shape what provokes responsiveness and what not, but that doesn't change the fact that something in an action, or a work, must be provocative if we are, in fact, provoked to respond.

24. The distinction between playing music and "playing" music might get fuzzy: what if the child continues hitting the keys of the piano but suddenly we hear a Beethoven sonata, or "Twinkle, Twinkle, Little Star"? What if the child stops splashing paint on the paper, takes up a brush, and paints a still life of the toys lying on the floor? And then each proceeds to go back to banging the piano or splashing paint, more or less seamlessly. I'm not sure what we would want to say in these circumstances, but they are exceptions—however philosophically important—to our everyday capacities to distinguish intelligible activity from more or less unintelligible behavior.

CHAPTER 4

1. A conceptual analysis of domination that clarifies Pettit's (and Iris Marion Young's) work can be found in Lovett 2001.

2. In later work Pettit uses "uncontrolled interference" rather than arbitrary interference, so as to avoid certain connotations of the term *interference*. In other words, interference that is not significantly controlled by the agent interfered with—control here meaning either permitting or being able to punish interference—is dominating. For the purposes of my argument, the difference is negligible. See Pettit 2012, 58.

3. On this point I disagree with Charles Larmore, who doesn't see freedom as nondomination in light of Pettit's theory of freedom as discursive control. See Larmore 2001, 230; 2003, 97–98.

4. At the end of his discussion of Berlin, Pettit suggests that Berlin was moving toward, even if not self-consciously, a republican conception of freedom as being a master in an institutionally carved out space of liberty (Pettit 2011, 714–716). However, Berlin could not accept Pettit's account of republican freedom because Berlin could not and would not admit that an agent can be actively interfered with and yet not have their liberty reduced. Berlin offers a very Nietzschean diagnosis of the trick of the "I" at work in positive liberty, and he would surely apply this diagnosis to Pettit's own theory of

republican freedom. In any case, the burden of this section of the chapter is to show that we have good grounds for being suspicious of the claim that one's freedom is not reduced by even authorized, controlled, contestable, or consented to interference.

5. It is because I am asking this question that Pettit's intriguing suggestions about how we can design a democratic, republican, contestatory citizenry that genuinely controls government will not be discussed here. My question is whether even in the best of circumstances, where citizens do actively and effectively influence the direction of government, we can still say that government interference—specifically coercion—does not reduce freedom. The question is, as it has been throughout this chapter, about what freedom is and whether political freedom *is* non-domination as Pettit argues. For Pettit's discussion of the institutional issues raised by his arguments, see the final two chapters of Pettit 2012.

6. That something like self-domination is on display in Pettit's work has already been noted in Chapter 3. "Orthonomy," while not autonomy, nonetheless is "the sort of self-rule in which you guide what you believe and desire, intend and do, by the values that you endorse, however valuation is construed" (Pettit 2012, 281). Orthonomy, as being ruled by the "right," does not necessarily require an independent, substantive moral standard. Orthonomy does require, however, the identification of the self with a subset of the beliefs and desires and evaluations one possesses, as well as the authority of what used to be known as "right reason." It is that reason—practical reason—that normatively grounds orthonomy and "imposes" rule upon the practically unreasonable self (see Pettit and Smith 1993).

7. The recurrence of this trope—the analogy between politics and nature—in arguments that intuitively suggest a reduction in freedom is worthy of investigation in its own right. Perhaps the most consistent critics of the naturalization of politics are Hobbes and Arendt. Hobbes, on the one hand, refuses to see even the "artificial man" that is the state as anything other than artifice, with its "body" analogized in terms of parts of a machine. Rousseau, on the other hand, imagines the political body in terms of actual body parts. The reliance on this trope, in any case, is something to be explored further.

8. In fact, the connection between Rousseau and Pettit might be even deeper, if entirely by chance. In *Emile*, Rousseau argues that there are two kinds of dependence, dependence on men and dependence on things. The former is, as all republicans agree, a bad thing, a form of domination. Dependence on things, however, "since it has no morality, is in no way detrimental to freedom and engenders no vices." Thus, "if there is any means of remedying this ill [dependence on men] in society, it is to substitute law for man and to arm the general wills with a real strength superior to the action of every particular will. If the laws of nations could, like those of nature, have an inflexibility that no human force could ever conquer, dependence on men would then become dependence on things again; in the republic all of the advantages of the natural state would be united with those of the civil state, and freedom which keeps man exempt from vices would be joined to morality which raises him to virtue" (Rousseau 1979, 85). The idea that nature is opposed to morality in such a way that a natural dependence on things

does not impinge on one's freedom is what Pettit is getting at in the idea that the imposition of the common good on an individual who "suffers" from that imposition is not domination: it is like a natural disaster. For Rousseau, an ideal republic would be one in which the civil law would be as effective—and non-dominating—as the laws of nature (like gravity), and thus the imposition of the general will would not violate freedom (just as gravity does not violate my freedom). When the law goes against my private interests, it is like a hurricane destroying my house, but not a violation of my freedom. This tendency to rely on the concept of the natural in its distinction from the moral and political is not explicit in Pettit's work, but it is perhaps an unsurprising, and telling, inheritance of a certain kind of republican theory.

9. For related observations that suggest Pettit has misconstrued the meaning of freedom, see Kukathas 2009; Larmore 2001, 239–240; Carter 2000, 45; 2008. Ian Carter is on to something when he notes that Pettit introduces a "moralized" conception of interference without domination, one that resonates with the moralization that takes place in Rousseau. A criticism quite close to mine in this chapter—one that sees the Rousseauianism in Pettit—can be found in Harbour 2012. For a "puzzling" example of what, for republicans, must be a non-dominating act of handcuffing an innocent person, see Talisse 2014, 124. Christian List argues that if we construe republican and liberal freedom modally, there is a strong probability that the robustness of republican freedom—its guaranteeing non-domination across possible worlds— might very well lead to a significant diminishment in its scope. This, List claims, is not a reason to reject freedom as non-domination, but it is a problem that must be resolved. See List 2006.

10. One answer to these questions might be a "supremacy clause": the common good is supreme, and can be enforced against the private interests of some individuals without dominating them. Or the answer might come in a more subtle, indeed Rousseauian form: "It is important to recognize the linkage between the internalization of republican norms and identification, because it reveals that civility is not just a matter of denying the personal self. It is also a matter of letting other identities take over in your person. It is a matter of owning heritages of experience and belief and intention that transcend your personal concerns" (Pettit 1997b, 259). This line of thinking tends toward patriotism and civic-mindedness, so much so that "if we cherish our own citizenship and our own freedom, we have to cherish at the same time the social body in the membership of which that status consists" (Pettit 1997b, 260; cf. Rousseau 1978, 2.7; 4.7; 4.8; 1985, 1–26). The ideal of civic virtue in republican thinking explains, presumably, the primacy of the common good and of the social body as a whole over private interest and the individual. The social body is the condition of possibility for freedom as non-domination, and pursuit of the common good is instrumental to achieving freedom as non-domination. Therein lies its priority: one cannot have freedom as non-domination vis-à-vis the state without the priority of the common good. However, M. Victoria Costa has argued that Pettit does not go far enough in his reliance on norms of civility, and that his neorepublicanism needs supplementation by a non-perfectionist account of personal virtue. See Costa 2009.

11. Norms of reason introduce into Pettit's account a normativity he generally tries to avoid. See Costa 2007, 298–299.

12. Although the context is very different, a similar point is made by Christopher McMahon when he argues that on Pettit's account of freedom as non-domination, any decision made according to proper procedures in a contestatory democracy will be, by definition, non-dominating. See McMahon 2005, 79. Pettit's response to McMahon is that he is misread by him, but to my mind, Pettit ignores one of the central problems McMahon raises, that of determining when someone is free in the sense of non-dominated. Pettit thinks of this as a factual matter because someone is dominated when the power of arbitrary interference by X does not track the avowable interests of, or is uncontrolled by, Y. The problem is that no matter how one construes interests, there are surely multiple interests we all have, many of which are in conflict with one another. Even if a citizen weighs all of their interests and chooses what, on balance, is the most rational interest to pursue, they still "repress" other interests. Even here there is a trick of the "I" and thus unfreedom. But when it comes to the state, the fact that a citizen, even though a policy undermines or constrains or conditions or blocks the satisfaction of one or many of their interests, must admit that they are free, that is non-dominated, simply because that policy satisfies at least one of their interests—a common interest—seems to me to admit that unfreedom is present. See Pettit 2006.

13. I have ignored Pettit's "easier" version of a conflict, where some individuals disagree about matters of less importance than moral and legal questions about such issues as gay marriage. See Pettit 1997b, 198.

14. For example, Harbour 2012.

15. The performative character of the Arendtian self has been discussed in various ways: see, for example, Moruzzi 2000; Dolan 1995; and Villa 1996, 89–94.

16. The term *disclosure* is central to the work of Heidegger and, at least here, Arendt seems to be following Heidegger. In *Being and Time* Heidegger defines "disclose" and "disclosedness" (and more broadly "disclosure") as, respectively, "to lay open" and "the character of having been laid open" (Heidegger 1962, 105; see also Heidegger 1982, 72). Although the concept undergoes modification in later works, the fundamental idea of disclosure remains the same: prior to the particular statements, perceptions, and experiences of an "ontical" region (for example, anthropology, physics, craftsmanship), a prior disclosure must "take place" in light of which the particular beings in that region can be encountered. For example, on a Heideggerian account, modern physical theory could emerge only on the basis of an understanding of the world and the objects in the world as a set of temporally and spatially unique objects confronting a knowing, representational subject (that is, a roughly Cartesian ontology). This doesn't make physics a "social construction," on Heidegger's account, but it does mean that physics rests on a prior disclosure of being that emerged in a specific time and place. To disclose is to "lay open" the world, to show the world as being in a specific way.

17. Otanes himself does not describe isonomy in these terms. Rather, Otanes—having lost in his attempt to institute isonomy as a regime—claims that *he* wants neither to rule nor to be ruled: in exchange for not ruling or being able to rule, he and his family

are not ruled. Otanes is granted his request, and thus while he and his family must obey the law, they need not obey the king. The house of Otanes is the only free house in Persia (Herodotus 1998, 3.83).

Arendt's appropriation of isonomy is strange not because she misreads Otanes—Arendt often creatively misreads the canon—but in the specifics of her misreading (see, for example, the discussion of isonomy in Vlastos 1953; and Monoson 2000, 33–37). The term *isonomy* also makes an important appearance in the famous Attic drinking tune "Song of Harmodious" (see, for example, Jones 2014; and Vlastos 1953, 339–344). Isonomy, Otanes claims, *is* the rule of the many under equality before the law and government by lot, not a condition of no-rule (Herodotus 1998, 3.80). In other words, isonomy is not, as Arendt claims, a condition of neither ruling nor being ruled, but Athenian democracy, which is, a form of rule. Otanes is, in fact, granted a life under a condition of no rule—neither ruling nor being ruled—insofar as he *withdraws* from the political. His desire neither to rule nor to be ruled leads him to leave the sphere of politics. And yet, Arendt takes isonomy to be, and to be a desirable, structure of "rule" for the political sphere. Moreover, it is unclear how Otanes and his family can be bound to obey the law but not bound to obey the king—unless, of course, law and politics are distinct. This is, to be sure, Arendt's position. But given the already apparent theoretical difficulties of imagining a political society in which isonomy "ruled," there are many problems ahead.

It is easy to criticize Arendt for her misreadings of traditional texts, but she has a reason for what she is doing. Arendt accepts the Heideggerian and Benjaminian claim that the tradition of western thought is broken, and thus we can no longer simply accept the claims of the past as they have been handed down to us over two millennia. Rather, we need to "rescue" the fragments of the tradition, read classic texts with new eyes, and try to recover what is essential in them, what essential experience they mark or reveal. If one wants to criticize Arendt's misreadings of the tradition, then one should begin by arguing against her two central claims: (1) the western tradition, starting with Marx, Kierkegaard, and Nietzsche and ending with the horrors of the 20th century, is irrevocably broken; and (2) the proper response to that break is to read *autrement*. I am sympathetic to claim 1 and wary of claim 2. For Arendt's own "method" of reading, see her essay on Walter Benjamin in Arendt 1983. For her discussion of the break in the tradition, see the first few chapters of Arendt 1993.

18. Andreas Kalyvas argues that Arendt's later work on the will sets up the possibility of reconstructing a theory of decision in her work. However, what Kalyvas has in mind is not the decision making and enforcement of a political body but the relationship between the willing and the Acting subject, where the former is, for Arendt, usually anti-political and the latter exists only when the will does not control Action. Kalyvas' argument rests on the idea that Arendt herself equated freedom as such with political freedom, which is a problematic identification. See Kalyvas 2004.

19. A good discussion and critical defense of Arendt's theory of council democracy can be found in Sitton 1987.

20. Arendt even suggests, in the last few pages of *On Revolution*, that it would be fine to have a political space occupied by a self-selected group of individuals who enter

the political because of a felt need to engage in the happiness of free public discussion, rather than any desire to rule (Arendt 1965, 281–284). Arendt appears to be fine with this, even recognizing that her political would put an end to general suffrage, although not the openness of the political to all.

CHAPTER 5

1. Derrida might be to blame for some of this because, as Paul Patton rightly argues, Derrida failed to engage contemporary accounts of democracy, specifically the liberal tradition that dominates analytic political philosophy. Had Derrida taken Rawls as seriously as Aristotle or Hegel, then perhaps political philosophers would have had no choice but to respond to a "deconstruction" of Rawls' work. See Patton 2007. For a good deconstructive reading of Rawls that affirms the Rawlsian project as an essential feature of a deconstructive approach to justice, see Bankovsky 2012.

2. This is an issue that Rawls does not address in his reply to Habermas.

3. This is the place to emphasize the important work of Charles Mills, whose work I came to, unfortunately, only after writing this chapter. My argument here is in line with Mills' persistent attempts to show the failure of Rawls (and other liberals) to take seriously the political system of white supremacy that has underwritten the modern world and much philosophical reflection on that world. See Mills 1997; 2017.

4. This part of Chapter 5 follows a line of argument parallel to a discussion in Davis 2011, 211–214. Davis' argument has shaped my thinking on this score.

5. This is a point powerfully made by, among others, Bernard Williams. See Williams 1985.

6. Derrida's commitment to law as the privileged institution for rendering justice (as well as a few other unconditional acts such as hospitality and forgiveness) can be seen in Derrida 1994, 83–85; 2001a, 22; 2005, 150; see also Beardsworth 2005.

7. My argument here is just about the opposite of Christophe Menke's reading of Derrida's "Force of Law" (Menke 2005). Menke wants to argue, first, that justice is deconstructible. This Derrida explicitly denies: "Justice in itself, if such a thing exists, outside or beyond law, is not deconstructible. No more than deconstruction itself, if such a thing exists. *Deconstruction is justice*" (Derrida 2002, 243). Derrida's hesitations about the existence of justice "in itself" are not meant to inform us that there is only a deconstructible form of justice, thus that justice *is* deconstructible. Derrida is simply being Derrida: if to exist is, following Kant, to be posited, positioned, present to perception, then justice does *not* exist because, as we will see, justice is *never* present. It is perhaps for that very reason that justice is not deconstructible. Now, it may be that Richard Rorty is right to call Derrida's claim that justice is undeconstructible, an experience of the impossible, and so on, "pointless hype," but that is different from claiming that, on Derrida's own account, justice is deconstructible (see Mouffe 1996, 41–42). Menke also argues that justice should *not* be understood as unrealizable, an understanding that he claims Derrida explicitly holds, although the evidence for this is invisible to me. Finally, Menke argues that justice should be understood as a force that makes law as justice possible but also interrupts law as justice, hence makes it

impossible. This is a more complicated issue, addressed in the following note. See Menke 2005, 602, 607.

8. Derrida here and elsewhere in "Force of Law" means this: justice is *without* force and thus law is necessary to enforce justice, to make justice effective, to realize justice. Menke argues that justice not only has force thanks to which justice can make law possible at the same time that it makes law impossible, but further that the force of justice is the "force of the normative" (Menke 2005, 607). There is something to this idea because the term *force* in Derrida's work often does play the double role of making possible and impossible at the same time. For example, in "Force and Signification"—a deconstruction of structuralist literary criticism—the term *force* is associated with creative power, quality, intensity, temporal rupture, *différance*, that which is other to language but makes language what it is; and is opposed to form, structure, teleology, preformationism, entelechy, and so on (Derrida 1978b, 3–30). Later, in "Signature, Event, Context," force takes on related associations. Written signs carry a force that "breaks with its context," a "breaking force [*force de rupture*]" that is the "very structure of the written text" (Derrida 1988, 9). Moreover, Derrida suggests that, at times, J. L. Austin substituted the "value of force, of difference of force (*illocutionary* or *perlocutionary* force)" for the opposition between true and false (Derrida 1988, 13). He adds that this is a distinctly Nietzschean move (Nietzsche is discussed at the end of "Force and Signification" as well). Derrida's Nietzsche is, among other things, a thinker of force and the difference of forces as well as force as difference, a line of thought inherited, I suspect, from Deleuze's *Nietzsche and Philosophy*, published in 1962 (see, for example, Deleuze 1983, 3–8, 39–44, 49–55; Derrida 2001b, 192–195).

Justice, in "Force of Law," does carry some of these connotations of force, but contrary to Menke, justice does *not* make law possible. Menke crucially misreads Derrida. The passage in "Force of Law" that Menke turns to for his claim that justice is the force that makes law (im)possible is not a discussion of justice as Derrida understand the term, but as Pascal understands the term, specifically "justice—in the sense of *droit* (right or law)" (Menke 2005, 607; Derrida 2002, 241). Justice doesn't make law because the *coup de force*, the performative force that makes law possible, is "neither just nor unjust": justice is absolutely heterogeneous to law even though law acts in the name of justice and justice demands that law make justice effective (Derrida 2002, 241). Justice demands that law enforce justice because justice *has no force*. If justice had force it would not need law. Worse, if justice were to make its phenomenal appearance in the world unmediated by law, we would have Walter Benjamin's divine justice, and that, for Derrida, is bad news.

9. That Derrida departs from the tradition in this sense does not mean he departs from the tradition entirely. See Vernon 2010. Derrida is also inheriting a Kantian tradition and, seemingly, a Jewish moral tradition, albeit these inheritances are inflected both through Pascal and through phenomenology and Levinas.

10. Derrida's early discussion of the Kantian Idea in his interpretation of Husserl's "Origin of Geometry" is helpful here. In the few pages Derrida devotes to the "Idea in the Kantian sense," we see many of the themes that shape the discussion of the Idea of justice.

For example, justice itself, as Idea, is "operative" rather than "thematic," that is, the form of the Idea can be phenomenologically intuited but not any content, and thus the Idea "is the basis on which a phenomenology is set up" (Derrida 1978a, 141). In other words, the Idea is not, as in Kant, simply (or at all) a concept that regulates our cognition, but (or also) that which opens the infinite task of science, mathematics, and philosophy as well as the formal structure of intentionality as such: without the formal Idea of, say, justice, concrete justice could not be experienced, be striven for, or be the responsibility of a finite, concrete, subject. A second key difference from Kant is that the Idea, for Husserl, is an "ideation" that constitutes an object, the Idea, as a creation. Ideas are not what Reason *discovers* through its need to think the unconditional, but what consciousness creates. This makes the constitutive act of creating the Idea "more historical" (Derrida 1978a, 135). The Idea in Husserl—and this goes for Derrida too, I believe—is not located in some *topos ouranios* outside of history, but is itself the historical event that opens or constitutes history as such. This is the paradox or aporia Husserl tries to think through and Derrida thinks with: the condition of possibility of history is not something ahistorical, atemporal, but is itself temporal, historical, and thus impure, contaminated by the very "thing" it makes possible. For the whole discussion see Derrida 1978a, 134–141.

11. See Critchley 1999, 12. For the relevant texts in Levinas as well as helpful secondary criticism, see Levinas 1969, especially 72–101,194–201; Derrida 1978b, especially 114–117, 126–131, 146–153; 1999; De Vries 2002, chap. 2, especially 149–187; 2005, 373–386, and chap. 9.

12. Derrida notes the connection between his argument in "Force of Law" and his analysis of the gift in *Given Time: I. Counterfeit Money* (Derrida 2002, 235, 254, 257; 1992). As readers of Derrida have learned to say, the conditions of possibility of the gift are the conditions of impossibility of the gift (Derrida 1992, 1–34). If justice is, to borrow a traditional phrase, "to give each what they are due," then the gift of justice must necessarily be an impossible gift. The interpretation of Derridean justice in terms of the gift was suggested to me by Paola Marrati's interpretation of the gift in Derrida (Marrati 2005, 190–197).

13. However, Derrida—in a very suggestive set of remarks—calls the reasonable (as opposed to the rational) the "wager" that some transaction exists between what, in "Force of Law," Derrida calls justice and law (Derrida 2005, 118–140, 151).

14. Derrida's hesitation toward the Kantian Idea is that it involves a temporality at odds with the temporality of justice, with justice's *à-venir*. As one can see most clearly in Kant's essays on perpetual peace and a cosmopolitan universal history, Ideas are never finally reached, but only asymptotically approached. The Idea opens up a history, but it is a history of waiting and progress. Yet, "justice, however unpresentable it remains, does not wait. It is that which must not wait. To be direct, simple, and brief, let us say this: a just decision is always required *immediately*, right away, as quickly as possible" (Derrida 2002, 255). The *à-venir* is not a "future present," T2 rather than T1, but a "to-come" that is, structurally, never a present moment. The *à-venir* is not the *avenir*.

15. I can't help thinking that Derrida is here alluding to the different "formulas" of the categorical imperative in Kant's *Groundwork*, which, nonetheless, are somehow meant to be simply different versions of the same thing.

16. Christophe Menke's argument that the third aporia cannot be explained in terms of a "practical conflict—a conflict in the practical requirements of a just decision"—seems wrong to me (Menke 2005, 600). The judge faces two requirements: first, more knowledge, more time, more evidence, more reasoning, interpretation, and the like; and second, as U.S. constitutional law has it, the defendant's right to a speedy trial—justice cannot wait, it must be rendered now. That being said, Menke is right that there are (at least) two possible ways to read the three aporias: as the conflict between normative requirements on judges and as the asymmetry between the demands of justice and practice itself.

17. I have not discussed the second half of Derrida's essay—a deconstructive reading of Benjamin's essay "Critique of Violence"—because it would require a separate chapter. However, Derrida's reading of Benjamin is consonant with the claims he makes in the first part of the essay, and as I read his critique, Derrida is attracted to "Critique of Violence" because Benjamin recognizes the singularity of justice and the a-legitimacy of a necessarily violent, positive legal order. What Derrida rightly fears in Benjamin is the messianic, apocalyptic implications of a singular divine justice that destroys law. This justice, as Benjamin himself knew, might be unrecognizable by human beings, or worse, indistinguishable from the most unjust, horrific violence. For Derrida, a singular justice must be instantiated in law, if for no other reason than to prevent the worst. Thus, the reading of "Force of Law" by McCormick cannot be right (see McCormick 2001; Corson 2001).

18. Specifically, Derrida emphasizes two aspects of Kant's moral thought. First, Derrida follows Kant's insistence that we can never know if we have truly acted morally because we can never finally know whether we have acted out of conformity to the law or out of duty to the law, or whether we have acted freely (Kant 1964, 4:458). Second, and for this reason, Derrida must also share some version of Kant's insistence on the "moving force of the pure representation of virtue" as "the most powerful incentive to the good" (Kant 1996, 5:152). In Kant the emphasis on purity of virtue and motive in morality accompanies, or is inculcated by, at least in part, ethical exercises or experiences in which shame and humiliation are involved. For example, "respect for the moral law" has a humiliating effect on feeling, albeit one in which the "lowering of pretensions to moral self-esteem—that is, humiliation on the sensible side—is an elevation of the moral—that is, practical—esteem for the law itself on the intellectual side" (Kant 1996, 5:78). Or, in the *Metaphysics of Morals*, in a synopsis of a "moral catechism": "It is the shamefulness of vice, not its harmfulness (to the agent himself), that must be emphasized above all" (Kant 1996, 6:483). Although Derrida discusses neither ethical learning nor moral affects, one suspects that "negative" affects might emerge in Derrida's ethics.

19. The internal structural link between justice and law would fall along the lines of the relation, discussed previously, between the "Idea in the Kantian sense" and the phenomenological experience that the Idea "makes possible": no experience of law without the non-phenomenological aporetic experience of the Idea of justice.

20. Anaximander's fragment is also the subject of a long essay by Heidegger (Heidegger 1974), but suffice it to say that Heidegger quickly removes any trace of "merely"

judicial or legal or ethical meanings in his translation. Derrida briefly engages Heidegger's essay in Derrida 1994, 23–29.

CONCLUSION

1. The classic texts here are Miller 1939 and 1956 and Bercovitch 1978, although there is a great deal of recent work on the jeremiad in American literature. I discuss these issues in the context of Arendt's *On Revolution* in Arnold 2014.

BIBLIOGRAPHY

Adorno, Theodor. 1973. *Negative Dialectics*. Translated by E. B. Ashton. New York: Continuum.

Affeldt, Steven G. 1998. "The Ground of Mutuality: Criteria, Judgment, and Intelligibility in Stephen Mulhall and Stanley Cavell." *European Journal of Philosophy* 6 (1): 1–31.

Agamben, Giorgio. 1998. *Homo Sacer*. Translated by Daniel Heller-Roazen. Palo Alto: Stanford University Press.

Akehurst, Thomas L. 2008. "The Nazi Tradition: The Analytic Critique of Continental Philosophy in Mid-century Britain." *History of European Ideas* 34:548–557.

Aquinas, Thomas. 2002. *Political Writings*. Edited by R. W. Dyson. Cambridge: Cambridge University Press.

Arendt, Hannah. 1965. *On Revolution*. New York: Viking Press.

Arendt, Hannah. 1968. *The Origins of Totalitarianism*. San Diego: Harcourt Brace.

Arendt, Hannah. 1969. *On Violence*. San Diego: Harcourt Brace.

Arendt, Hannah. 1972. *Crises of the Republic*. San Diego: Harcourt Brace.

Arendt, Hannah. 1978a. *The Life of the Mind: Thinking*. San Diego: Harcourt Brace.

Arendt, Hannah. 1978b. *The Life of the Mind: Willing*. San Diego: Harcourt Brace.

Arendt, Hannah. 1983. *Men in Dark Times*. San Diego: Harcourt Brace.

Arendt, Hannah. 1993. *Between Past and Future*. New York: Penguin Books.

Arendt, Hannah. 1998. *The Human Condition*. Chicago: University of Chicago Press.

Arendt, Hannah. 2005. *The Promise of Politics*. New York: Schocken Books.

Aristotle. 1976. *Ethics*. Translated by J.A.K. Thomson. London: Penguin Books.

Aristotle. 1992. *Politics*. Translated by T. A. Sinclair. London: Penguin Books.

Arnold, Jeremy. 2012. "A Response to Martel's '*Amo: Volu ut sis*: Love, Willing, and Arendt's Reluctant Embrace of Sovereignty.'" *Philosophy and Social Criticism* 38:609–617.

Arnold, Jeremy. 2014. "Arendt's Jeremiad: Reading *On Revolution* in a Time of Decline." *Review of Politics* 76:361–387.

Arnold, Jeremy. 2017. *State Violence and Moral Horror.* Albany: State University of New York Press.

Austin, J. L. 1975. *How to Do Things with Words.* Cambridge: Harvard University Press.

Austin, J. L. 1979. *Philosophical Papers.* Oxford: Oxford University Press.

Bailyn, Bernard. 1992. *The Ideological Origins of the American Revolution.* Cambridge, MA: Harvard University Press.

Bankovsky, Miriam. 2012. *Perfecting Justice in Rawls, Habermas and Honneth.* London: Bloomsbury.

Barber, Benjamin. 2006. "The Politics of Political Science: "Value-free" Theory and the Wolin–Strauss Dust-Up of 1963." *American Political Science Review* 100:539–545.

Barry, Brian. 1995. "John Rawls and the Search for Stability." *Ethics* 105:874–915.

Bavister-Gould, Alex. 2013. "Bernard Williams: Political Realism and the Limits of Legitimacy." *European Journal of Philosophy* 21:593–610.

Beaney, Michael. 2013. *The Oxford Handbook of the History of Analytic Philosophy.* Oxford: Oxford University Press.

Beardsworth, Richard. 2005. "In Memorium Jacques Derrida: The Power of Reason." *Theory and Event* 8 (1). doi:10.1353/tae.2005.0001

Bearn, Gordon C. F. 1998. "Sounding Serious: Cavell and Derrida." *Representations* 63:65–92.

Benhabib, Seyla. 2003. *The Reluctant Modernism of Hannah Arendt.* Lanham: Rowman & Littlefield.

Benjamin, Walter. 1978. *Reflections.* Edited by Peter Demetz. New York: Schocken Books.

Bennett, Jane. 2010. *Vibrant Matter.* Durham: Duke University Press.

Bentham, Jeremy. 1988. *The Principles of Morals and Legislation.* Amherst: Prometheus Books.

Berg-Schlosser, Dirk. 2006. "Political Science in Europe: Diversity, Excellence, Relevance." *European Political Science* 5:163–170.

Bercovitch, Sacvan. 1978. *The American Jeremiad.* Madison: University of Wisconsin Press.

Bergson, Henri. 1992. *The Creative Mind.* Translated by Mabelle L. Anderson. New York: Citadel Press.

Berlin, Isaiah. 1969. *Four Essays on Liberty.* Oxford: Oxford University Press.

Berlin, Isaiah. 1999. *Concepts and Categories.* Princeton: Princeton University Press.

Bevir, Mark, and Jason Blakely. 2010. "Analytic Ethics in the Central Period." *History of European Ideas* 37:249–256.

Botwinick, A., and W. E. Connolly, eds. 2001. *Democracy and Vision.* Princeton: Princeton University Press.

Buck-Morss, Susan. 1977. *The Origin of Negative Dialectics.* New York: Free Press.

Buckle, Stephen. 2004. "Analytic Philosophy and Continental Philosophy: The Campbell Thesis Revised." *British Journal for the History of Philosophy* 12:111–150.

Bufacchi, Vittorio, ed. 2009. *Violence: A Philosophical Anthology.* New York: Palgrave Macmillan.

Campbell, Richard. 2001. "The Covert Metaphysics of the Clash Between 'Analytic' and 'Continental' Philosophy." *British Journal for the History of Philosophy* 9:341–359.

Carnap, Rudolf. 1959. "The Elimination of Metaphysics Through the Logical Analysis of Language." In A. J. Ayer, ed., *Logical Positivism*. New York: Free Press.

Carter, Ian. 2000. "A Critique of Freedom as Non-domination." *The Good Society* 9:43–46.

Carter, Ian. 2008. "How Are Power and Unfreedom Related?" In Cecile Laborde and John Maynor, eds., *Republicanism and Political Theory*, 58–82. Malden: Blackwell..

Cavell, Stanley. 1969. *Must We Mean What We Say?* Cambridge: Cambridge University Press.

Cavell, Stanley. 1988. *In Quest of the Ordinary*. Chicago: University of Chicago Press.

Cavell, Stanley. 1989. *This New Yet Unapproachable America*. Albuquerque: Living Batch Press.

Cavell, Stanley. 1990. *Conditions Handsome and Unhandsome*. Chicago: Chicago University Press.

Cavell, Stanley. 1992. *The Senses of Walden*. Chicago: University of Chicago Press.

Cavell, Stanley. 1999. *The Claim of Reason*. New York: Oxford University Press.

Cavell, Stanley. 2004. *Cities of Words*. Cambridge, MA: Harvard University Press.

Cavell, Stanley, Cora Diamond, John McDowell, Ian Hacking, and Cary Wolfe. 2008. *Philosophy and Animal Life*. New York: Columbia University Press.

Christiano, Thomas. 2008. *The Constitution of Equality*. Oxford: Oxford University Press.

Christiano, Thomas. 2009. "Debate: Estlund on Democratic Authority." *Journal of Political Philosophy* 17:228–240.

Coady, C.A.J. 2008. *Morality and Political Violence*. Cambridge: Cambridge University Press.

Coates, Ta-Nehisi. 2014. "The Case for Reparations." *The Atlantic*, June 2014. https://www.theatlantic.com/magazine/archive/2014/06/the-case-for-reparations/361631/

Connolly, William E. 1987. *Politics and Ambiguity*. Madison: University of Wisconsin Press.

Connolly, William E. 1995. *The Ethos of Pluralization*. Minneapolis: University of Minnesota Press.

Connolly, William E. 2000. *Why I Am Not a Secularist*. Minneapolis: University of Minnesota Press.

Connolly, William E. 2005. *Pluralism*. Durham: Duke University Press.

Connolly, William E. 2008. *Capitalism and Christianity, American Style*. Durham: Duke University Press.

Corson, Ben. 2001. "Transcending Violence in Derrida: A Reply to John McCormick." *Political Theory* 29 (6): 866–875.

Costa, M. Victoria. 2007. "Freedom as Non-Domination, Normativity, and Indeterminacy." *Journal of Value Inquiry* 41:291–307.

Costa, M. Victoria. 2009. "Neo-republicanism, Freedom as Non-domination, and Citizen Virtue." *Politics, Philosophy & Economics* 8:401–419.

Cover, Robert. 1986. "Violence and the Word." *Yale Law Journal* 95:1601–1629.

Critchley, Simon. 1999. *The Ethics of Deconstruction*. Edinburgh: Edinburgh University Press.

Critchley, Simon. 2001. *Continental Philosophy: A Very Short Introduction*. Oxford: Oxford University Press.

D'Agostini, Franca. 2001. "From a Continental Point of View: The Role of Logic in the Continental/Analytic Divide." *International Journal of Philosophical Studies* 9:349–367.

Dascal, Marcelo. 2001. "How Rational Can a Polemic Across the Analytic-Continental 'Divide' Be?" *International Journal of Philosophical Studies* 9:313–339.

Davidson, Donald. 2001. *Essays on Actions and Events*. Oxford: Oxford University Press.

Davis, Ryan W. 2011. "Justice: Metaphysical After All?" *Ethical Theory and Moral Practice* 14:207–222.

Deleuze, Gilles. 1983. *Nietzsche and Philosophy*. Translated by Hugh Tomlinson. New York: Columbia University Press.

Deleuze, Gilles. 1994. *Difference and Repetition*. Translated by Paul Patton. New York: Columbia University Press.

Derrida, Jacques. 1978a. *Edmund Husserl's "Origin of Geometry": An Introduction*. Translated by John P. Leavy Jr. Lincoln: University of Nebraska Press.

Derrida, Jacques. 1978b. *Writing and Difference*. Translated by Alan Bass. Chicago: University of Chicago Press.

Derrida, Jacques. 1986. "Declarations of Independence." *New Political Science* 7:7–15.

Derrida, Jacques. 1988. *Limited Inc*. Translated by Samuel Weber. Evanston: Northwestern University Press.

Derrida, Jacques. 1992. *Given Time: 1. Counterfeit Money*. Translated by Peggy Kamuf. Chicago: University of Chicago Press.

Derrida, Jacques. 1994. *Specters of Marx*. Translated by Peggy Kamuf. London: Routledge.

Derrida, Jacques. 1995. *The Gift of Death*. Translated by David Wills. Chicago: University of Chicago Press.

Derrida, Jacques. 1999. *Adieu*. Translated by Pascale-Anne Brault and Michael Naas. Stanford: Stanford University Press.

Derrida, Jacques. 2000. *Of Hospitality*. Translated by Rachel Bowlby. Stanford: Stanford University Press.

Derrida, Jacques. 2001a. *Cosmopolitanism and Forgiveness*. Translated by Mark Dooley and Michael Hughes. London: Routledge.

Derrida, Jacques. 2001b. *The Work of Mourning*. Translated by Pascale-Anne Brault and Michael Naas. Chicago: University of Chicago Press.

Derrida, Jacques. 2002. "Force of Law." In Gil Anidjar, ed., *Acts of Religion*. New York: Routledge.

Derrida, Jacques. 2005. *Rogues*. Translated by Pascale-Anne Brault and Michael Naas. Palo Alto: Stanford University Press.

de Vries, Hent. 2002. *Religion and Violence*. Baltimore: Johns Hopkins University Press.

de Vries, Hent. 2005. *Minimal Theologies*. Translated by Geoffrey Hale. Baltimore: Johns Hopkins University Press.

de Vries, Hent. 2006. "From 'Ghost in the Machine' to 'Spiritual Automaton': Philosophical Meditation in Wittgenstein, Cavell, and Levinas." *International Journal of Philosophy and Religion* 60:77–97.

Diamond, Cora. 2003. "The Difficulty of Reality and the Difficulty of Philosophy. *Partial Answers* 1:2:1–26.

DiSalvo, Daniel. 2013. "The Politics of Studying Politics: Political Science Since the 1960s." *Society* 50:132–139.

Dolan, Frederick. 1995. "Political Action and the Unconscious: Arendt and Lacan on Decentering the Subject." *Political Theory* 23:330–352.

Donahue, Thomas J., and Paulina Ochoa Espejo. 2016. "The Analytical-Continental Divide: Styles of Dealing with Political Problems." *European Journal of Political Theory* 15:138–154.

Douglass, Robin. 2016. "Hobbes and Political Realism." *European Journal of Political Theory*, 1–20. Online First. doi: 10.1177/1474885116677481

Dreyfus, Hubert. 1991. *Being-in-the-World*. Cambridge, MA: MIT Press.

Dworkin, Ronald. 1986. *Law's Empire*. Cambridge, MA: Harvard University Press.

Eckstein, Harry. 1956. "Political Theory and the Study of Politics: A Report from a Conference." *American Political Science Review* 50:475–487.

Eldridge, Richard. 1986. "The Normal and the Normative: Wittgenstein's Legacy, Kripke, and Cavell." *Philosophy and Phenomenological Research* 46 (4): 555–575.

Erman, Eva, and Nick Möller. 2015. "Political Legitimacy in the Real Normative World: The Priority of Morality and the Autonomy of the Political." *British Journal of Political Science* 45:215–233.

Estlund, David. 2009a. "Debate: On Christiano's *The Constitution of Equality*." *Journal of Political Philosophy* 17:241–252.

Estlund, David. 2009b. *Democratic Authority: A Philosophical Framework*. Princeton: Princeton University Press.

Farr, James. 1988. "The History of Political Science." *American Journal of Political Science* 32:1175–1195.

Fenves, Peter. 2001. "Derrida and History: Some Questions Derrida Pursues in his Early Writings." In Tom Cohen, ed., *Jacques Derrida and the Humanities: A Critical Reader*, 271–295. Cambridge: Cambridge University Press.

Flathman, Richard E. 1980. *The Practice of Political Authority*. Chicago: University of Chicago Press.

Flathman, Richard E. 1992. *Willful Liberalism*. Ithaca: Cornell University Press.

Flathman, Richard E. 1993. *Thomas Hobbes: Skepticism, Individuality and Chastened Politics*. Newbury Park: Sage.

Flathman, Richard E. 1998. *Reflections of a Would-be Anarchist*. Minneapolis: University of Minnesota Press.

Flathman, Richard E. 2003. *Freedom and Its Conditions*. New York: Routledge.

Flathman, Richard E. 2010. "In and Out of the Ethical: The Realist Liberalism of Bernard Williams." *Contemporary Political Theory* 9:77–98.

Foucault, Michel. 1988. *Madness and Civilization*. Translated by Richard Howard. New York: Random House.

Friedman, Michael. 2000. *The Parting of the Ways*. Chicago and LaSalle: Open Court.

Gadamer, Hans-Georg. 1998. *Truth and Method*. Translated by Joel Weinsheimer and Donald G. Marshall. New York: Continuum.

Galison, Peter. 1990. "Aufbau/Bauhaus: Logical Positivism and Architectural Modernism." *Critical Inquiry* 16:709–752.

Galston, William A. 2010. "Realism in Political Theory." *European Journal of Political Theory* 9:385–411.

Gasché, Rodolphe. 1986. *The Tain of the Mirror*. Cambridge, MA: Harvard University Press.

Gasché, Rodolphe. 1994. *Inventions of Difference*. Cambridge, MA: Harvard University Press.

Gaus, Gerald. 1996. *Justificatory Liberalism*. Oxford: Oxford University Press.

Geuss, Raymond. 2005. *Outside Ethics*. Princeton: Princeton University Press.

Geuss, Raymond. 2008. *Philosophy and Real Politics*. Princeton: Princeton University Press.

Geuss, Raymond. 2010. *Politics and the Imagination*. Princeton: Princeton University Press.

Glendinning, Simon, ed. 1999. *The Edinburgh Encyclopaedia of Continental Philosophy*. London: Routledge.

Glock, Hans-Johann. 2008. *What Is Analytic Philosophy?* Cambridge: Cambridge University Press.

Gordon, Peter E. 2010. *Continental Divide: Heidegger, Cassirer, Davos*. Cambridge, MA: Harvard University Press.

Gorr, Michael. 2005. "*A Theory of Freedom: From the Psychology to the Politics of Agency* by Philip Pettit." *Philosophy and Phenomenological Research* 70:498–501.

Grant, J. Tobin. 2005. "What Divides Us? The Image and Organization of Political Science." *Political Science and Politics* 38 (3): 379–386.

Gunnell, John G. 1988. "American Political Science, Liberalism, and the Invention of Political Theory." *American Political Science Review* 82:71–87.

Gunnell, John G. 2006. "Dislocated Rhetoric: The Anomaly of Political Theory." *Journal of Politics* 68:771–782.

Gunnell, John G. 2010. "Professing Political Theory." *Political Research Quarterly* 63:674–679.

Habermas, Jürgen. 1975. *Legitimation Crisis*. Translated by Thomas McCarthy. Boston: Beacon Press.

Habermas, Jürgen. 1983. *Philosophical-Political Profiles*. Translated by Frederick G. Lawrence. Cambridge, MA: MIT Press.

Habermas, Jürgen. 1990. *The Philosophical Discourse of Modernity*. Translated by Frederick G. Lawrence. Cambridge, MA: MIT Press.

Habermas, Jürgen. 1995. "Reconciliation Through the Public Use of Reason: Remarks on John Rawls's Political Liberalism." *Journal of Philosophy* 92:109–131.

Habermas, Jürgen. 1996. *Between Facts and Norms*. Translated by William Rehg. Cambridge, MA: MIT Press.

Hall, Edward. 2015. "Bernard Williams and the Basic Legitimation Demand: A Defence." *Political Studies* 63:466–480.

Hammer, Espen. 2002. *Stanley Cavell: Skepticism, Subjectivity and the Ordinary*. Cambridge: Polity Press.

Haney, Craig. 2002. "The Psychological Impact of Incarceration: Implications for Post-Prison Adjustment." In *From Prison to Home: The Effect of Incarceration and Reentry on Children, Families, and Communities*, 77–92. Papers from the "Prison to Home" project.

Haney, Craig. 2003. "Mental Health Issues in Long-Term Solitary and 'Supermax' Confinement." *Crime & Delinquency* 49:124–156.

Harbour, Michael David. 2012. "Non-domination and Pure Negative Liberty." *Politics, Philosophy & Economics* 11:186–205. Hart, H.L.A. 1955. "Are There Any Natural Rights?" *Philosophical Review* 64:175–191.

Hart, H.L.A. 1961. *The Concept of Law*. Oxford: Oxford University Press.

Hartz, Louis. 1991. *The Liberal Tradition in America*. Orlando: Harcourt.

Hegel, G.W.F. 1977. *Phenomenology of Spirit*. Translated by A. V. Miller. Oxford: Oxford University Press.

Hegel, G.W.F. 1997. *Reason in History*. Translated by Robert S. Hartman. Upper Saddle River: Prentice-Hall.

Heidegger, Martin. 1962. *Being and Time*. Translated by John Macquarrie and Edward Robinson. San Francisco: Harper & Row.

Heidegger, Martin. 1974. "The Anaximander Fragment." Translated by David Ferrell Krell. *Arion* 1:576–626.

Heidegger, Martin. 1982. *The Basic Problems of Phenomenology*. Translated by Albert Hofstadter. Bloomington: Indiana University Press.

Herodotus. 1998. *The Histories*. Translated by Robin Waterfield. Oxford: Oxford University Press.

Hobbes, Thomas. 1997. *Leviathan*. New York: Norton.

Honig, Bonnie. 1991. "Declarations of Independence: Arendt and Derrida on the Problem of Founding a Republic." *American Political Science Review* 85:97–113.

Honig, Bonnie. 1993. *Political Theory and the Displacement of Politics*. Ithaca: Cornell University Press.

Honig, Bonnie. 2009. *Emergency Politics: Paradox, Law, Democracy*. Princeton: Princeton University Press.

Horton, John. 2010. "Realism, Liberal Moralism, and a Political Theory of Modus Vivendi." *European Journal of Political Theory* 9:431–448.

Horton, John. 2012. "Political Legitimacy, Justice and Consent." *Critical Review of International Social and Political Philosophy* 15:129–148.

Jefferson, Thomas. 1984. *Writings*. New York: Library of America.

Jones, Gregory S. 2014. "Voice of the People: Popular Symposia and the Non-elite Origin of the Attic *Skolia*." *Transactions of the American Philological Association* 2:229–262.

Jubb, Robert, and Enzo Rossi. 2015. "Political Norms and Moral Values." *Journal of Philosophical Research* 40:455–458.

Kalyvas, Andreas. 2004. "From the Act to the Decision: Hannah Arendt and the Question of Decisionism." *Political Theory* 32:320–346.

Kant, Immanuel. 1964. *Groundwork of the Metaphysic of Morals*. Translated by H. J. Paton. New York: Harper & Row.

Kant, Immanuel. 1983. *Perpetual Peace and Other Essays*. Translated by Ted Humphrey. Indianapolis: Hackett.

Kant, Immanuel. 1996. *Practical Philosophy*. Translated by Mary J. Gregor. Cambridge: Cambridge University Press.

Kant, Immanuel. 1998. *Critique of Pure Reason*. Translated by Paul Guyer and Allan Wood. Cambridge: Cambridge University Press.

Kaufman-Osborn, Timothy. 2010. "Political Theory as Profession and as Subfield." *Political Research Quarterly* 63:655–673.

Kettler, David. 2006. "The Political Theory Question in Political Science, 1957–1967." *American Political Science Review* 100:531–537.

Klosko, George. 1987. "The Principle of Fairness and Political Obligation." *Ethics* 97:353–362.

Klosko, George. 1993. "Rawls's 'Political Philosophy' and American Democracy." *American Political Science Review* 87:348–359.

Klosko, George. 2004. "Multiple Principles of Political Obligation." *Political Theory* 32:801–824.

Knowles, Dudley. 2003. "A Theory of Freedom: From the Psychology to the Politics of Agency by Philip Pettit." *Philosophical Quarterly* 53 (212): 473–476.

Krause, Sharon. 2012. "Plural Freedom." *Politics & Gender* 8:238–245.

Kripke, Saul. 1981. *Naming and Necessity*. London: Blackwell.

Kropotkin, Peter. 2002. *Anarchism*. Mineola: Dover Books.

Kukathas, Chandran. 2009. "One Cheer for Constantinople: A Comment on Pettit and Skinner on Hobbes and Freedom." *Hobbes Studies* 22:192–198.

Larmore, Charles. 2001. "A Critique of Philip Pettit's Republicanism." *Philosophical Issues* 11:229–243.

Larmore, Charles. 2003. "Liberal and Republican Conceptions of Freedom." *Critical Review of International Social and Political Philosophy* 6:96–119.

Leiter, Brian, and Michael Rosen. 2007. *The Oxford Handbook of Continental Philosophy*. Oxford: Oxford University Press.

Levinas, Emmanuel. 1969. *Totality and Infinity*. Translated by Alphonso Lingis. Pittsburgh: Duquesne University Press.

Levinas, Emmanuel. 1998. *Otherwise Than Being*. Translated by Alphonso Lingis. Pittsburgh: Duquesne University Press.

Levy, Neil. 2003. "Analytic and Continental Philosophy: Explaining the Differences." *Metaphilosophy* 34:284–304.

List, Christian. 2006. "Republican Freedom and the Rule of Law." *Politics, Philosophy & Economics* 5:201–220.

Locke, John. 1988. *Two Treatises of Government*. Cambridge: Cambridge University Press.

Lovett, Francis N. 2001. "Domination: A Preliminary Analysis." *Monist* 84:98–122.

MacIntyre, Alasdair. 1984. *After Virtue*. Notre Dame: Notre Dame University Press.

Magid, Henry M. 1955. "An Approach to the Nature of Political Philosophy." *Journal of Philosophy* 52:29–42.

Markell, Patchen. 2006. "The Rule of the People: Arendt, *Archê*, and Democracy." *American Political Science Review* 100:1–14.

Marrati, Paola. 2005. *Genesis and Trace*. Translated by Simon Sparks. Stanford: Stanford University Press.

Martel, James. 2008. "*Amo: Volo ut sis*: Love, Willing and Arendt's Reluctant Embrace of Sovereignty." *Philosophy and Social Criticism* 34:287–313.

McCormick, John. 2001. "Derrida on Law; or Poststructuralism Gets Serious." *Political Theory* 29 (3): 395–423.

McMahon, Christopher. 2005. "The Indeterminacy of Republican Policy." *Philosophy & Public Affairs* 33:67–93.

Menke, Christophe. 2005. "Ability and Faith: On the Possibility of Justice." Translated by Howard Rouse. *Cardozo Law Review* 27:595–612.

Miller, Fred D., Jr. 2007. *A History of the Philosophy of Law from the Ancient Greeks to the Scholastics*. Dordrecht: Springer.

Miller, Perry. 1939. *The New England Mind: The Seventeenth Century*. Cambridge: Cambridge University.

Miller, Perry. 1956. *Errand into the Wilderness*. New York: Harper Torchbooks.

Mills, Charles. 1997. *The Racial Contract*. Ithaca: Cornell University Press.

Mills, Charles. 2017. *Black Rights/White Wrongs*. New York: Oxford University Press.

Monoson, Sara. 2000. *Plato's Democratic Entanglements*. Princeton: Princeton University Press.

Moruzzi, Norma Claire. 2000. *Speaking Through the Mask*. Ithaca: Cornell University Press.

Mouffe, Chantal. 1996. *Deconstruction and Pragmatism*. London: Routledge.

Mouffe, Chantal. 2005. *The Democratic Paradox*. London: Verso.

Mulhall, Stephen. 1994. *Stanley Cavell: Philosophy's Recounting of the Ordinary*. New York: Oxford University Press.

Mulhall, Stephen. 1997. "Promising, Consent, and Citizenship: Rawls and Cavell on Morality and Politics." *Political Theory* 25 (2): 171–192.

Mulhall, Stephen. 1998. "The Givenness of Grammar: A Reply to Steven Affeldt." *European Journal of Philosophy* 6 (1): 32–44.

Nietzsche, Friedrich. 1974. *The Gay Science*. Translated by Walter Kaufmann. New York: Vintage Books.

Nietzsche, Friedrich. 1989. *Beyond Good and Evil*. Translated by Walter Kaufmann. New York: Vintage Books.

Nino, C. S. 1983. "A Consensual Theory of Punishment." *Philosophy & Public Affairs* 12 (4): 289–306.

Norris, Andrew. 2002. "Political Revisions: Stanley Cavell and Political Philosophy." *Political Theory* (30) 6: 828–851.

Norris, Andrew. 2006. *The Claim to Community*. Palo Alto: Stanford University Press.

Norris, Christopher. 1989. "Philosophy as *Not* Just a Kind of Writing: Derrida and the Claim of Reason." In Reed Way Dasenbrock, ed., *Redrawing the Lines: Analytic Philosophy, Deconstruction, and Literary Theory*, 189–203. Minneapolis: University of Minnesota Press.

Nozick, Robert. 1969. "Coercion." In Sydney Morgenbesser, Patrick Suppes, and Morton White, eds., *Philosophy, Science, and Method: Essays in Honor of Ernest Nagel*, 440–472. New York: St. Martin's Press.

Owen, David. 1999. "Cultural Diversity and the Conversation of Justice: Reading Cavell on Political Voice and the Expression of Consent." *Political Theory* 27 (5): 579–596.

Passerin D'Entrèves, M. 1994. *The Political Philosophy of Hannah Arendt*. London: Routledge.

Patton, Paul. 2007. "Derrida's Engagement with Political Philosophy." In Mark Bevir, Jill Hargis, and Sara Rushing, eds., *Histories of Postmodernism*, 149–169. New York: Routledge.

Patton, Paul. 2010. *Deleuzian Concepts: Philosophy, Colonization, Politics*. Palo Alto: Stanford University Press.

Pettit, Philip. 1995. "The Virtual Reality of 'Homo Economicus.'" *Monist* 78 (3): 308–329.

Pettit, Philip. 1996. *The Common Mind*. Oxford: Oxford University Press.

Pettit, Philip. 1997a. "Republican Theory and Criminal Punishment." *Utilitas* 9:59–79.

Pettit, Philip. 1997b. *Republicanism*. Oxford: Oxford University Press.

Pettit, Philip. 2001a. *A Theory of Freedom*. Oxford: Oxford University Press.

Pettit, Philip. 2001b. "Two Sources of Morality." *Social Philosophy and Policy* 18:102–128.

Pettit, Philip. 2004. "The Common Good." In Keith Dowding, Robert E. Goodin, and Carole Pateman, eds., *Justice and Democracy: Essays for Brian Barry*, 150–169. New York: Cambridge University Press.

Pettit, Philip. 2006. "The Determinacy of Republican Policy: A Reply to McMahon." *Philosophy & Public Affairs* 34:275–283.

Pettit, Philip. 2007a. "Joining the Dots." In Geoffrey Brennan, Robert Goodin, Frank Jackson, and Michael Smith, eds., *Common Minds: Themes from the Philosophy of Philip Pettit*, 215–338. Oxford: Oxford University Press.

Pettit, Philip. 2007b. "Neuroscience and Agent Control." In Don Ross, David Spurrett, Harold Kincaid, and G. Lynn Stephens, eds., *Distributed Cognition and the Will*, 77–91. Cambridge, MA: MIT Press.

Pettit, Philip. 2011. "The Instability of Freedom as Non-interference: The Case of Isaiah Berlin." *Ethics* 121:693–716.

Pettit, Philip. 2012. *On the People's Terms*. Cambridge: Cambridge University Press.

Pettit, Philip. 2013. "Two Republican Traditions." In Andreas Niederberger and Philipp Schink, eds., *Republican Democracy: Liberty, Law and Politics*, 169–204. Edinburgh: Edinburgh University Press.

Pettit, Philip. 2017. "Political Realism Meets Civic Republicanism." *Critical Review of International Social and Political Philosophy* 20 (3): 331–357.

Pettit, Philip, and Michael Smith. 1993. "Practical Unreason." *Mind* 102:53–79.

Pettit, Philip, and Michael Smith. 1996. "Freedom in Belief and Desire." *Journal of Philosophy* 93 (9): 429–449.

Pitkin, Hanna. 1965. "Obligation and Consent—I." *American Political Science Review* 59 (4): 990–999.

Pitkin, Hanna. 1972. *Wittgenstein and Justice*. Berkeley: University of California Press.

Pitkin, Hanna Fenichel. 1981. "Justice: On Relating Private and Public." *Political Theory* 9:327–352.

Pitkin, Hanna Fenichel. 1988. "Are Freedom and Liberty Twins?" *Political Theory* 16:523–552.

Plato. 1968. *The Republic*. Translated by Allan Bloom. New York: Basic Books.

Plato. 1997. *Complete Works*. Indianapolis: Hackett.

Rancière, Jacques. 1999. *Disagreement*. Translated by Julie Rose. Minneapolis: University of Minnesota Press.

Rancière, Jacques. 2009. "The Aesthetic Dimension: Aesthetics, Politics, Knowledge." *Critical Inquiry* 36:1–19.

Rawls, John. 1971. *A Theory of Justice*. Cambridge, MA: Harvard University Press.

Rawls, John. 1996. *Political Liberalism*. New York: Columbia University Press.

Rawls, John. 1999a. *Collected Papers*. Cambridge, MA: Harvard University Press.

Rawls, John. 1999b. *The Law of Peoples*. Cambridge, MA: Harvard University Press.

Rawls, John. 1999c. *A Theory of Justice*. Rev. ed. Cambridge, MA: Harvard University Press.

Rawls, John. 2000. *Lectures on the History of Moral Philosophy*. Cambridge, MA: Harvard University Press.

Rawls, John. 2001. *Justice as Fairness: A Restatement*. Cambridge, MA: Harvard University Press.

Raz, Joseph. 1981. "Authority and Consent." *Virginia Law Review* 67 (1): 103–131.

Raz, Joseph. 2009. *The Authority of Law*. Oxford: Oxford University Press.

Rockmore, Tom. 2004. "On the Structure of 20th Century Philosophy." *Metaphilosophy* 35:466–478.

Rorty, Richard. 1982. *Consequences of Pragmatism*. Minneapolis: University of Minnesota Press.

Rossi, Enzo. 2012. "Justice, Legitimacy, and (Normative) Authority for Political Realists." *Critical Review of International and Social Philosophy* 15:149–164.

Rossi, Enzo, and Matt Sleat. 2014. "Realism in Normative Political Theory." *Philosophy Compass* 9/10:689–701.

Rousseau, Jean-Jacques. 1978. *On the Social Contract*. Translated by Judith R. Masters. Boston: Bedford/St. Martin's Press.

Rousseau, Jean-Jacques. 1979. *Emile, or On Education*. Translated by Allan Bloom. New York: Basic Books.

Rousseau, Jean-Jacques. 1985. *The Government of Poland*. Translated by Willmoore Kendall. Indianapolis: Hackett.

Ryle, Gilbert. 1929. "Review of *Sein und Zeit* by Martin Heidegger." *Mind* 38:355–370.

Ryle, Gilbert. 2009. *Critical Essays*. London: Routledge.

Sagar, Paul. 2016. "From Scepticism to Liberalism? Bernard Williams, the Foundations of Liberalism and Political Realism." *Political Studies* 64:368–384.

Sangiovanni, Andrea. 2008. "Justice and the Priority of Politics to Morality." *Journal of Political Philosophy* 16:137–164.

Sangiovanni, Andrea. 2016. "How Practices Matter." *Journal of Political Philosophy* 24:3–23.

Scheuerman, William E. 2013. "The Realist Revival in Political Philosophy, or: Why New Is Not Always Improved." *International Politics* 50:789–814.

Schmitt, Carl. 1996. *The Concept of the Political*. Translated by George Schwab. Chicago: University of Chicago Press.

Searle, John R. 1958. "Proper Names." *Mind* 67 (266): 166–173.

Shusterman, Richard. 1997. "Putnam and Cavell on the Ethics of Democracy." *Political Theory* 25 (2): 193–214.

Simmons, A. John. 1993. *On the Edge of Anarchy.* Princeton: Princeton University Press.

Simmons, A. John. 2001. *Justification and Legitimacy.* Cambridge: Cambridge University Press.

Simons, Peter. 2001. "Whose Fault? The Origins and Evitability of the Analytic-Continental Rift." *International Journal of Philosophical Studies* 9:295–311.

Sitton, John F. 1987. "Hannah Arendt's Argument for Council Democracy." *Polity* 20:80–100.

Skinner, Quentin. 1969. "Meaning and Understanding in the History of Ideas." *History and Theory* 8:3–53.

Sleat, Matt. 2007. "Making Sense of Our Political Lives—On the Political Thought of Bernard Williams." *Critical Review of International Social and Political Philosophy* 10:389–398.

Sleat, Matt. 2010. "Bernard Williams and the Possibility of a Realist Political Theory." *European Journal of Political Theory* 9:485–503.

Smith, Rogers M. 1997. "Still Blowing in the Wind: The American Quest for a Democratic, Scientific Political Science." *Daedalus* 126:253–287.

Soames, Scott. 2003a. *Philosophical Analysis in the Twentieth Century.* Vol. 1, *The Dawn of Analysis.* Princeton: Princeton University Press.

Soames, Scott. 2003b. *Philosophical Analysis in the Twentieth Century.* Vol. 2, *The Age of Meaning.* Princeton: Princeton University Press.

Sophocles. 1991. *Three Tragedies.* Translated by David Grene. Chicago: University of Chicago Press.

Sreedhar, Susanne. 2008. "Defending the Hobbesian Right of Self-Defense." *Political Theory* 36:781–802.

Staiti, Andrea. 2013. "Philosophy: *Wissenschaft* or *Weltanschauung*? Towards a Prehistory of the Analytic/Continental Rift." *Philosophy and Social Criticism.* doi: 10.1177/0191453713494972

Stone, Julius. 1965. *Human Law and Human Justice.* London: Stevens & Sons.

Strawson, Peter. 1959. *Individuals.* Garden City: Anchor Books.

Stroud, Barry. 1980. "Reasonable Claims: Cavell and the Tradition." *Journal of Philosophy* 77 (11): 731–744.

Talisse, Robert B. 2014. "Impunity and Domination: A Puzzle for Republicanism." *European Journal of Political Theory* 13:121–131.

Vernon, Richard. 2010. "Pascalian Ethics? Bergson, Levinas, Derrida." *European Journal of Political Theory* 9:167–182.

Villa, Dana. 1996. *Arendt and Heidegger: The Fate of the Political.* Princeton: Princeton University Press.

Vlastos, Gregory. 1953. "Isonomia." *American Journal of Philology* 74:337–366.

von Rautenfeld, Hans. 2004. "Charitable Interpretations: Emerson, Rawls, and Cavell on the Use of Public Reason." *Political Theory* 32 (1): 61–84.

Wellmer, Albrecht. 2000. "Arendt on Revolution" In Dana Villa, ed., *The Cambridge Companion to Hannah Arendt*, 220–241. Cambridge: Cambridge University Press.

Wellmer, Albrecht. 2001. "Hannah Arendt on Judgment: The Unwritten Doctrine of Reason." In Ronald Beiner and Jennifer Nedelsky, eds., *Judgment, Imagination, and Politics*, 165–182. Lanham: Rowman & Littlefield.

Wenar, Leif. 2004. "The Unity of Rawls's Work." *Journal of Moral Philosophy* 1:265–275.

White, Hayden. 1978. *Tropics of Discourse*. Baltimore: Johns Hopkins University Press.

White, Hayden. 1987. *The Content of the Form*. Baltimore: Johns Hopkins University Press.

Williams, Bernard. 1981. *Moral Luck*. Cambridge: Cambridge University Press.

Williams, Bernard. 1985. *Ethics and the Limits of Philosophy*. Cambridge, MA: Harvard University Press.

Williams, Bernard. 1997. "Moral Responsibility and Political Freedom." *Cambridge Law Journal* 56:96–102.

Williams, Bernard. 2005. *In the Beginning Was the Deed*. Princeton: Princeton University Press.

Williams, Michael. 1996. *Unnatural Doubts*. Princeton: Princeton University Press.

Wittgenstein, Ludwig. 1958. *Philosophical Investigations*. Translated by G.E.M. Anscombe. Upper Saddle River: Prentice Hall.

Wolfe, Cary. 1994. "Alone with America: Cavell, Emerson, and the Politics of Individualism." *New Literary History* 25 (1): 137–157.

Wolff, Robert Paul. 1969. "On Violence." *Journal of Philosophy* 66:601–616.

Wolin, Sheldon. 1969. "Political Theory as a Vocation." *American Political Science Review* 63:1062–1082.

Wolin, Sheldon. 1983. "Hannah Arendt: Democracy and the Political." *Salmagundi* 60:3–19.

Wood, Gordon S. 1998. *The Creation of the American Republic: 1776–1787*. Chapel Hill: University of North Carolina Press.

INDEX